The Protocol of Neferyt

THE JOHNS HOPKINS NEAR EASTERN STUDIES
Hans Goedicke, General Editor

Hans Goedicke, *The Report about the Dispute of a Man with His* Ba
J. J. M. Roberts, *The Earliest Semitic Pantheon*
John D. Schmidt, *Ramesses II: A Chronological Structure for His Reign*
David Lorton, *The Juridical Terminology of International Relations in Egyptian Texts through Dyn. XVIII*
Bernard Frank Batto, *Studies on Women at Mari*
Hans Goedicke, *The Report of Wenamun*
Hans Goedicke and J. J. M. Roberts (eds.), *Unity and Diversity: Essays in the History, Literature, and Religion of the Ancient Near East*
Patrick D. Miller, Jr., and J. J. M. Roberts, *The Hand of the Lord: A Reassessment of the "Ark Narrative" of 1 Samuel*
Thomas W. Mann, *Divine Presence and Guidance in Israelite Traditions: The Typology of Exaltation*
Hans Goedicke, *The Protocol of Neferyt*

The Protocol of Neferyt

(The Prophecy of Neferti)

Hans Goedicke

Manufactured in the United States of America

The Johns Hopkins University Press, Baltimore, Maryland 21218
The Johns Hopkins Press Ltd., London

Library of Congress Catalog Card Number 76-47371
ISBN 0-8018-1905-9

Library of Congress Cataloging in Publication Data

Goedicke, Hans.
The protocol of Neferyt: The prophecy of Neferti.

(The Johns Hopkins Near Eastern studies)
Includes bibliographical references and index.
1. Prophecy of Neferti. 2. Egyptian literature—History and criticism. I. Prophecy of Neferti. 1977. II. Title. III. Series: Johns Hopkins University. Near Eastern studies.
PJ1571.G6 893'.1 76-47371
ISBN 0-8018-1905-9

Contents

PREFACE

The present study grew from the investigation of a number of select passages. In the course of the work it became increasingly apparent that a piecemeal approach to this literary text could not do justice to its merits. It became necessary to incorporate the entire text in order to present an encompassing picture of it. It presented eventually a welcome opportunity to tackle another representative of the high literature of ancient Egypt, and it became gradually clearer that the bulk of literary texts represents an interrelated oeuvre of one or two great writers. It is hoped that the present study will further the discussion about ancient Egyptian literature and will eventually help to secure its place among the great literary achievements of mankind. Needless to say, a study of this kind cannot hope or claim to have exhausted all problems connected with the text, but it is sincerely hoped that this will further the discussion to the benefit of Egyptology.

I wish to thank Gerald Kadish for some useful remarks and especially David Lorton for the help he has extended. My thanks go also to Jack Goellner, director of the Johns Hopkins University Press, for many years of fruitful collaboration, and to Mrs. Joanne Hildebrandt for typing the manuscript.

INTRODUCTION

What survives of the secular literature of ancient Egypt is a small number of texts. It is impossible to establish conclusively whether they are indicative of the scope of the literary production or whether they are the incidental survivors of the adversities of time and men. The fact that some of the texts, or at least parts of texts, are preserved in numerous copies indicates that they were esteemed long after they were originally written. Again, the causes of later appreciation remain uncertain except that they served as models of good style and were used in the education of pupils. Whether later generations concerned themselves only with the literary qualities of the writings of the past, or whether the contents of the texts were significant in their selection, cannot be said. The pattern of survival of literature from ancient Egypt is incalculable, because most of the extant material comes from the workmen's village of Deir el-Medineh, which was hardly typical of the level of intellectual activity in the land. To use it as a measuring device would be like evaluating the literature of a country from the schoolbooks of a village school.

Among the surviving literary texts from ancient Egypt, "The Prophecy of Neferti" has received less attention in Egyptological discussion than other texts. The main copy of the text is contained in Papyrus 1116 B recto in the Ermitage Museum, Leningrad. This, the only complete version, is augmented by two writing tablets (Cairo 25224 and BM 5647) and twenty ostraca, all available in a synoptical integrated edition in W. Helck, *Die Prophezeiung des Nfr.tj, Kleine ägyptische Texte*, Wiesbaden, 1970.[1] The existence of the complete version in the Ermitage Museum was announced by W. Golenischeff in 1876.[2] It was almost forty years before the text was published in an appropriate edition with photographs, transcription, and translation.[3] Previously, the most extensive variant, the writing board

Cairo 25224, was the basis for a translation by H. Ranke.[4] One year after the *editio princeps* A. H. Gardiner,[5] who had participated in the preparation of the transcription of the Ermitage Papyrus, offered a rendering in English accompanied by sundry notes. A. Erman included the text in *Die Literatur der alten Ägypter*, 1923, 152-157 but, in line with the character of the work, abstained from philological discussions and omitted a number of the more difficult passages. An article by Struve dealing with the text[6] has found little recognition. The text is incorporated in such general works as G. Roeder, *Altägyptische Erzählungen und Märchen*, 1927, 113-117; G. Lefèbvre, *Romans et contes égyptiens de l'époque pharaonique*, 1949, 96-105, and J. A. Wilson in J. B. Pritchard, *Ancient Near Eastern Texts*, 1955, 444-446. The first intensive discussion of the text was done by G. Posener,[7] who demonstrated political motives for its composition. He also inaugurated the philological study of the text by discussing a number of passages that had defied previous translators or that he desired to elucidate. At almost the same time the text was studied by S. Hermann[8] from the viewpoint of literary criticism, although he did not face the prevailing philological problems.

The publication by Helck finally provided a complete, sound edition of the extant text material. His concerns are more epigraphic than philological, although his edition includes a translation and some notes. The philological problems contained in the text were tackled in earnest by W. Barta, *Zu einigen Textpassagen der Prophezeiung des Neferti*, MDIK 27, 1971, 35-45. His meritorious comments deal with a wide range of difficult passages, providing grammatical and lexicographical comments. More recently, translations of the text were included in two surveys of ancient Egyptian literature: R. O. Faulkner, in W. K. Simpson, ed., *The Literature of Ancient Egypt*, 1972, 234-240; and Miriam Lichtheim, *Ancient Egyptian Literature*, vol. I, 1973, 139-145, which includes a number of comments.

As a result of the relatively late date of the *editio princeps* compared with most of the other great literary texts, Papyrus Ermitage 1116 B is not fully incorporated into the materials of the Berlin Wörterbuch. The lack of an exhaustive study of the text is further responsible for the fact that the text is largely unutilized in the grammatical studies of classical Egyptian, although it contains some important material in this respect.

THE NATURE OF THE TEXT

In publishing the text for the first time, Golenischeff described its contents as that of "une prophétie, qui revêt tout à fait le charactère d'une prophétie messianique." That such an evaluation was bound to trigger reactions of one type or another is not surprising. The term "prophecy" is for many charged with a particular set of value connotations, so there was ample fuel for the ensuing controversies. Much ado was made about whether the text is truly prophetic or whether it is merely predicting future events, as well as about whether its concern with social and political problems deserves the label "prophetic." Whereas, Gardiner, *Admonitions of an Egyptian Sage*, 15 ff. and JEA 1, 1914, 100 f., insisted on the predictive nature of the text and denied any prophetic aspects comparable to Biblical prophetism, Breasted, *Development of Religion and Thought in Ancient Egypt*, 1912, 212, note 1, stressed the similarities and considered the text a document of "Messianism nearly fifteen hundred years before its appearance among the Hebrews." A similar view is held by Lanczkowski[9] in his study of prophecy in ancient Egypt. In his view, "der Text hat ganz den Charakter einer prophetischen Vorhersage im Sinne der Verkündigung eines messianischen Herrschers" who will reestablish the political sovereignty of Egypt. Beyond this primarily political objective, Lanczkowski sees also a religious motivation to advocate a religious renewal in the name of Amun. That it prophesies future disasters that would end with the reign of Amenemhet I is Otto's[10] interpretation of the text, although he does not touch on the question of the prophecy's nature. A somewhat differing view was taken by M. Lichtheim,[11] for whom "the work is a historical romance in pseudo-prophetic form." This view, based on Posener's[12] interpretation of the text as political literature, is now widely accepted,[13] so the question of the "prophetic" character of the text is no longer posed.

The presently dominant interpretation of the text as political literature is designed to eliminate any basis for positing a prophetic character. Although it is true that it would be impossible to consider the text as "prophetic" in the sense of predicting future events through visionary abilities, it is equally unjustifiable to take the text flatly as political propaganda. There is nothing in the text to support the claim[14] that the text was written on behalf of the king to justify and corroborate his usurpation. As will be discussed later, the text belongs to the very early reign of Amenemhet I, but this would not in itself have warranted any political justification by literary means.

The text itself makes it quite clear that it does not aspire to be "prophetic" or pseudoprophetic. The statement, "While I shall say what is before me (i.e., what I anticipate), I cannot foretell things before they have come" in line 26[15] is unequivocal in that Neferti, who has to be identified with the poet himself, does not claim or pretend the gift of supernatural abilities enabling him to predict the future. He portrays himself rather as a rational human being able to anticipate developments and events on the basis of past experience without insisting on their inevitability. There is no claim of any divine or supernatural inspiration, and the problems raised in the deliberations nowhere touch questions beyond the human realm. A divine plan in history or an eschatological purpose of history is not an underlying premise, but history is seen as happening in the mundane world. Men are its principal actors, although the impact of nature is allotted its due role. The political and social evils are not considered reflections of moral shortcomings or divine punishment for sinfulness or neglect of a divine plan but are rationally analyzed for their causes and effects.

The work has been classified as representative of a pessimistic literature triggered by the collapse of the Old Kingdom state and society,[16] which "produced a sense of messianic salvation" to overcome the prevailing predicaments by the appearance of a savior king in the person of Imeny, scil. Amenemhet I. However, there is no discernible dramatic build-up in the text, which would seem required as a contrast to the desired "messianic salvation." The long line of undesirable and unpleasant situations and events is enumerated with a striking matter-of-factness with no bemoaning or moralizing. There is nothing pessimistic in the listing of the facts, which are considered conceivable prospects based on prior experience. The text thus does not create the particular emotional climate for a "messianic salvation."

Erman, *op. cit.*, 152, had already spoken about the predominantly political character of the text. There can be no doubt that it is deeply concerned with Amenemhet I, the first ruler of the Twelfth Dynasty.[17] For Erman the writer of the work was on intimate terms with this king, whom he glorified for posterity by juxtaposing the glory of the monarch with terrors of various kinds that had occurred immediately preceding him but during the writer's lifetime. The political aspect and its stimulating influence on the contemporary literature is the approach pursued by Posener.[18] For him the work originated in the immediate vicinity of Amenemhet I and was possibly inspired directly by him as a vehicle of promulgating his rulership and his political ideas. The affiliations with the past, in particular the connection with Snofru, who was viewed as the ideal king, Posener considers as a design for the sanctioning of Amenemhet I's assuming the rule in Egypt. Little is said about the probable achievements of the king, which Posener takes as an indication that the work was created at the beginning of the king's reign, because the text is "une présentation d'un nouveau roi et non un bilan d'un règne." From the emphasis extended to the solution of the problems with the bedouin and the safeguarding of the eastern Delta, Posener assumes that the consolidation of the frontiers was the initial task of the newly crowned Amenemhet I and that the founding and completion of the defensive works in the Wadi Tumilat provided a propitious opportunity for a propaganda effort especially intended for the eastern Delta. However, we have no indication that the king was especially concerned with the defense of the eastern Delta at the beginning of his reign. As there is some evidence that his early reign saw some resistance in Upper Egypt,[19] it would seem unlikely that the king would first have turned to a task that could only have been peripheral when compared with the problem of secure control of the South. Further, it would seem unlikely that Amenemhet I had to woo the inhabitants of the northern frontier region by propaganda, especially after he had taken measures to ward off infiltration by undoubtedly undesirable foreigners.

The political aspect was even more emphasized in the recent treatment by Faulkner,[20] for whom "Ammenemes I . . . gained his throne by usurpation from the ruling family of the Mentuhotpes, and to ensure his position used a certain amount of written propaganda." M. Lichtheim, *op. cit.*, 139, considers the work "a historical romance in pseudo-prophetic form." In her judgment it reflects the successful early years of Amenemhet I's reign, which is contrasted with "the artificial gloom of the prophecies of disasters that would precede the redemption." She considers "the theme 'national distress' . . . an intellectual problem that became a literary topos." Consequently the events described in the text do not, in her view, require a specific factual basis but are merely a general reference to the periodically occurring phenomenon of civil disorder.

Even if Amenemhet I was a usurper, disregarding the constitutional aspects it is difficult to imagine for whom any political propaganda by the king might have been intended and how it could have strengthened his position. Those opposing him in the early years of his reign would hardly have been inspired to change their attitude and opposition, and the supporters hardly needed a "historical romance" to convince them. To invent an "artificial gloom" to develop a literary topos of "national distress" without factual cause would have struck any contemporaries as rather odd and would have made the king appear a liar, one who could not be trusted and did not deserve support. There can be no doubt that the text was written for contemporaries, who were fully familiar with the events, and not for readers in a distant future. The difficulties are described simply and factually; the account requires the experience of having lived through them. We have no reason to presume civil disorder as a "periodically occurring phenomenon," nor would it seem likely that it would be treated as literary fiction by ancient Egyptians. Mythological language would in such a case have provided a vehicle of expression rather than an enumeration of factual situations.

In contrast to this approach, which centers in the person of a contemporary of Amenemhet I and the events mentioned in the text, S. Herrmann[21] considers the text a literary compilation ("literarisches Sammelwerk") utilizing numerous selections derived from other sources. In his opinion the work does not assume the character of a prophecy, because only a limited number of passages contain constructions in future tense. For him the historic-political setting is only an external frame, while the center is a dialogue of a man with his heart and with the creator god, bemoaning the prevailing conditions. As a result of an excessively applied literary criticism, the unity and uniqueness of the text as a literary creation evaporate together with the personality of an individual writer and his particular set of concerns. Instead of the work of a creative individual, the text would become a representative of a literary genre whose aims are so general that they are no longer particular to a certain time and the historical or intellectual developments occurring in it. The ingenious dissecting lacks any justification, because the work certainly is coherent and self-contained and does not have the apparent inconsistencies that would suggest possible redaction. In addition, the philological base on which the operation rests is in many cases speculative and indefensible.

The text, to let it speak for itself, is presented as the transcript made by King Snofru of the statements made by one of his subjects. This person is not one of the king's intimate followers, but is introduced to him by the court-council because of his outstanding merits. This exceptional man, whose pronouncements are considered so valuable that the king writes them down, has all the features of an individual. He is introduced to the king as one who was "valiant with his arm" as a youth, "excellent with his fingers" as a scribe, i.e., as an accomplished official, and as one "who has greater wealth than any peer of him." This individuality based on achievements is matched by the personal attention King Snofru extends to him, which culminates in the specification of the author in the introduction of his transcribed statements (ll. 17-18). His legal residence is stated to be the Heliopolitan district, his professional and religious affiliation is with the cult of Bastet, and he is "a knowledgeable man of the East." The degree of these specifications fosters the conclusion that a specific individual ought to be pictured as the source of the discourses about the events in the land. The emphasis on details and the space they occupy in the relatively short text make it improbable that the speaker in whose mouth the pronouncements are put is the fictitious product of a writer's mind. The speaker hardly participates in the events described, which in turn makes it improbable that we have here a social type and not a personality. Throughout, the speaker remains the narrator of a chain of events, which he considers to be potential prospects until the country finds its inner balance again. The discourse about anticipated developments is followed by the emphatic recommendation of steps to avoid the potential adversities.

Since we are thus compelled to accept as a historical person the speaker to whom the pronouncements are credited, the next step must be the delineation of his identity. The name of the speaker had long been read Nefer-rehu[22] when Posener, RdE 8, 1951, 174, changed the reading to 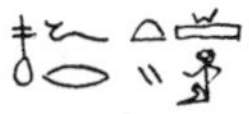 on the basis of O Turin 9596, and it is now generally accepted as *Nfr.ty*. At the time the name was attested only in a single occurrence as a feminine name in the New Kingdom.[23] In support of Posener's reading Hornung[24] published a fragment, probably part of a doorway, dating to the late Sixth Dynasty. The name  could be read *Nfrti*, except that its formation as a masculine name is not convincing. The doubts are strengthened by the attested male name , which can only be read *Nfr-ỉt* "may the father be good."[25] Although it is impossible to trace the name beyond the end of the Old Kingdom to establish a link with Snofru, there seems no doubt that the author of the pronouncements codified by the king is identical with  *Nfry,*[26] listed in Pap. Chester

Beatty III vs 3.6 together with *Ḫty* in an enumeration of the great sages and writers of the past.[27] Posener's reading of the name is certainly a major improvement, but it does not explain the consistent use of  , which must be surprising in a name *Nfrti*. It must also be noted that the Turin ostracon has  and not  . In view of this spelling, 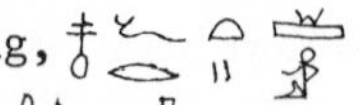 , I surmise the original form of the name to have been  with a subsequent metathesis. This name is attested in El Bersheh I pl. 18 as a male name[28] dating to the very early Middle Kingdom. The identification with this name provides an explanation not only for the inclusion of the "book-roll" in the name but also for the Ramesside form *Nfry*. The reading of the name as *Nfryt* (Neferyt) is maintained in the discussion below.

The later traditions leave no doubt that Neferyt was a historical person and that he was considered one of the great sages and writers of the past. As almost all of the names quoted for them in the Ramesside Period, with the notable exception of Kaires, have been proved to belong to historical personalities, it is only appropriate to consider Neferyt in the same vein. Pap. Chester Beatty III makes no effort to assign him to any specific period, because the account is basically ahistorical. Neferyt *(Nfry)* is mentioned together with *Ḫty*, who is denoted as the greatest of them all, i.e., of the persons listed. He can safely be dated to the beginning of the Twelfth Dynasty,[29] primarily to the reign of Amenemhet I and living into the reign of Sesostris I but dying before him. Neferyt's affiliation with Khety provides a basis for placing the two in close chronological proximity. Such a date is corroborated by the indications provided by the text itself. From them it transpires that, at the time of its composition, Amenemhet I was king of the South only and had not yet become ruler of the entire country, as he subsequently did, possibly on the prodding of Neferyt.

The literary text, as is usual with the great literary documents of ancient Egypt, bears no identifying title. Its commonly used description as "Prophecy" is, of course, modern.[30]

The work is generally subdivided into three parts:[31] the frame-story, the description of adverse social and political conditions, and the prophecy of a savior king who will bring renewed glory after a period of decline. Although such a structuring might seem self-evident, the varying sizes of the three parts should cause wonder. The presumed frame-story at the court of King Snofru is not taken up again in the text after

Neferyt's pronouncements are completed, so it is an introduction rather than a truly encompassing narrative. At the same time, the situation as established at the beginning is assumed to be prevailing throughout the long monologue of Neferyt. It is several times (ll. 35, 38, 44, 47, 54, 55) interrupted by direct addresses to the recording scribe, i.e., the king. The account of the difficulties in the country occupies and far exceeds the space allotted to the revelation of a savior, which is considered the goal of the work. The pronouncement of a savior king is awarded the least space, and his identity and accomplishments remain curiously veiled. Equally striking is the lack of any kind of apotheosis of this future king to end the text. It seems rather to close with a self-assertion by Neferyt about the veracity of his sayings, which will later bring him recognition and esteem. The modesty displayed by Neferyt throughout his monologue strangely contrasts with this final assertion.

The lack of balance within the infrastructure of the text is difficult to reconcile with the postulated purpose of the work "to support the new regime" of a usurper (Faulkner). Is the situation really this simple? There can be no doubt that the text was written in the time of Amenemhet I. That a literary text could have had any substantial influence in strengthening the king's position seems rather doubtful. If we consider the possibilities of distribution, it would seem improbable that it could affect a sizable number of people. Those to be influenced would have to be the educated, because the population at large was hardly in a position to read the text. To postulate major resistance to the rule of Amenemhet I by the educated is in itself an improbable thesis. It becomes even more so when we take into consideration that Amenemhet I pursued a much more even-handed policy for the entire country than the Theban Eleventh Dynasty rulers, who displayed exclusive interest for the South, their original domain, and totally neglected the North. Although Menthuhotep II assumed the Horus-name *Sm3-t3wy* "Uniter of the Two Lands," he and his successors acted rather like conquerors of the North but made no efforts to improve its conditions. No monument of a king of the Eleventh Dynasty has been found north of Asyut,[32] which seems a telling indication of the parochial political attitude of this group of rulers.

If the purpose of the work had really been to eulogize Amenemhet I after he had established himself as ruler of the entire country, the appearance of the king's name in a prominent way would be only logical, as would be the choice of a more rhapsodic form similar to the Hymns to

Sesostris III[33] or the praises of the king in Sinuhe B 46-75. Once Amenemhet I was established as king, there could be no reason to hedge about his personality. These arguments, to be posited against the thesis that the work aims to strengthen Amenemhet I's political position, apply equally--if not more strongly--to the related thesis that it was written under the direction or the influence of the king himself. Why should Amenemhet I have seen fit to hide his light under a bushel or behind a straw man by omitting any reference to his considerable political accomplishments?

Another feature has been completely disregarded in the discussion of the original aim of the work. Although the term *kmt* "the black land" occurs several times in the text (11. 26, 33, 36, 67), it is not used to denote "Egypt" as a geopolitical unit; this applies also to the recurrently used term *t3* "land," which is applied only to a specific area at Egypt's eastern fringe and is not used as a reference to the entire country.[34] To postulate that Amenemhet I tried to demonstrate his abilities by concentrating on his accomplishments in the limited area of the easternmost Delta is as implausible as to assume that these were his only political successes. Equally improbable is a postulation of any major interest on the part of Thebes--which was, after all, his base of power in that remote part of Egypt after the Eleventh Dynasty rulers had shown total neglect of it. If we accept the conditions as described in the text, it would have been most surprising if Amenemhet I met any indigenous resistance by resident "Egyptians" in the region concerned. Indeed, the repulsion and checking of bedouin infiltration could hardly have brought him any opposition from an Egyptian population. The text is unequivocal in its disdain of and objection to the "Asiatics," so that Amenemhet I should have been greeted there as a savior and would not have needed any propaganda to strengthen his position in the part of the country with which the text is exclusively concerned.

An analysis of the motives postulated for the compilation of the work rules out the possibility of its being a piece of political propaganda in support of a new king, as well as the possibility of the king's direct influence in the formulation. This approach leads to a methodological "short circuit," making the text either a superfluous exercise in vainglory when there was ample political success or a piece of artistic literature in the form of a "historical romance" in the face of towering reality.

Thus the origin of the text in the immediate vicinity of the king or under his direct influence, as envisaged since Erman, proves an avenue to the nowhere, and an entirely new approach is required. There is no indication in the text of any contact by Neferyt with the court of Amenemhet I or of any direct affiliation between the two. The frame is set at the court of Snofru, which is no doubt a "romanticism," in so far as this term is applicable at all. However, it has to be emphasized that Snofru is mentioned as being deceased, to judge from the epithet *m3ᶜ-ḫrw*. This kind of retrospection occurs also in Pap. Westcar in regard to Zoser (I 14), Neb-ka (I 19; III 18; IV 1,8,14), Snofru (IV 19; VI 16, 19), and Khufu (I 12; IV 13; VI 18; VII 6,21, etc.) and could be considered an anachronism, at least concerning King Khufu, at whose court the entire event is set. The officials whose stories are quoted are all contemporaries of Khufu, which produces a historical consistency not found in our text. No effort is made to describe Neferyt as a contemporary of Snofru. Later tradition affiliates him with the sage Khety, whose acme at the beginning of the Twelfth Dynasty can be considered certain.[35] Since there is no reason to doubt Neferyt's contemporaneity with Amenemhet I, are we to believe that the Egyptians would have been indifferent to this blatant anachronism, especially at the time the work was composed? Or should we take refuge in postulating the involved intellectual process of fictional unreality, i.e., that Neferyt, whose authorship has to be accepted, presents his deliberations as if he had been called to the court of King Snofru of the Fourth Dynasty? I find it difficult to envisage an Egyptian oblivious of the intervening six centuries, just as the incompatibility of Neferyt and the court of Snofru would have been fully apparent to any contemporary.

If Neferyt wrote the work without a royal commission from Amenemhet I, what could have been his motives and why did he use the anachronistic setting? His official introduction, allegedly heading the transcript of his pronouncements to the king, describes him as "a knowledgeable man of the East" (l. 17), "concerned about what is happening in the land" (l. 18) and "bringing to mind the condition of the East." These concise phrases give a picture of Neferyt's role in the text as a self-appointed advocate of the problems prevailing in Egypt's eastern border region. He was brought to the king as a man of learning and accomplishment who would give the king true and challenging information without flattery and without regard for his own purpose. This role appears to be the motive behind the composition of the text. Neferyt apparently was brought to the king to inform him about the deteriorated situation in the East, which would deserve the king's attention. Consequently, it is necessary to assume that Neferyt's pronouncements were made to Amenemhet I and that they were intended to spur the king to action.

On this basis we can gain a fairly exact date for the composition of the text, which can be understood either as the transcript of an audience or as a memorandum or petition submitted by Neferyt to the king. It has to fall in the very early part of the reign of Amenemhet I, when he was king only of the South (see p.35f.). The text contains an admonition to assume the double crown and thus the rule of both parts of the country, with the implied obligation to protect the eastern frontier. That the historical setting of the text is the very early reign of Amenemhet I is supported by the lack of any reference to Sesostris I, who was coregent beginning with the twentieth year of his father. These considerations, combined with the probability that Amenemhet I eventually included in his regnal count all his years as king and not only those spent as ruler of all of Egypt, suggest dating the origin of the text before year 10, i.e., 1981 B.C. Such a date would provide sufficient time for Amenemhet I's rule as king of the South, in which capacity he is challenged by Neferyt to assume the kingship of the Two Lands and to attend to the situation on the eastern border. At the time of his death some twenty years later the control over the East was fully established and a fortification system there a fact, to judge from the information provided by the Sinuhe story. The suggestions made by Neferyt would have required some time to be translated into action, which would be easily accommodated by the proposed schedule.

If our text is not a *post eventum* glorification of Amenemhet I, but rather the transcript of an initiative advanced by a concerned subject who was trying to interest the king of the South in the problems of the eastern border region, i.e., the area of the Wadi Tumilat, why is it set at the court of Snofru, and why did Neferyt not address himself directly to King Amenemhet I? When we place ourselves in the historical situation, the disguise becomes transparent. At the time of his presentation Neferyt could not have been sure of the reaction he might encounter. The romantic disguise modified the possibilities of adverse reaction, if this should have been the case.

If we pose the thesis that Neferyt used the historical setting as a kind of safeguard, the lacking completion of the frame-story after the monologue becomes understandable. However, we still have to explain the choice of Snofru as the king to whom Neferyt addresses his admonitions, as well as the name *ʾImny* for the king of the South who is challenged to take both crowns and rule the united country. Concerning the former there is a distinct desire to establish a link with the past, as will be shown later (p. 53f.) this in itself, however, does not explain the choice of Snofru. It is generally assumed[36] that the esteem in which Snofru was held during the Twelfth Dynasty is responsible for his role in our text. However, Snofru's fame was dormant after Pepi I, and his numerous mentions and his renewed funerary cult commence with Sesostris I, at the earliest in the late reign of Amenemhet I.[37] As far as can be determined, Snofru did not hold any special position in the early to middle part of Amenemhet I's reign but attained it not before the very end of the reign. Neferyt, therefore could not have been influenced by an already existing esteem for the Fourth Dynasty king. The mention of Snofru thus should be credited exclusively to Neferyt's ingenuity, and it is conceivable, though beyond substantiation, that he might have been instrumental in the Middle Kingdom interest in Snofru. That Snofru had pursued any active policy in the East is uncertain, although it is likely, to judge from Methen's inscription.[38] This might have been the specific historical reason for Neferyt's choice or attachment, but it would hardly suffice as reason for an elaborate introduction of his concerns about the situation in the East to a king whose reaction he was not entirely sure of. Although the historical aspect carried its unquestionable impact, the invoking of King Snofru appears to have had a second aspect as well. Not only was Snofru apparently the first lawgiver in ancient Egypt,[39] but the king's name as "he who makes proper" contains a specific statement as well. Because of the absence of an article--definite or indefinite--in classical Egyptian, the invocation of *nswt-bit Snfrw* can also be understood as "a king who makes proper," which then would be not a name but a moral statement. I have the impression that the mention of Snofru's name in the introductory account was motivated by this implicit pun, by which Neferyt challenged the king to be "one who makes proper," i.e., to ameliorate the situation in the East.

Although there is no way of proving the use of an elaborate pun based on the mention of Snofru, the particular nature of the other royal name quoted in our text supports such a thesis. Imeny is certainly an oblique reference to Amenemhet I, as it is now generally accepted.[40] However, the name is spelled and determined as if it were an imperfective active participle, "the hiding one."[41] In this case another pun is involved, referring to the envisaged and hoped-for savior king as "hiding," in addition to the possibility of applying the designation to the king as the hypocoristic form of his name.[42] Since Neferyt could not anticipate the king's reaction to his memorandum and had to be prepared for a rejection, he tried to mellow the possible reaction by the use of a pun.

The outcome of the discussion thus far can be summarized as follows: The text should be attributed to an individual named Neferyt, who composed it at the beginning of the Twelfth Dynasty. According to the writer's own statements that he can say only what he foresees but that he is not practicing divination, the text does not contain a "prophecy" of future events but is an elaboration of existing conditions in the eastern border region and potential dangers resulting therefrom. The central concern of the text is in no way a glorification of Amenemhet I to strengthen his rule. It is rather a challenge by a concerned citizen to move the king of the South to assume the rule of the Two Lands and to take an interest in the problems besetting the East, so as to change and improve the situation there. In order to reflect the nature of the composition more appropriately than the customary "Prophecy of Neferty" does, "The Protocol of Neferyt" is suggested here as a new designation of the text.

THE LITERARY FORM

The text makes use of two literary devices to enhance its impact. The introduction follows the literary pattern commonly labeled "Königsnovelle"[43] by introducing an instigating event, which happened at the royal court as a result of the king's concern. Different from the setting used in the Papyrus Westcar, in which Khufu is portrayed as suffering from boredom,[44] Snofru is depicted as a conscientious ruler who fully partakes in the governing of the country. In the daily court-council, affairs of state as well as the daily administrative routine are discussed. Only after the regular business in completed does the king request that some outstanding man be brought in to inform him about matters "which could extend the view of his majesty" (ll. 7-8). This desire is in line with the characterization of Snofru (or a Snofru, i.e., "one who makes proper") as a ruler whose concern for the country does not end with his official obligations: he is shown as trying to expand his understanding of the problems facing the country and contribute to their solution. Khufu, in contrast, is depicted in the Papyrus Westcar as pursuing entertainment. Whereas Snofru seeks the counsel of his subjects, Khufu is not interested in advice and, when confronted therewith, "becomes very sad" (Pap. Westcar 9,12) and has to be reassured.

The similarity in the setting between our text and the stories of the Papyrus Westcar is so striking that a common author appears a feasible thesis. At the same time there are marked differences in the language; Papyrus Westcar displays distinct vernacularisms.[45] However, these differences in the language are not necessarily a reflection of a chronological development but could equally well be attributed to differing literary aims.

As far as can be seen the "Königsnovelle," i.e., the assigning of a symptomatic role to a historical king,[46] has its earliest representatives in the Protocol of Neferyt and in the Stories of Papyrus Westcar.[47] Other literary texts of the early Twelfth Dynasty use the frame-story as a literary device[48] but do not use the royal setting, except for the Berlin Leather Roll,[49] in the formulation of which an accomplished author, either Neferyt or Khety, must have participated.

The other literary device applied in our text is that of a transcription of verbal statements. The same is found in the Complaints of the Peasant. However, unlike the latter, which is recorded for a king,[50] our text is presented as the king's personal transcript of his subject's sayings (l. 16). This remarkable feature serves two purposes: it increases the weight of the pronouncements, and it illustrates the benevolence of King Snofru to his subject in line with the other characterizations of Snofru.

The king's alleged transcript commences with a summary, probably influenced by chancery practices.[51] It consists of Neferyt's qualifications, including his legal affiliations for census purposes (cf. p.68) and the motive for his address to the king. This concern is specified as "what is happening in the land" and "the condition of the East," with a progression from the general to the specific. It is followed by the particular reason for disquiet, which runs through the text like a red thread--namely, the unchecked infiltration of "Asiatics" and its adverse consequences on the orderly administration of this part of the country. The conspicuous emphasis with which the question of the Asiatics is treated, from the introductory remarks to Neferyt's sayings and to his concluding admonition to reconstruct the fortifications for checking their movements, makes it evident that this problem is the sole concern of the text. Seen in the context of political problems faced in Amenemhet I's early reign, the Asiatic infiltration could hardly have been more than one among many and most likely was not the gravest for the country in its entirety. Thus, even the successful resolution of the problem would have been no more than the accomplishment of one of many tasks and could not serve as a *sine qua non* to demonstrate and strengthen the king's position.

That Neferyt's aim was to arouse the interest of the king of the South in the eastern border region, which apparently was Neferyt's home or close to it, transpires from his opening words. They express the wish and hope, "May my heart (scil. mind) stir your bemoaning this land." Consequently, what follows has to be understood as reflections on or descriptions of developments, as well as wishes or suggestions for their correction. The building of the "Walls-of-the-Ruler" is thus to be seen as a recommendation to remedy the prevailing troubles, which at the time of the audience had not been accomplished. Neferyt makes it absolutely clear that the task to be faced is a formidable one, because the administration in the region concerned had totally collapsed (11. 22f.).

The situation had not erupted accidentally but had resulted from a prevailing extreme drought. We are undoubtedly right to view it as the ultimate cause that inspired Neferyt to turn to the king for relief from the intruders, whose presence aggravated the already difficult situation.

This drought, which is mentioned again later (1. 51) with an assurance that even the worst has an eventual end, serves as a major theme in the composition. It is against this background that Neferyt makes his deliberations concerning prospects. As he emphasizes, these are not predictions (1. 26) but possibilities; he states them as "what is before me." The bleak situations he describes thus are not prognostic but are foreseeable without being inescapable. The lengthy discourse (11. 26-54) delineates numerous situations, which are arranged in a progression. They are far too numerous and varied to have actually occurred in the few years separating the Eleventh Dynasty and the Twelfth Dynasty.[52] Likewise, Neferyt could not possibly have been in a position to anticipate all the potential prospects he mentions without some experience, personal or traditional, to draw from. If we have to assume that the anticipation of the events mentioned is derived from their previous occurrence, the deliberations of Neferyt take on the character of reflecting history.[53] Because of the number and the nature of the events described, it seems necessary to see them as having been spread over a longer period. Thus the events Neferyt talks about to the king are a selection of what had the greatest adverse impact on the eastern border region and what he fears might occur again. That he draws from past experiences is corroborated by the recurrent assertion (ll. 38, 44, 47, 55) *di.ỉ n.k* "I (can) produce for you," i.e., "I (can) show you."

If this part of the text, which I see as a "historical" reflection similar to Merikare^{c} P. 69-110,[54] covers more than a few years immediately preceding the ascent of Amenemhet I as ruler of the Two Lands, the next task is to define the extent of the period in question and, if possible, establish its limits. The historical section begins with a description of a drought, and the same kind of event stands at its end, forming a link with the prevailing situation. The reference to the drought in the early years of Amenemhet I[55] is the basis for stepping into the past, when a similar disaster occurred. It seems a justifiable assumption that Neferyt was a man of years at the time of his audience with the king.[56] If we place this event prior to Amenemhet I's tenth regnal year,[57] a man of sixty would have been a youth before Menthuhotep II overthrew the Heracleopolitan dynasty and became lord of all Egypt. Neferyt's life can thus be assumed to have reached back well into the Tenth Dynasty, about which we know practically nothing. A disastrous famine apparently occurred in the late Ninth Dynasty, and the memory of it lingered on into the Tenth and Eleventh dynasties. If this famine, the consequences of which appear to be the basis of Neferyt's concern, occurred during the Heracleopolitan Period, the other events alluded to--especially the attacks by Asiatics, their breaking through existing defenses, the desolation of the eastern border region, civil war, social upheaval, and administrative mismanagement--are too numerous and devoid of direct causal connections to allow their concentration in a limited period of time. On this basis it becomes possible to see in the historical section of The Protocol of Neferyt a reflection of the history of part of the First Intermediate Period and its effects on Egypt's eastern border.

This incorporation of historical events into a literary composition is paralleled in the Instructions for King Merikare^{c}, a text that also displays concern for the situation in the East. Otherwise the two texts differ substantially: the latter adheres to the genre of wisdom literature with its moral concerns,[58] whereas the Protocol of Neferyt deals only with political questions. A comparison between these dissimilar texts, although they are of very close date of origin, is difficult to make. Semantic affinities exist to some degree, but they are not so pronounced that common authorship is a compelling conclusion. The uncertainty concerning the beginning of the Instructions for King Merikare^c increases the obstacles to making a comparison. At the same time there are distinct similarities, in particular the historical setting, the marked concern for the East, and the advising of the King by a commoner (P. 138 ff.). Because King Merikare^c most likely lived very late in the Tenth Dynasty,[59] the text affiliated with his name could not have been written much before the end of the Heracleopolitan Period. This brings the Instructions for King Merikare^c into a period when Neferyt could very well have been alive and grown up. His reputation as a "writer (sš = scribe) . . . excellent with his fingers" (l. 10) would make perfect sense as a reference to Neferyt's earlier career as a "writer," which in likelihood had been interrupted by the victory of the Theban Eleventh Dynasty, as these rulers do not seem to have had much interest in the arts. Although certainty cannot be attained on the basis of the information available, the thesis of common authorship by Neferyt of the Instructions for King Merikare^c and our text has its appeal and would explain his esteemed role among the writers of the past during the Ramesside Period. That the two texts were most probably found together could be considered support of such a thesis. The two texts, however, would have to be envisaged as representing different periods in Neferyt's work and life. Since it seems unlikely that the name of a Heracleopolitan king was promulgated in a literary work during the Eleventh Dynasty and, furthermore, since a posthumous reference to Merikare^c would seem far-fetched in view of his apparently limited historical significance,[60] it seems appropriate to attribute the Instructions to the king whose name they bear,[61] i.e., to the end of the Tenth Dynasty. Nor is there any reason to question the identity of Imeny and Amenemhet I, which establishes the time-frame of the Protocol of Neferyt in his reign and, for reasons already elaborated, in its early stage. Chronologically this produces a span of approximately forty-five to fifty years, which does not seems excessive as part of a man's life.

Aside from the fact that our text appears to be the earliest attestation of the "Königsnovelle" as a literary device, it is also significant for its literary form as a codification of verbal pronouncements. The verbal instruction is, of course, the form typical for the wisdom literature,[62] and its codification is mentioned once in the Instructions of Kagemni[63] (pap. Prisse II 4f.): "all that is written in this book, heed it as if I speak. Do not go beyond what has been set down." According to it the adages of the sage were codified and transmitted in this form. The most extensive application of the transcript as a literary form is, of course, the Story of the Eloquent Peasant, whose rhetorical talents were the reason that his nine formal petitions were transcribed by order of King Nebkaure^{c}-Khety. A connection with Neferyt's *oeuvre* is a distinct possibility but, without a penetrating study of the entire text, it would be premature to voice an opinion.

Outside the closely interrelated group of Middle Egyptian literary texts, Neferyt appears to have had some belated influence in connection with a neoclassical renaissance in the Nineteenth Dynasty, particularly in the reign of Ramesses II. There seem to be distinct reflections of our text in the dedicatory inscription and in the Kuban stela. It is paralleled by the interest during the Nineteenth Dynasty in the writers of the past and their works. The majority of ostraca containing our text date from the Ramesside Period.[64]

This later esteem could have stemmed from the finesse and liveliness of the text. In order to challenge his listener, Neferyt resorts to direct address and rhetorical questions (l. 24). Several times the flow of the discourse is interrupted for a return to the listener, an address to him directly (ll. 38, 44, 47, 55, and especially 35). It is noteworthy that these interruptions increase toward the end of Neferyt's monologue. The use of anticipated objections and their presentation in the form of quotes likewise serves to enliven the presentation (l. 38). There are adages incorporated, which either are current maxims or are formulated to suit the context (ll. 42, 43-44, 53, 54-55). The description of the collapse of social order (ll. 40ff.) has distinct affinities with the formulations in the Admonitions of an Egyptian Sage. It is at present impossible to decide, however, if this similarity holds any significance. In the concluding section the author becomes rhapsodic and addresses the future subjects of King Amenemhet I, promising joy to the loyal and terror to the treacherous.

The mastery with which these stylistic techniques are employed is truly impressive. Even more stunning, though less conspicuous to a cursory survey, is the finesse of the wording and the precision in the movement of the train of thought.

In order to provide clarity and comprehension, the long historical section is divided into parts, the beginning of each marked by a *rubrum*.[65] This device yields a structure in which the different stages of reflected history are separated. Each section opens with a theme-setting statement, which is subsequently substantiated by additional pronouncements describing progressive stages. They are arranged in such a fashion that each new passage is based on the closing point of its predecessor until the description of the past condition is completed. Consequences resulting from situations are sometimes included in the discourse.

Considerable artistry is displayed in the employment of complex puns and parallelisms. The most elaborate application of this technique is in ll. 26-28. The statement about the drying up of the major watercourses is followed by two passages, one saying that the water can be crossed on foot, the other that one will have to seek water for sailing. This tripartite structure, which has the concern for "water" as its center, is paralleled by a similarly structured group of three passages concerning "riparian land." Not only does the key word (*wḏb*) occur in all three parts, but two of the passages are intricately intermeshed by arranging the three words as A B C and b C A, the difference between B and b being a phonetic pun.

An allusion, probably of political nature, is the statement that "the south wind will ward off the north wind, so that heaven consists of only one wind" (ll. 28f.). While it makes perfect sense as a description of the meteorological conditions during the drought, the *double entendre* plays on the one-sided political situation in the country during the Eleventh Dynasty. The same kind of wordplay applies to the reference concerning *3pdw ḏrḏr* (l. 29) "foreign birds," which can also be read as "foreign migrants" because of a phonetic pun.

Equally impressive is the artistry in the composition of Section VII, where two different subjects are masterfully juxtaposed. First, the disappearance of the good fortune of hunters and fishers is discussed, as are its adverse effects on the dismal supply situation. The peaceful use of knives by fishers and hunters has its counterpoint in the military attack launched by Asiatics, who overrun the existing fortifications in their drive to descend into Egypt. Their success is attributed, not to superior strength, but to the lack of coordination and foresight by those who should have been responsible for the defense. This failure is contrasted and alleviated by Neferyt's assurance of his personal vigilance against a possible recurrence of such events.

The foreign attack led to devastation, and the "game of the desert drinking from the watercourses" is pictured, utilizing again a metaphor in reference to the foreigners, in addition to involving the metaphorical significance of water as the source of life. Although it is not stated explicitly, it transpires that the undesirable foreigners are still in the eastern border region and that their departure--and the forestalling of another intrusion--are hopes but not facts. It is significant that at this point Neferyt emphasizes again his inability to prognosticate the future, despite his ability to recognize the prevailing dilemma.

As a result of neglect by the authorities, the situation has deteriorated to a degree that internal fighting can be anticipated; the land is in a state of anarchy. The terror of domestic fighting is vividly portrayed in Section IX, and the abysses of human nature are mercilessly explored. As a means to effect the strongest possible impression, identically composed sentences are strung together, using contrasting themes to further the impact, as in ll. 40-42:

> When one will make arrows of copper
> one will request bread with blood
> one will laugh at the outcry for pain
> one will not weep for a death
> one will not spend a night hungry for a death.

In addition, there is the technique of interlacing the elements by basing a new statement on a word occurring in the foregoing one. Similar artistry is displayed in the observation (ll. 42-43):

> man's heart (*ỉb*) is concerned with himself--
> one will not do the post mortem presently--
> the mind (*ỉb*) has totally gone away from it.

This structuring of the individual sections is in no way monotonous. Whereas Sections VII-IX close with personal appeals by Neferyt to his listener, the direct approach is placed in the center of Section X, showing that the organization of the text is not formalistic but is, rather, an outcome of the train of argumentation. Thus the central position of the personal appeal in Section X serves as the dividing line between the general considerations about the breakdown of law and the distortions that follow it. The personal statement in between has the immediacy of individual experience.

The strength of the formulation unquestionably lies in the inner continuity of the arguments, where point follows point with inescapable logic. The arrangement of logical pairs falls under this heading, as in (ll. 50-51):

> While the land diminishes, its administrators
> are numerous. While it dries up, its servants are
> rich.

The clarity of perception and the lucidity of its expression applies equally to the description of phenomena in nature. There are several examples in the text. One concerns the gradual drying up of the water supply (l. 28):

> The riparian land will silt up the water-place
> until what is in the water-place is riparian land

which describes dramatically the diminishing of the water-hole owing to the drought. The relation of moist land and water-place is reversed in the two passages, thus aptly reflecting the transformation.

Two other examples concern the sun and its particular appearance during the drought and the accompanying heat:

> The sun is covered and does never shine (clearly),
> so that people can see (ll. 24f.).

The observation of the haze caused by the intensive heat is paralleled by:

> One can not live as long as clouds are always
> covering who is being red (i.e., the sun) (l. 25).

referring to the red sun covered by haze, which is typical of drought conditions.[66] The second description of the sun during the drought is more detailed (ll. 51-53):

> Re^{c} removed himself from men:
> He shines
> and the daytime exists,
> but one knows not that noon happened,
> and one is not able to calculate his shadow.
>
> The face (of the sun) is not clear when one looks,
> nor do the eyes fill with water,
> as he (i.e., the sun) is in the sky like the moon.

The section seems self-explanatory and is an impressive sample of the clarity in the observation of meteorological and physiological phenomena.[67]

The third part of the text has an entirely different character from the rest. The request that the king of the South come to the rescue of the suffering country has distinct poetical features. Curious is the formalism at this point, as reflected in the "he" form. This feature is found similarly in Sinuhe B 51 ff. and again in the Nineteenth Dynasty.[68] The invitation to the king of the South to become ruler of all of Egypt is described as a universal desire for changing the prevailing situation. It uses the nautical metaphors of "grasping the oar" and "turning the rudder,"[69] which seem to contain a further allusion to Menthuhotep II and the developments he brought about. The invitation to the king is combined with an admonition to contemporaries to realize the blessings that will come to them, as well as the necessity to subjugate those who are unwilling to embrace a return to order, which applies also to the foreigners and their obligation to respect Egypt's frontiers.

Although the need for order justifies the application of force to attain it, this should not lead to wanton persecution. The admonition to the subjects is followed by one to the king, emphasizing the role of authority rather than suppression to gain respect, although the latter would be in accordance with the letter of the law. The stress on consideration for the shortcomings of men, but also the need for authoritative action, is found similarly in the Instructions for King Merikare^{c}[70] and can to some degree be compared to the pardon Sinuhe eventually receives from the king.[71] The advice on how to resolve the political realities in the eastern border region culminates with two specific recommendations: one proposes the rebuilding of the frontier fortifications to ward off any recurrence of Asiatic infiltration; the other illustrates the depth of the political and human wisdom of Neferyt. While he is opposed to any infiltration, he realizes the need of the bedouin to water their herds in order to bring them through the summer. He thus recommends that they be admitted but only after due supplication and under strict supervision. The custom of allowing bedouin to bring their herds into the Wadi Tumilat during the summer seems to have its beginning in Neferyt's recommendation to King Amenemhet. We find this practice still alive in the Nineteenth Dynasty more than eight centuries later.[72]

The political recommendations are concluded with two adages, one addressed to the king, the other to his subjects. The first is the adjuration to establish order and expel chaos, which is found in almost identical formulations in Ptolemaic times.[73] The second is the assurance that service for the king is profitable for the one who performs it, as stated likewise in Ptahhotep.[74]

The gradually emerging quality of the "Protocol" and its author Neferyt inspires appreciation and respect for this individual and his literary achievement. Can one say that Neferyt, though critical of himself, also realized his capacity to think and to formulate his thoughts in words, and justly foresaw that

> the educated one will pour water for me when he realizes that what I said, happened (ll. 70f.)?

THE HISTORICAL SECTION

The largest part of our text is devoted to Neferyt's deliberations about anticipated developments. As discussed earlier, these are not prophecies by divine inspiration or by a supernatural talent for prognostication, but are descriptions of developments considered possible on the basis of previous experience. The anticipated events thus are a reflection of past history and as such can be considered a summary account of events that happened during a protracted lifetime just prior to the early part of Amenemhet I's reign. Since the time in question is a period about which the available information is particularly limited, any additional information that helps to elucidate it is welcome. Although we have in the text a reflection of historical events that occurred during the later part of the so-called First Intermediate Period, the text should not be taken as a historical narrative. There is a conspicuous intent to discuss the recent past for the new king, but this does not make it descriptive history. If we nevertheless venture to extract historical information from Neferyt's deliberations, we have to be aware of the limitations implicit in such an attempt. First, this is a literary and not a historical text. Whatever historical information it contains serves the overall aims of the composition and is not primarily intended as objective history. Rather, events are alluded to in general terms for their intrinsic rather than their historical significance.

It is equally important to realize the narrowly defined geographical concern of the text and the deliberations it contains. Events are mentioned only because of their impact on the eastern fringe of the Delta, specifically the Wadi Tumilat. In order to avoid drawing a lopsided historical picture, this limitation requires attention. At the same time, the proximity of this area to "Asia" and the reflection of events that did not concern only "Egypt" proper but reached beyond the Isthmus of Suez, make the text a particularly welcome source of information. Lastly, the fact has to be taken into consideration that we have before us a personal view, namely that of Neferyt. That his deliberations about past events are motivated by his desire to entice the king of the South to assume the rule over all of Egypt and come to the succor of the northeastern frontier region is certainly significant. Although this subjectivity might seem reason to reject outright the value of the historical information, what truly "objective" history exists at all? Since history is a reflection of human minds on events, the subjectivity of any historical endeavor is only human.

The reflection on the past is instigated by its similarity to the prevailing physical conditions in the eastern border region. Reference is made to drought at the beginning (11. 24ff.) and at the end (11. 51ff.) of the historical section. The two events are conflated to some degree, but the occurrence of two different afflictions cannot be doubted. The drought at the time Neferyt had his audience or formulated the text serves as a reminder of a similar event in the past and of its consequences. We have thus to presume two occurrences of severe drought within a lifetime or thereabouts, of which the latter occurred in the early part of Amenemhet I's reign, Droughts were a recurrent experience in ancient Egypt,[75] and it is natural to attempt to identify the allusions in our text with mentions of famine in other sources. We know virtually nothing about agricultural conditions in the Northeast of Egypt, as practically the entire text material at our disposal concerns Upper Egypt. Because of the geographical differences between Upper Egypt and the Delta, hydrographic irregularities in the form of a low Nile would affect the two parts of the country differently. A low Nile would be detrimental in the South but would not necessarily have an equal impact in the North. Only severe droughts with extensive heat and evaporation would seriously affect the North.

We do not have any specific information about a famine during the reign of Amenemhet I in our primarily Upper Egyptian sources.[76] This may be accidental, especially in view of the fact that inscriptions dating to his reign are rare. It thus must remain an unsettled question whether the drought described in the text as contemporary with Amenemhet I's early years affected only the Delta or had an equally strong impact on Upper Egypt.

References to famine before the Twelfth Dynasty are numerous,[77] and our next task must be to try to bring them into a chronological scheme. A famine is assumed to have occurred in the late Eleventh Dynasty in the reign of Seankhkare^{c} Menthuhotep III, twenty years before Amenemhet I, based on Ḥeḳanakhte II 2-5:[78] "Do not worry about me! See! I am well and alive! See, you are one who could eat until he was sated or hunger until his eyes were closing. See! The entire land might die, but you shall not hunger!" This translation differs from that of James[79] and Baer,[80] who consider this section as a description of prevailing conditions and not as epistemological assurances. By taking the Old Perfective *mwt* as a stative and rendering "the entire land is dead," an irreconcilable contradiction is produced, because Ḥeḳanakhte and his mother Upi, the recipient of the letter, are obviously alive, and so is his household. If it is thus necessary to see here a dramatic assurance in the face of minor adversities, it should be read *n<n> ḥḳr*[.*ṯn*] "you shall not hunger," following a protasis stating a fictitious condition. Consequently the passage reflects, not a famine, but difficulties not much beyond the normal. However, it does make reference to a famine in the past, the memory of which apparently lingered on for Ḥeḳanakhte's mother.[81] There is no indication of when this dreaded famine occurred, except that it was sometime in the past. Ḥeḳanakhte apparently had not been afflicted personally by it or had been too young to have his memory scarred by the experience. At the time of writing the letter, i.e., year 8 of Seankhkare^{c} Menthuhotep III (± 2002 B.C.), Ḥeḳanakhte was obviously an established person of some age. The suffering of his mother under the famine could easily have been fifty or more years earlier, which would bring the event into the reign of Antef III--Horus Nakht-Neb-tep-nefer[82] (2069-2061 B.C.), when a famine did occur, as attested by Cairo 20502:[83] "I was one who knew how to find a solution when it was lacking on the day of making plans, convincing of speech in the council of the dignitaries, self-controlled on the day of misery . . . Horus Nakht-Neb-tep-nefer, 'Son-of-Re^{c}' Intef, the great one, may he live eternally, said about my plan for supplying this city. . . ." Though not explicit, the mention of a town, presumably Abydos, makes it virtually certain that the allusion concerns a famine.[84] This event would fall approximately ninety years before the writing of Neferyt's text, which is still within the limits of a living tradition.

There are several other mentions of famine whose chronological relation to one another has to be established. Khety I (Siut V 9, 19) states, "I was rich in grain when the land was in a bind" (*ṯs*) and "I was a vigilant one about what was said to him, self-controlled during the miserable years." The date of the tomb is absolutely certain. Khety II (Siut IV) fought for the Heracleopolitan king Merikare^{c} against the Thebans, probably not long before Menthuhotep II's final victory in his thirty-fifth regnal year (2026 B.C.). Khety II (Siut IV) has thus to be considered a contemporary of Menthuhotep II.[85] This probably applies also to his father Tefib (Siut III), who mentions in his tomb-inscriptions, not a famine, but extensive fighting.[86] Khety I (Siut V) is not much separated in time from the two other owners of inscribed tombs at Siut and is probably to be placed a generation earlier.[87] This would make part of his life concurrent with the reign of Horus Nakht-Neb-tep-nefer.

The devastation caused by famine is reflected in the inscription of *Ḏ3ri* (l. 3):[88] "I was a great provider of their house in the year of courage (*snb-ỉb*), as I provided one whom I did not know as well as one whom I knew." His date can be established from another stela of the man now in Cairo $\frac{12}{22} \Big| \frac{4}{9}$,[89] which mentions Horus *W3ḥ-^{c}nḫ* Intef II and contains a reference to the man's efforts "to procure food for the entire land" (i.e., the Thebaïs). This specification expands the chronological range of the "Great Famine" as falling in part into the reign of Horus *W3ḥ-^{c}nḫ*, following fighting between the Theban rulers and the Heracleopolitan kings. This date of the famine in the late reign of Horus *W3ḥ-^{c}nḫ* and early part of that of Horus Nakht-Neb-tep-nefer, i.e., ca. 2075-2065 B.C., can accomodate all the other references to severe famine we have from Upper Egypt.

Of particular significance are the inscriptions of *ᶜnḫ.ty.fy* at Moᶜalla,[90] which report fighting in Upper Egypt against the emerging Theban coalition and also a severe famine (IV 1-30):

> The hereditary prince count plenipotentiary royal knight lector priest overseer of troops overseer of foreigners, overseer of mercenaries, chief administrator of the districts of Edfu and Hieraconpolis Ankhtyfy-nakht, he says: "I gave bread to the hungry, cloth to the naked. I anointed the unanointed, shod the barefoot. I gave a wife to the one who had no wife. I sustained the towns of Hefat, Hormer . . . (where) heaven was overcast and the earth was in the [South] wind, when the hungry one came across to (me) because of the sand-bank of Apophis: the South approached with its people and the North came with its children. When a trading caravan brought the prize of Upper Egyptian grain, I sold it, (so) (my) Upper Egyptian grain went southward as far as Wawat, and north as far as the Thinite district. The entire Upper Egypt was dying from hunger; every man was eating his children; (but) I never allowed a death in this district from hunger. When I gave a seed-loan of Upper Egyptian grain, I did not charge interest. This is not to be found by a previous ruler; never has any overseer of troops of this district done the like. But I sustained the region of Elephantine, and I sustained the Kôm Negan during those years after Hefat and Hormer were satisfied. This is not to be found by any previous father (= ancestor). I acted (as) a mountain for Hefat and as a cool shadow for Hormer." Ankhtyfy said: "While this entire land became locusts in swarming, one going north, the other going south, I never created a fugitive from this district to another--I truly."

Of particular interest in this account is the emphasis on the meteorological phenomenon of the overcast sky, which occurs also in our text (ll. 24ff. and 52f.) and the adverse wind mentioned in IV 9, which it is tempting to restore into *ṯ3w rsy* as in our text, l. 28.

From Ankhtyfy's region comes also the stela of ꞽIti,[91] who claims, "I have sustained Gebelein in the miserable years, when 400 men were in its alimentation.[92] I did not take possession of a man's daughter and I did not take possession of his land . . . I gave Upper Egyptian grain to Hermonthis and Moᶜalla after Gebelein was provided for. While the Thebaïs travelled North and South, I never let Gebelein travel to another district." Although these claims contradict those of Ankhtyfy, it nevertheless can be taken as certain that the two inscriptions refer to the same event.

From Thebes comes the inscription of *Rḥwy*,[93] who was "overseer of priests" of the Amun-temple and who claims, "I supply the grain for the Amum temple in the miserable years and contract slaughtering[94] to give a portion for the offering tables at the beginning of the month and to establish (provisions) at the beginning of the year."[95] Closely related is the inscription of *Snni* (Cairo 20500),[96] which reports, "I measured out Upper Egyptian grain for the supply of this town in the gateway (of the house) of the count overseer of priests *Ḏfi* during the miserable years of courage."[97] From Gebelein and apparently of the same period is the inscription of *Ḥḳ3-ꞽb* (BM 1671),[98] in which it is stated: ". . . I supported this entire city with Upper Egyptian grain during (the) years until I ran out of supplies."[99]

From Dendera comes a statement concerning famine among the inscriptions of *Sn-nḏsw*,[100] which are dated to the Heracleopolitan Period:[101] *ꞽw grt rnpwt ksn(w)t ḫpr.ti n(.ꞽ) snb-ꞽb(.ꞽ) ḏnn(.ꞽ)*. . . . "and when the miserable years happened to (me), I was courageous and dammed up. . . ." The lacking context impairs our understanding of the passage and its significance;[102] it is, however, important as yet another reference to "miserable years" during the Heracleopolitan Period not long before the Theban ascendancy. Chronologically related is the inscription of *Nfr-ꞽw* (MMA 12.183.8),[103] which contains an oblique reference to famine. The address to the living ones opens with two assurances: "I nourished ones greater than me in the time I contracted slaughter (*ꞽw sm.n(.ꞽ) ᶜ3w r(.ꞽ) rnpt nt ḫtm(.ꞽ) rḫs*), and I acted greatly with my arm as far as (i.e., including) children. It was (my) excellence which acted for me, as I was aggrandized more than those greater than (me)." The few statements bristle with difficulties concerning the rendering.[104] Significant for our discussion is the claim to have supplied people, young and old, during a period of distress.

Of the same date but very vague is a passage in the tomb of Mery I at Hargasa:[105] ". . . *prt*-season . . . who were confident that Upper Egyptian grain will arrive. I sustained the poor ones. . . ." From Gebelein comes the stela of a certain *Mrr*,[106] who also makes reference to his actions during difficult times (ll. 8-10): "I sustained my brethren and sisters. I buried those who had died and sustained those who were alive, wherever I settled during this affliction which occurred. I leased their fields and all their *kôms* in town and field." The designation used in reference to the "affliction" is *ṯs*, lit. "sandbank," which is a recurrent metaphor for low water,[107] to the Egyptians synonymous with famine.[108] The expression is so general in nature that it seems unlikely that it was used or coined under the immediate impact of a famine. This suggests that the inscriptions in which it occurs were formulated *post eventum*.

The numerous references, though not particularly explicit, provide a coherent picture. A famine, which was of extreme severity, lasted for a number of years. Although it is described as though it had lasted unabatedly, it is not clear whether we have to assume a number of consecutive years of famine conditions or whether the adversity varied in its severity. It is best attested for southern Upper Egypt but can be ascertained for Middle Egypt as well. There is no indication that it also affected the Delta, but the thesis that the reference to extreme drought in the Delta made by Neferyt should be equated with the attested Upper Egyptian affliction can be taken as a justifiable proposition. While none of the references bears a specific date, there is enough circumstantial evidence to narrow the date of this great famine to a fairly limited range of time, although the memory of it lingered on for many years.[109] On the basis of Ḥeḳanakhte II vs. 3 (see above p. 26) the event should have occurred within the lifetime of a person who was still alive under Menthuhotep II--Nebhetepreᶜ. As there is no indication of a famine during the reign of this king and, furthermore, the events mentioned in connection with the famine exclude a dating to this reign, the famine should be assumed to have happened in the reign of Antef II--Wakh-ᶜankh or Antef III--Nakht-Neb-tep-nefer.

From the military events mentioned in the inscriptions of Ankhtyfy at Moᶜalla it can be assumed that he was involved in the early stages of the Theban secession; this implies for our problem that the great famine should be placed as early as possible in the Eleventh Dynasty. For evidence of a date in the reign of Antef II--Wakh-ʿankh as the setting of the great famine, we have the information contained in the inscription of *D3ri* and others mentioning problems of supply.[110] It must, however, be noted that the late inscriptions of Antef II--Wakh-ʿanhk, such as the "dog-stela" (Cairo 20512) and the stela of Thethi (BM 164), make no reference to famine but report only political expansion. This would suggest that the "great famine" was already sufficiently removed that it could be disregarded. On the other hand, if the famine was as catastrophic as the texts make us believe, a more lasting impact can be expected. Furthermore, a devastating famine that lasted for several years would affect any society so deeply that it would hardly be able to conduct warfare and pursue political expansion for at least a generation. On the basis of this consideration and in view of the subsequent political developments, the great famine would have to be envisaged as having occurred earlier, i.e., either in the reign of Antef I--Seher-tawy or, more likely, in the early years of Antef II--Wakh-ʿankh, i.e., ca. 2100 B.C. This, however, is difficult to reconcile with the date range computed on the basis of Ḥekanakhte II vs. 3. In order to overcome this seeming contradiction it appears necessary to assign the great famine to the early reign of Antef II--Wakh-ʿankh and to pose that another, though minor, famine occurred in the reign of Antef II--Nakht-Neb-tep-nefer or possibly even as late as the early years of Menthuhotep II.[111] The latter could very well have been within the memory of Neferyt, who certainly would not have been alive in the early Eleventh Dynasty. Summing up the rather bewildering evidence, two ways to explain it seem feasible. One is that a great famine occurred in the early part of the Eleventh Dynasty and, corresponding to it, in the Heracleopolitan Tenth Dynasty, the remembrance of which lingered on. The other is that there were two distinct droughts, one in the early Eleventh Dynasty, the other in the reign of Antef II--Wakh-ʿankh or possibly during the early years of Menthuhotep II, which is also reflected in the inscriptions of Khety I (Siut V). The latter thesis seems better suited to account for the widely spread chronology and also allows a connection with the account of Neferyt.[112] Finally, a minor drought occurred at the time Neferyt presented his concerns to King Amenemhet I, inspiring a comparison with the more severe drought experienced in the past and the consequences to which it had led.

According to Neferyt's account, the cause of the famine was an extreme drought that affected the entire hydrography of the Delta, eliminating the existing sources of water supply and silting them up. Not only did the Nile have insufficient water, but the calamity was also combined with extreme heat, aggravated by desert winds. Although it is not mentioned explicitly, it transpires that this disastrous affliction had abated long before Neferyt's audience with Amenemhet I. It can be taken for granted that a natural disaster of the indicated magnitude was not without consequences necessitating extensive reorganization, which is the main concern of Neferyt's presentation. This, of course, would primarily involve a reopening of the water supply in order to make possible a reorganization of the easternmost part of the Delta, especially the Wadi Tumilat. Neferyt does not mention this necessity in detail. His silence on this point suggests a restoration of the water supply before the reign of Amenemhet I, for the events described cannot be envisaged without water. Consequently, the water supply must have been restored once the drought had ended. While we have no contemporary historical record concerning such a deed, we find it reflected in Merikare^{c} (P. 99), *šd mḏnit r . . . s smḫ gs.s (r) Km-wr mk sy m hp n ḫ3styw* "dig a canal so that it . . ., fill it as far as Lake Timsah, as it is the lifeline for the foreigners (desert dwellers)."[113]

A drought of the severity indicated by our text would hardly have been limited to the Delta but must have affected the adjoining regions in the East and the West as well. The first to feel the impact would be those living on the fringes of civilization as hunters or as bedouin. The former seem to have had ethnic, but not social, connections with the society of Egypt; the bedouin (*Styw*) however, were treated as an ethnically separate group.[114] The adverse circumstances forced both groups, who had pursued their livelihood at the edge of Egypt's domain, to seek shelter inside Egyptian territory, thus increasing the difficulties already existing for the sedentary population.[115]

Clearly distinct from these familiar and basically harmless groups were the *^{c}3mw* "Asiatics." Whereas the others were seeking a haven in Egypt to survive during the calamity, the Asiatics are described as attackers in a military sense. There is no indication that this aggression occurred in temporal proximity to the famine. Although the possibility of instigation by the drought is conceivable, there is no support for it in the available account. It thus seems justified to consider it a separate event. There is no indication that it was a recurrent phenomenon, and so we seem right to postulate on specific military attack and intrusion by Asiatics.

This event, which has to be carefully distinguished from the recurrent temporary infiltration by nomads into the eastern Delta to seek refuge from the impact of the summer heat on the areas in which they grazed their flocks, is clearly described as a military attack, which was at least partly successful because of Egypt's weakness as a result of the drought. The approximate date can be established by using the drought as *eventum post quod*, which allows an assignment to the early Tenth Dynasty. As there is no mention of a prior attack,[116] this event can be used as the pivot in the delineation of the political relations between Egypt and Asia, i.e., the Negev and southern Palestine. First of all, it contradicts the widely held thesis that Asiatics invaded Egypt at the end of the Sixth Dynasty and that they caused the fall of the Old Kingdom and the alleged turmoil of the First Intermediate Period.[117] The sequence of events as arranged in the Protocol of Neferyt places the invasion at a relatively late point in the First Intermediate Period, falling in the Tenth Dynasty.

The arrival of aliens in search of land is mentioned in Admonitions 3, 1 *pḏwt rwty ỉi.ti n Kmt* "alien foreigners have come for arable land,"[118] which might be taken to refer to a more serious intrusion than the recurrent--if not annual--entry by bedouin. The information gained from the Admonitions is limited by the broken context to the fact of an intrusion. Somewhat more substantial information can be gathered from the Instructions for King Merikare^{c}," where two references can be found. Merikare^{c} (P. 83), "The East is full of foreigners and its taxes are lacking" refers to a state of affairs in which foreigners had settled in the East and had become a burden on its administration. It is not clear how the foreigners came there, so it is difficult to evaluate the historical implication of the passage. It certainly resembles the concerns voiced by Neferyt about the state of affairs prior to the attack by the Asiatics.[119] Whereas this passage concerns the economic and administrative impact of foreigners, Merikare^{c} (P. 94-97) has distinct military overtones:[120] "As I live (scil. I swear)--as long as I existed and those foreigners were in their walled fortification, my (?) troops did open and attack them, as I caused the Delta to strike them." Although it is not entirely certain, it seems that Merikare^{c}'s predecessor Khety had made attempts to reverse the situation in the Delta and had brought the intruders under control. It apparently was also he who instigated the fortification of the eastern

Delta to forestall a recurrence of such an intrusion.[121]

The section describing a surprise attack against a fortification by intruders (ll. 33-34) makes it necessary to presuppose the existence of defense fortifications. It is not clear if the episode is based on a past experience or if it serves as a general observation that a surprise attack is feasible because of the adverse conditions.

The effect of the foreign invasion is described as disastrous for the eastern Delta and its population, which is decimated. This situation is also mentioned in Admonitions 3, 2, where the mention of foreign intruders is followed by *nn ms wn rmṯ m st nb* "there are no (Egyptian) people in any place." The description Neferyt gives in ll. 35-36 is very similar.[122]

A completely unrelated development in the account is the outbreak of internecine fighting, with all its extreme brutality. The historical events mirrored by these passages apparently are the battles that eventually led to the overthrow of the Heracleopolitan rulers by the Theban Eleventh Dynasty. The pictures in which the situation is cast are gloomy indeed and resemble those contained in the Admonitions of an Egyptian Sage.[123] It is tempting to equate the two accounts and connect them with the same events. Although the general background is fairly clear, it remains ambiguous what stage in the conflict between South and North the descriptions reflect. It is likely that it was not the final military decision in the fight, but the events finally leading to it.[124]

The administrative breakdown is to be attributed either to the Eleventh Dynasty rulers or to the Heracleopolitan kings. It seems that it should be applied rather to the former and that the victorious Thebans had little, if any, regard for the law of the country whose sole masters they had become. The rulers in the distant Thebes might have tried to carry out the necessities of government, but their liegemen seem to have taken a different attitude, trying to benefit from their situation as much as possible. The disintegration affects especially the execution of law (ll. 47ff.).

Demagoguery, the impact of which is particularly spurned, is also a topic in Merikare^c (P. 23-24 and 27). It is most tempting to assume that the two passages have the same concern, but the formulation is much too general to allow any specification of a historical person or event. From the few details that can be gleaned, the reference could be suspected to refer to a socioeconomic movement primarily in the North, aiming for a redistribution of economic resources.[125]

The outcome of the administrative breakdown is an increase in the officialdom, with many drawing advantages from their political situation, very much to the detriment of the country. Similar allusions are contained in the Instructions for King Merikareᶜ,[126] and one gets the impression that this revolutionary age coincides with the earlier years of Menthuhotep II before he overcame the Heracleopolitans. The possibility of using promises of social reform in his fight with the North is not beyond reason, but it lacks substantiation.[127] The indications in the Instructions for King Merikareᶜ rule out the possibility that the references concern events after the fall of the Heracleopolitans. Although a connection with the events at the very end of the Eleventh Dynasty is not totally impossible, it would require the Instructions for King Merikareᶜ to have been written, not under Heracleopolitan rule, but later, and to have used the setting in the past as a literary device.

The past immediately prior to Neferyt's audience with Amenemhet I appears to be alluded to in two references. One concerns the rule by a weakling in command, which probably applies to Nebtawyreᶜ-Menthuhotep IV, the last of the Eleventh Dynasty Kings.[128] According to Neferyt's description, the general situation had deteriorated to such a degree that eschatological hopes were the only thing that kept men alive.[129] The other is the occurrence of another drought, though less severe than the earlier one, which added to the impact of the socioeconomic upheaval.[130]

It is in the context of these sufferings that Neferyt turned to Amenemhet I and asked him to come to the aid of the tormented country. The legal background of Imeny, whose mother apparently was from Elephantine,[131] is denoted as "the Residence," possibly referring here to Thebes, although it is possible that Imeny at the time was residing at Heracleopolis or even at Memphis. According to the wording, the ruler to whom Neferyt addresses his admonitions was at that time "King of the South" (*nswt n rsy*); only later did he become king of the Two Lands by assuming the double crown, to which Neferyt entices him. The necessity of envisaging two different stages in the royal career of Amenemhet I opens new aspects. The inscription on an offering table in the Alexandria Museum[132] concerns a king named *Ḥr S ḥtp-ỉb-t3wy Nbty S ḥtp-ỉb-t3wy Ḥr-nwb Sm3 Nswt-bit S ḥtp-ỉb-R s3-Rᶜ ʾImn-m-ḥ3t*. Daressy assigned the piece to the Thirteenth Dynasty, and he was followed in doing so by Gauthier.[133] Only Pieper[134] advocated associating the inscription with Amenemhet I in view of the identity of nomen and prenomen. The deviation from Amenemhet I's titulary concerns the other three names. While Amenemhet I has otherwise *Wḥm-mswt* as his Horus and Nebty-name, the inscription has instead *Sḥtp-ỉb-t3wy* "he who (will) satisfy the desire of the Two Lands." This name is strikingly similar to the king's prenomen *Sḥtp-ỉb-rᶜ* and would make perfect sense as the political program of a king setting out to overcome a schism in the country. *Wḥm-mswt* "creation shall be repeated" or "repeater of creation"[135] would seem a rather ambiguous formulation for a political program in the face of the situation Amenemhet I encountered at the beginning of his reign. *Sḥtp-ỉb-t3wy* would seem more appropriate for that time. *Wḥm-mswt*, which is attested from the king's twenty-third year on, makes good sense at a later stage in the king's reign, when the reunification of the country was accomplished. When *Wḥm-mswt* is rendered as "he who will carry out the birth(s)," it can be taken as a promise to bring the beginnings of a new era to fruition. When seen in this way, the coining of the name *Wḥm-mswt* would make good sense only after the foundations for the rebuilding of Egypt after the trauma of the First Intermediate Period were laid out. The twentieth year of the king's reign was an especially important one, for it was then that he had his son Sesostris appointed coregent. This event, which equals a consolidation of the rule, could very well have been the occasion for changes in the titulary of the senior ruler as well.

The early reign of Amenemhet I was not without political problems caused by opposition in Upper Egypt. The threats in the later part of the text (ll. 62-65) reflect reality. Although we know nothing about any actions against Asiatics or Libyans,[136] we learn about internal struggles from Khnumhotep I in his tomb at Beni Hasan.[137] He reports (Urk. VII 12, 3) about accompanying the king on a campaign against the South. The details given are not specific, but it seems that the campaign was primarily conducted against foreign elements, which had settled in Upper Egypt and had usurped power at the expense of the indigenous population and its lawful government.

Once the resistance was broken, the authority held by the king--symbolized by the uraeus on his forehead--would keep any discontented ones in check.[138] This loyalistic outlook is held as a desirable prospect for the king, to entice him to assume the rule of all of Egypt. However, it is combined with the admonition to wield the authority wisely and without causing undue hardship. Such a policy of firm authority without resorting to excessive force is likewise advocated in the Instructions for King Merikare^{c}.[139] The order that Neferyt advocates is one in which the servant loyal to the king can make a career, an idea also expressed in the Instruction of Ptahhotep.[140]

The particular concern of Neferyt throughout his admonitions to the king is the safety and the defense of the easternmost Delta, in particular the Wadi Tumilat. This topic is introduced again at the end of the text with the recommendation that the fortification system "Walls-of-the-Ruler" be rebuilt. Since fortification already existed in the area in question in the Heracleopolitan Period, the reference (1. 66) can only be interpreted as being prospective and concerning a reconstruction rather than an entirely new building. This implies that the fortifications were not yet started when Neferyt had his audience with Amenemhet I but that he strongly recommended their construction. A span of roughly twenty-five years is provided for the construction of fortifications and the setting up of the organization supporting them, because by the end of Amenemhet I's reign, when Sinuhe passed through the Wadi Tumilat (Sinuhe B 17-19), they were fully operative. These fortifications were intended to forestall a recurrence of invasion by Asiatics. The move, however, was not intended to eliminate the other problem in the eastern Delta, namely, the temporary entry of bedouin during the summer heat to water their flocks. Neferyt proposes that they be admitted after due supplication, and he appears to have proposed a system, which is attested again under Merneptah eight centruies later.[141]

The king apparently took Neferyt's advice in this regard and, seemingly, in others as well. The actions at this time were strictly defensive, as was the policy of Sesostris I, according to the words used by Sinuhe.[142] Too many problems within the country required attention. Whatever causes might have instigated the onslaught by Asiatics against the Delta, the Egyptian king did not interfere there; it was apparently left to Palestine to resolve whatever problems were besetting it.

[1] Since its publication only one additional ostracon has been published: O DeM 1261 by Posener, *Catalogue des ostraca hiératiques litteraires de Deir el Medineh* II (Documents des Fouilles XVIII), pl. 68.

[2] Le papyrus Nr. 1 de St. Petersburg, ZAS 14, 1876, 107-111.

[3] Les papyrus hiératiques no. 1115, 1116A, et 1116B de l'Ermitage Impérial à St.-Petersbourg, 1913, pls. 23-25.

[4] In H. Gressmann, *Altorientalische Texte zum Alten Testament* I, 1909, 204-06; the text was translated anew for the second edition, 1926, 46-48.

[5] *New Literary Works from Ancient Egypt* II, Pap. Petersburg 1116B, recto, JEA 1, 1914, 100-05.

[6] *Zapiski Kollegii Vostokovedov pri Aziatskom Mouseie Rossiiskoi Akademii Naouk* 1, 1925, 210-17.

[7] *Littérature et politique dans l'Egypte de la XIIe dynastie*, 1956, 21-60 and 145-57; previous, *idem*, RdE 5, 1946, 255 and RdE 8, 1951, 171-74.

[8] *Untersuchungen zur Überlieferungsgestalt mittelägyptischer Literaturwerke*, Inst. für Orientforschung, Veröffentlichung Nr. 33, 1957.

[9] *Altägyptischer Prophetismus*, Ägypt. Abhandlungen 4, 1960, 97.

[10] *Handbuch der Orientalistik*, ed. B. Spuler, 1. Band, 2. Abschnitt: Literatur,[2] 1970, 144.

[11] *Ancient Egyptian Literature* I, 1973, 139.

[12] See above note 7.

[13] See also H. Brunner, *Grundzüge einer Geschichte der altägyptischen Literatur*, 1966, 53ff.

[14] In particular Posener, Faulkner.

[15] See below p. 81.

[16] Cf. especially Wilson, *loc. cit.*, 444; similarly Otto, *loc. cit.*, 144; Posener, *op. cit.*, 28.

[17] Struve, *loc. cit.*, 218, proposed to identify *ᴵImny* with Amenemhet II on tenuous grounds, a suggestion that has found no acceptance; see the discussion of Posener, *op. cit.*, 23f. The identification was first proposed by E. Meyer, *Geschichte des Altertums* I, 2 § 280A.

[18] *Op. cit.*, 60, "La Prophétie de Neferty, inspirée par le roi ou par son entourage, exploite les goûts, les souvenirs, les craintes et les espoirs des hommes de ce temps pour mettre en valeur les premières initiatives d'Aménémès Ier et pour consolider son autorité encore précaire"; similarly Brunner, *op. cit.*, 53-56.

19 See Urk.VII 12, 3ff.; W. C. Hayes, *The Middle Kingdom* (CAH), 35f.

20 *Loc. cit.*, 234.

21 *Op. cit.*, 37.

22 Golenischeff, ZAS 14, 1876, 109 considered reading it *Nefer-her* but abandoned it in his edition of the text. The form *Nfr-rḥw* was introduced by Gardiner, who transcribed it 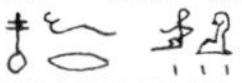 , in which form it is listed in H. Ranke, *Ägyptische Personennamen* I, 197, 20, where it is affiliated with *S3t-Nfr-rḥw* in Cairo 20142 d.

23 Ranke, *op. cit.*, 204, 8.

24 *Neferti im Alten Reich*, ZAS 84, 1959, 157 f. A possible parallel is ASAE 16, 1917, 212.

25 A. Fakhry, *Sept Tombeaux 17*, which is of late Old Kingdom date.

26 Posener, RdE 8, 1951, 174, note 12, proposed reading it *Nfrti* ( ) in support of his transcription of the other form of the name. However, this would produce an unusual male name, so that Gardiner's reading *Nfry* (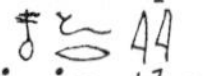) remains more convincing; cf. Gardiner, *Hieratic Papyri in the British Museum* III, pl. 19.

27 Gardiner, *op. cit.*, 39. For Ḫty and his role as an author, cf. Goedicke, *The Report About the Dispute of a Man with His Ba*, 5 ff.

28 Cf. Ranke, *op. cit.*, 203, 15.

29 See Goedicke, *op. cit.*, 6f., *idem*, *The Berlin Leather Roll* (P. Berlin 3029), *Festschrift zum 150jährigen Bestehen des Berliner Ägyptischen Museums*, 104.

30 It was first introduced by Golenischeff, ZAS 14, 1876, 107ff., and has found universal acceptance.

31 Cf. Posener, *Littérature et politique*, 22; Brunner, *op. cit.*, 53.

32 The fragment of a private double statue mentioning King *Sᶜnḫ-k3-rᶜ* found at the Khataᶜna is not an "official" monument, and its raison d'être in that place is obscure; cf. Petrie, Tanis II, pl. XLII.

33 See Goedicke, *Remarks on the Hymns to Sesostris III*, JARCE 7, 1968, 23ff.

34 Cf. Posener, *op. cit.*, 36f., who discusses the distinct limitations of the text's concern and considers it possible, though hypothetical, that "Heliopolis pouvait avoir son prétendant au trône de l'Egypte" or that Amenemhet I encountered special difficulties to establish himself in the eastern Delta.

35 See Goedicke, *The Report About the Dispute of a Man with His Ba*, 5ff.

36 See Posener, *op. cit.*, 29ff.; Brunner, *op. cit.*, 53.

37 See D. Wildung, *Die Rolle ägyptischer Könige im Bewusstsein ihrer Nachwelt I*, MAS 17, 116ff., in particular also his listing of the priests of

Snofru during the Middle Kingdom, 124ff.

38 See Goedicke, *Die Laufbahn des Mṯn*, MDIK 21, 1966, 1ff., especially 70.

39 See below p. 54.

40 See Posener, *op. cit.*, 22ff.

41 Posener, *op. cit.*, 27 explains *ʾImny* as a nisbeh, "celui qui appartient à Amon," disregarding the determinative  in Ermitage 58 and OGardiner 331, which contradicts such an interpretation. This determinative (Gardiner, Sign List A 4) is normal with *ỉmn* "to hide" but out of place in a derivate from the god Amun. The thesis of *ʾImny* as derivate from Amun was expanded by Lanczkowski, *op. cit.*, 98, into an anticipation of a religious reformation at the beginning of the Twelfth Dynasty.

42 As we have no records of Amenemhet I's early years, the possibility cannot be ruled out that "Ameny" was in use when the later Amenemhet I was king only of the South. Ameny as hypocoristic for Amenemhet is attested; cf. Newberry, *Beni Hasan I*, pl. VII = Urk.VII 17,4,9 and 7,12.

43 For this literary genre see A. Hermann, *Die ägyptische Königsnovelle*, LAS 10, 19, 38; S. Herrmann, *Die Königsnovelle in Ägypten und in Israel*, Wiss. Zeitschr. Univ. Leipzig 3, 1953/4, Heft 1, 51-62; Posener, *op. cit.*, 30f.; 137ff.; Otto, *loc. cit.*, 172ff.

44 That Khufu asks to be entertained is probably a slant on his personality of which later Egyptians did not particularly approve; cf. the careful probing of the king's character and its juxtaposition with Snofru by Posener, *op. cit.*, 11ff.; 30f.

45 The Pap. Westcar has been dated to the Second Intermediate Period, but recently an assignment to the Twelfth Dynasty has become customary; cf. Brunner, *op. cit.*, 46ff.; Spiegel, *Handbuch der Orientalistik* I, 2^2 158. For the vernacularisms, considered as early occurrences of Late Egyptian features, see Kroeber, *Die Neuägyptizismen vor der Amarnazeit*, 1970, 22f., who assigns the text to the Second Intermediate Period.

46 See the definition of this literary genre by S. Herrmann, *op. cit.*, 11.

47 Otto, *loc. cit.*, 173, sees in Fischer, *Inscriptions from the Coptite Nome*, An.Or. 40, 112ff., fig. 16 a/b, pl. 37, a forerunner of this literary genre in the Eleventh Dynasty, because the text cites some direct speeches. However, the "Königsnovelle" is more than a frame for royal statements. The latter can be found incorporated already in tomb inscriptions of the Old Kingdom (e.g., Urk.I 42, 151, 232, 9-11) and the Heracleopolitan Period (e.g., Siut IV 19) and thus should be separated from a discussion of the "Königsnovelle."

48 See Goedicke, *Die Geschichte des Schiffbrüchigen*, Äg.Abh. 30, 1ff.

49 Goedicke, *The Berlin Leather Roll* (P. Berlin 3029), *Festschrift zum 150jährigen Bestehen des Berliner Ägyptischen Museums*, 87-104.

50 Peasant B 1,80 "Then it shall be brought to us in writing so that we can hear it."

51 Cf. Goedicke, *Diplomatical Studies in the Old Kingdom*, JARCE 3, 1964, 31-41; *idem, Four Hieratic Ostraca of the Old Kingdom*, JEA 54, 1968, 23ff., in particular 26.

52 This is the view expressed by Posener, *op. cit.*, 24: "Si on tient compte du fait que le tableau pessimiste peint par le voyant contient, à n'en pas douter, une part d'exagération, on voit qu'il n'y a pas incompatibilité entre ce que recouvre la vision prophétique et la situation réelle au passage entre la XIe et la XIIe dynasties." That the poet or writer concentrates the events to make their bearing more transparent is not necessarily an exaggeration, but is rather to be seen as "poetical truth" *versus* historical description.

53 It is in this vein that Posener takes it.

54 See in particular Scharff, *Der historische Abschnitt der Lehre für König Merikarê*, SAW, München, 1936, 8.

55 See below p.

56 Advanced age is implicit in the description of him by the courtiers (ll. 9-11): "there is a renowned lector priest of Bastet . . . a citizen is he, valiant with his arm, a scribe is he, excellent with his fingers, a wealthy one is he, who has greater wealth than any peer of his."

57 Rulers in ancient Egypt never saw it necessary to separate their years of rule according to differing constitutional conditions. Just as those who spent their early years as coregents of their predecessor included those years in the final count of their regnal years, it can be taken for granted that a change in the extent of jurisdiction would be disregarded in the counting of regnal years and that all years of rulership would be treated alike.

58 This is evident first of all in the arrangement as a teaching of a father to his son, which is the basic pattern in the Wisdom Literature; cf. Brunner, *Die Lehren, Handbuch der Orientalistik* I 2^2 114f. At the same time, the Instructions for King Merikare occupy a special place in the genre of Wisdom Literature, as they blend moral with political issues.

59 See Goedicke, *Probleme der Herakleopolitenzeit*, MDIK 24, 1969, 136-43.

60 He might have been the one defeated by Menthuhotep II, and in this role he would hardly have warranted any special esteem by posterity.

61 Previously, in *The Report about the Dispute of a Man with His Ba*, 7f., I considered this wisdom text, together with the Eloquent Peasant and the Report about the Dispute of a Man with His Ba as an *oeuvre* of Khety dating to the early Twelfth Dynasty. While I see no reason to change my opinion of Khety, I am now more inclined to accept the existence of a wave of major literary creativity in the late Heracleopolitan Period, possibly all to be assigned to Neferyt.

62 In the Instruction of Ptahhotep reference is made only to verbal transmission and not to a written form; cf. Ptahhotep 38, 628.

63 Despite its attribution to Kagemni, who is usually identified with the well-known vizier of the Sixth Dynasty, I am no longer convinced that

this wisdom text is actually the work of this official. Kagemni, who inscribed his tomb with adages in the nature of Wisdom Texts (see Edel, *Die Biographie des K3j-gmjnj* [Kagemni], MIO 1, 1953, 210ff.), is not mentioned later among the sages of the past in Pap. Chester Beatty IV vs. 3, 5-7 or in a Nineteenth Dynasty stela listing famous men (Yoyotte, BSFE 11, 1952, 67-72). The Instruction of Kagemni is dated to King Snofru, when he succeeded his predecessor Huni. This is undoubtedly an anachronism, and Posener, RdE 6, 1951, 31ff., suggested that the text was written by a certain Kaires, possibly a contemporary of Ptahhotep, a view followed principally by Yoyotte. The dominant role of Snofru is noteworthy and would not suit a Sixth Dynasty date except at the very end of the reign of Pepi I, when there was a short-lived interest in the Fourth Dynasty king. It is not before the early Twelfth Dynasty that there is a substantial interest in Snofru. The possibility of dating the Instruction of Kagemni after the Old Kingdom receives support from the designation of Snofru as *nswt mnḫ* "beneficent king," which is also used in our text (1. 1).

[64] See Helck, *op. cit.*, 59f; Posener, *op. cit.*, 146f.

[65] Cf. Posener, *Sur l'emploi de l'encre rouge dans les manuscrits égyptiens*, JEA 37, 1951, 75-80.

[66] Descriptions of the recent severe drought in sub-Saharan Africa use similar language; cf. *National Geographic*, April 1977, pp. 544ff.

[67] Cf. Fischer, *Further Evidence for the Logic of Ancient Egyptian: Diminishing Progression*, JARCE 10, 1973, 5-9; see also Junker, *Die Götterlehre von Memphis*, AAW Berlin, 1939, 23, 69; Goedicke, The Inscription of *Ḥr-wr-r*ᶜ, MDIK 18, 1962, 14-25.

[68] Cf. Grapow, *Anreden* II, 59f. It is noteworthy that this kind of formulation occurs again with Ramesses II (Kitchen, *Ramesside Inscriptions* II, 258ff.) and his successor.

[69] Nautical comparisons are recurrent in the Eloquent Peasant, e.g., B 1, 171, 190, 267 et al.

[70] Merikareᶜ P. 45ff.

[71] Cf. Sinuhe B 181ff.

[72] Pap. Anastasi VI 51ff.; Caminos, *Late Egyptian Miscellanies*, 293ff.

[73] Wb.II 405, 11; see de Buck, *La littérature et la politique sous la douzième dynastie égyptienne*, *Symbolae van Oven* 1946, 1ff.; Cf. also the adage closing of the Berlin Leather Roll. Goedicke, *The Berlin Leather Roll*, (P. Berlin 3029), Festschrift zum 150jährigen Bestehen des Berliner ägyptischen Museums, 103.

[74] Ptahhotep 588f. "A son who hears is a follower of Horus; it goes well with him when he has listened."

[75] See in particular Vandier, *La famine dans l'Égypte ancienne*, Cairo, 1936.

[76] A famine is mentioned by *ᵓImny* for the reign of Sesostris I (Urk.VII 16,

8-16). This event is probably to be identified with the low Nile said to have occurred in a "twenty-fifth regnal year" in U.C. 14333. Different from my previous date (JEA 48, 1962, 27), I now follow Schenkel's attribution of the text to the reign of Sesostris I, especially in view of the similarity with Louvre C.167; see, JEA 50, 1964, 6f.

77 See Vandier, *op. cit.*, 100-113; also B. Bell, *The Dark Ages in Ancient History: I, The First Dark Age in Egypt*, AJA 75, 1971, 1-26.

78 James, The Ḥekanakhte Papers, 32f., pl. 5; Baer, *An Eleventh Dynasty Farmer's Letter*, JAOS 83, 1963, 1-19; cf. also B. Bell, *loc. cit.*, 16f.

79 *Op. cit.*, 32, "Do not worry about me. See! I am healthy and alive. See! you are that one who ate until he was satisfied and hungered until his eyes sunk (in his head) (?) See! the whole land is perished while [you] are not hungry!"

80 *Loc. cit.*, 7, "Don't worry about me. I am well and alive! Now, you are (like) the man who ate until he was satisfied when he was hollow-eyed with hunger. The entire land is dead, but [you] have not been hungry."

81 I wonder whether Hetepet, the second lady to whom the letter is addressed, is not Ipi's sister and thus Ḥeḳanakhte's aunt. The esteem shown her and the closeness in the mention suggests such an interpretation.

82 *Nḫt-nb-tp-nfr*, the traditional rendering of the name, can only be understood as "Strong/victorious will be the lord of a good beginning." The name suggests previous difficulties that the political program of the ruler, as expressed by the royal nomen, promises to alleviate.

83 Lange and Schäfer, *Grab- und Denkmalsteine des Mittleren Reiches* (CCG) 93; Schenkel, *Memphis--Herakleopolis--Theben*, Äg.Abh. 12, 109f; Vandier, *op. cit.*, 112.

84 Schenkel, *ibid.*, suggests that Cairo 20503 is to be joined with Cairo 20502, which corroborates the thesis of a famine, because the second text mentions [*sᶜnḫ.n.ỉ*] *niwt rnpt ḳsnt n-mrwt nfr rn.(ỉ)* "I [supplied] the town in the miserable year so that my name might be good"; cf. Vandier, *op. cit.*, 113.

85 Cf. Schenkel, *Frühmittelägyptische Studien*, 24; Brunner, *Die Texte aus den Gräbern der Herakleopolitenzeit von Siut*, Äg.Forsch. 5 38f.

86 Siut III 16 ff.; cf. Brunner, *op. cit.*, 18; Schenkel, *Memphis--Herakleopolis--Theben* 69ff.

87 Brunner, *op. cit.*, 39.

88 Petrie, Qurneh pl. II-III; Speleers, *Recueil des inscriptions égyptiennes* 15, no. 65; Clère and Vandier, *Textes de la Première Période Intermédiaire* (TPPI), § 19; Schenkel, *op. cit.*, § 73.

89 Petrie, *op. cit.*, pl. II-III; Clère and Vandier, *op. cit.*, § 18; Schenkel, *op. cit.*, § 72.

90 Vandier, Moᶜalla, *Bibl. d'Etude* 18, Inscr. no. 10, pp. 220ff.; Kees,

Orientalia 21, 1952, 86ff.; Schenkel, *op. cit.*, § 37; Vandier, *La Famine* 105.

91 Cairo 20001; Lange and Schäfer, *op. cit.*, III, Taf. 1; Daressy, RT 14, 18, 21; Vandier, *Mélanges Maspero I*, 66, 137-45; Breasted, *Ancient Records* I, §§ 457-59; Kees, *Kulturgeschichte* 41; Schenkel, *op. cit.*, § 39; *idem*, *Frühmittelägyptische Studien*, § 60 g-m.

92 Breasted, and following him Vandier, took *zz3* as "détresse," while Schenkel, *op. cit.*, 57, note c, renders it "Ratlosigkeit." There is no cognate to justify such an interpretation, and the view taken in Wb. III 474,14 in rendering it "alimentation" seems more convincing, especially since it is affiliated with *ss3* in Wb.IV 275.

93 Petrie, *op. cit.*, pl. X; Clère and Vandier, *op. cit.*, § 7; Vandier, *La famine*, 109; Schenkel, *op. cit.*, § 18.

94 Vandier, *La famine*, 109, had rendered *ḫtm rḫz* as "un contrat ayant été fait pour un sacrifice d'animaux," while Schenkel, *op. cit.*, § 18, gives for it "in Notjahren, wo man das Schlachtstück (?) versiegelt (?), um am Monatsanfang für die Opfertische zu spenden und um am Jahresbeginn zu spendieren." *Rnpwt ksn(w)t* refers to a specific period of misery and should not be considered a recurrent event for which standard measures of amelioration existed. Fischer, *Dendera in the Third Millenium B.C.*, 207f., in discussing MMA 12.183.8 (see below p. 29), prefers rendering *ḫtm rḫz* as a figurative expression for famine meaning literally "closing the pouch." *Ḫtm* occurs in the same inscription in the preceding line with the meaning "to contract," which makes it improbable to have here a widely different application of the verb. Furthermore, as the famine is already indicated by *rnpwt ksn(w)t*, a second expression denoting this adversity would be redundant and meaningless. The emphasis on *Rḥwy's* exactitude in carrying out his obligation in the face of grave difficulties would also remain unexpressed.

95 *Wpt* denotes the "opening day" in both occurrences, first of a month, second of a year; see Černý, *The Words for the First and Last Day of a Month*, ASAE 51, 1951, 444-46. Schenkel, *ibid.* is principally right, while Vandier, *op. cit.*, 109, connected both specifications with "le jour de la fête de l'ouverture de l'année." 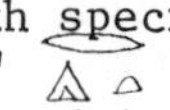 is to be taken as *r* + infinitive; for the infinitive *dit*, cf. Edel, Altägyptische Grammatik § 687. For *ᶜ* "portion" of food, see Wb.I 158,6. 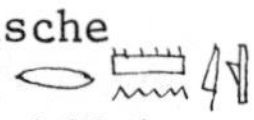 is, parallel to *r dit*, also *r* + infinitive; for *mny* "to establish with *(m)*," see Wb.II 74, 15-16; Sinuhe B 78f.; Merikare P. 61, where it is used parallel to *pr* and *s3ḥ*. The latter suggests that *mny* has the connotation of an administrative commitment established at the beginning of the year concerning the amount of provisions to be supplied during the year.

96 Lange and Schäfer, *op. cit.*, III, Taf. XXXIV; Clère and Vandier, *op. cit.*, § 9; Schenkel, *op. cit.*, § 20; Vandier, *La famine*, 111f.

97 The text appears to have an indirect genitive **rnpwt ksn(w)t nt snb-ib*, although this makes little sense. I wonder if *nt* is not a dittography, so that it should read **m rnpwt ksn(w)t snb ỉb(.ỉ) ỉr.n(.ỉ) m tp-nfr* ". . . in the miserable years. My heart was always well (i.e., I was courageous) when I acted properly. . . ."

98 Polotsky, JEA 16, 1930, 194-99, pl XXIX; Vandier, *op. cit.*, 107; Schenkel, *op. cit.*, § 40.

99 Polotsky, *op. cit.*, 194-96 rendered ". . . for many (?) years, not to speak of the . . .," assuming an occurrence of the particle *rs-si* after *rnpwt*. A different view was taken by Schenkel, *op. cit.*, 59, note d, who read *rnpwt rs-si ḥri.ỉ r zḫnwt* ". . . sogar in Jahren, in denen ich (selbst) fern von Vorräten war." While his rendering "stores" for *zḫnwt* seems convincing, I see no reason for the particle *rs-si* in this place; the proposed rendering would require a construction with an Old Perfective that would have to have some kind of introduction. I prefer to render *r sḥr(.ỉ)*, taking it as *r* + passive *sḏm.f*, thus rendering it literally "until I was made distant from stores."

100 Petrie, Dendereh pl. X, 4; Schenkel, *op. cit.*, § 125; Fischer, *op. cit.*, 162, fig. 31.

101 Fischer, *op. cit.*, 187, who dates him "close to Dynasty XI."

102 Schenkel, *op. cit.*, p. 139, renders "Es waren nämlich (?) schlimme Jahre der Hungersnot gekommen . . ."; similarly Fischer, *op. cit.*, 162, "there came miserable years of famine." However, *ḫpr* cannot be an Old Perfective as both translators apparently assume, because *rnpt* is feminine, making it necessary to take 𓈖𓏏 as a metathetical spelling for 𓏏𓈖, i.e., *ḫpr.ti n(.ỉ)*. For *ḫpr n* "to happen to somebody," cf. Wb.III 262, 16; Hatnub Gr. 14,8; JEA 47, 1961, 7.

103 Hayes, *Scepter of Egypt* I, 139f; fig. 82; Fischer, JARCE 2, 1963, 19; Schenkel, *op. cit.*, § 26; Fischer, *Dendera in the Third Millenium B.C.*, 206ff.

104 *ꜥ3w* is juxtaposed here with *ẖrdw*, so that it denotes here primarily "elders"; cf. JARCE 3, 1964, 28; otherwise *ꜥ3w* is paired with *nḏsw* (Petrie, *Dendereh*, pl. IX; Cairo 20503) and with *šri* (Cairo 20507); cf. Fischer, WZKM 57, 1961, 69-71; *idem*, JARCE 10, 1973, 5. *R mn m* was taken by Hayes, *ibid.*, as an infinitival construction "in order to be established among my children." He was followed by Schenkel, *ibid.*, as "um unter meinen Kindern fortzudauern," while Fischer, *op. cit.*, 208 favored a construction *r* + *sḏm.f* "that I might remain among my children." To nourish the elders in order to endure among one's own children strikes me as an illogical proposition. Therefore, I take *r-mn-m* as the compound prepositional expression "as far as" and understand it figuratively as having inclusive force. An inscription cited by Fischer *op. cit.*, 206, note 813, *ỉw ḥ3.n(.ỉ) r m33 rmṯw r-mn-m ẖrdw* "I strove so that the people including the children could see" corroborates this rendering.

In the participial statement, I follow Fischer, Kush 9, 1961, 52, note 10, in reading it *ỉ3k(.ỉ)* "my power," rather than posing a phonetic *ỉkr* > *ỉḳ3* as Schenkel proposes, or Fischer, *Dendera in the Third Millenium B.C.*, 208, who sees here an obscure deity *ỉḳ(w)*. To credit a deity with the accomplishing of personal deeds would be a most unusual formulation, especially for the time the inscription was written.

All translators take 𓋴𓏏 as the impersonal object, but it lacks an antecedent. I take 𓋴𓏏 rather as a writing for the particle *st*. That the form *st* is not restricted to cases where a pronoun follows was pointed out by Edel, *Altägyptische Grammatik*, § 852. The dependent sentence thus reads *sꜥ3.ỉ r ꜥ3w r.ỉ* with *ꜥ3w (ỉ)r.ỉ* "greater ones than me" as a comparative.

Although all translators have taken as a writing for *srw* "officials," it has to be pointed out that the designation *sr* is written with the sign . Consequently, it is necessary to read as *wrw*. The Old Perfective *mtr* is written with the plural ending -*w* spelled out, while *(i)r(y)t(.i)* "that which concerns me" is its object. For the spelling of *(i)r(y)t*, see Edel, *op. cit.*, 347, 2. The passage should be read *wrw mtrw (i)r(y)t(.i)* and not **wrw m mtr wi* as Fischer, *Dendera in the Third Millenium B.C.*, proposes.

105 Petrie, Athribis pls. VI-XII; Urk.I 266,10-11; Schenkel, *op. cit.*, § 28; Fischer *op. cit.*, 162, note 703. For the dating of the text see Fischer, *op. cit.*, 130, note 574. Sethe restored *rnpwt* [ ] , which has been accepted but which I find doubtful, despite my inability to forward another restoration.

106 Černy, *The Stela of Merer in Cracow*, JEA 47, 1961, 5-9 and pl. I; Schenkel, *op. cit.*, § 42; M. Lichtheim, *Ancient Egyptian Literature*, I 87f.

107 Cf. Vandier, *La famine*, 74ff.; *idem*, *Studies in Egyptology and Linguistics in Honor of H. J. Polotsky*, 10. Turin 1310, which is discussed there, reads, however, *nḫt n.f ṯzw nyw t3* "the land-troops were victorious for him," and there is no allusion to famine whatsoever.

108 Cf. William Willcocks and James I. Craig, *Egyptian Irrigation*,[3] 1913, 237; cf. Pliny, *Nat. Hist.* V, 10; see also Kees, *Das alte Ägypten* 1955, 22ff.

109 B. Bell, *loc. cit.*, 7ff., is misled in taking the text as reflecting only contemporary events. After all, they were not written as historical records, but as funerary texts. Consequently, she wishes to spread the texts over a period of three-quarters of a century and hypothesizes more than one famine resulting from the "decline of the Neolithic Wet Phase"; cf. also Butzer, *Die Naturlandschaft Ägyptens während der Vorgeschichte und der Dynastischen Zeit*, Mainz, Abh., Math.-naturw.Kl. 1, 1959. Her early date, particularly the Eighth Dynasty, is probably influenced by the widespread notion that the Old Kingdom collapsed in turmoil and that the Admonitions of an Egyptian Sage reflect the accompanying events. This is, however, an unfounded assumption, and there are few signs, aside from possible dynastic troubles, that any major political disruption occurred at the end of the Sixth Dynasty; cf. Goedicke, *Zur Chronologie der sogenannten "Ersten Zwischenzeit,"* ZDMG 112, 1963, 239-54.

110 See above p. 27.

111 Such a thesis could help explain the absence of major political action during this time.

112 This, however, does not resolve the problem of where to place the events described in the Admonitions of an Egyptian Sage. While they are similar enough to allusions in the Protocol of Neferyt that a dating of the Admonitions to the Second Intermediate Period can be rejected, a more precise place in the period between the Sixth and the Eleventh dynasties must await a renewed study of the text.

113 I follow principally W. A. Ward, *Egypt and the East Mediterranean World*,

1971, 30f. It would seem that the proposed canal was to serve two purposes. First, the supplying of water to bedouin without letting them enter into Egyptian territory, as Neferyt proposes (ll. 67ff.); second, a protection of the frontier against incursion, as in the New Kingdom; for this frontier canal, see *American Scientist* 63, 1975, 542-48.

114 There is no specification of the ethnic affiliation of those who make their living by hunting and fishing in the "exotic lakes," i.e., Lake Ballah and Lake Timsah, while "the bedouin roaming the land" clearly are a different group. Completely unconnected with them are the people called Asiatics (*^{c}3mw*), who are portrayed as attackers and whose action is triggered by strife affecting them. For *styw*, cf. Adm. 15, 1; further Sinuhe B 25, where the term is used in reference to bedouin in the eastern Wadi Tumilat, also B 17, where the purpose of the "Walls-of-the-Ruler" is specified as "warding off the bedouin." Other occurrences are Hammamat no. 17 and Cairo $\frac{24|5}{28|5}$ (Habachi, MDIK 19, 1963, 39, fj. 17).

115 L. 32.

116 Merikare^{c} P. 91-98 speaks of skirmishes with Asiatics (*^{c}3mw*) dating back into the distant past. However, the comparison in P. 97f. "do not trouble yourself about him (for) the Asiatic is a crocodile on his riverbank; he will snatch at a single person but will not seize a town of many inhabitants" (see Ward, *op. cit.*, 29f.) implies that no major fight as suggested by Neferyt had occurred at the time of Merykare^{c}'s predecessor. This could be used as the basis for a thesis that a major attack by Asiatics occurred between Merikare^{c} and the beginning of the Twelfth Dynasty. Whether Menthuhotep II's claim of military success against *Styw* is in any way connected with this event remains obscure; for the inscription from Gebelein, see Habachi, King Nebhepetre^{c} Menthuhotp, MDIK 19, 1963, 39, fig. 17, pl. XI b; Schenkel, *op. cit.*, § 325.

117 In particular P. Lapp, *Dhahr Mirzbaneh Tombs* 94ff.; *idem, Palestine in the Early Bronze Age, Near Eastern Archaeology in the Twentieth Century, Essays in Honor of Nelson Glueck,* 1970, 123; also Wilson, *The Burden of Egypt,* 111; K. Kenyon, *Archaeology in the Holy Land,* 1960, 135, 159. Similarly also Helck, *Die Beziehungen Ägyptens zu Vorderasien im 3. und 2. Jahrtausend v. Chr.,* 43.

118 I take *kmt* here in its literal meaning "arable land" (see p. 82) and not as denoting Egypt, as is commonly done. As the approach would be with hostile intention, *ỉỉ* would have to be construed with *r* if the reference were to an attack; the construction with *n* introduces, rather, the purpose of the coming.

119 Ll. 31f.

120 Volten, *Zwei altägyptische politische Schriften,* An. Aeg. IV, 1945, 51, rendered "Aber da ich lebte und noch war, (dann) waren aber die Barbaren wie eine Festungsmauer. Meine Truppen haben (indessen) eine Bresche in sie gebrochen. Ich liess sie Unterägypten betreten"; Faulkner, in *The Literature of Ancient Egypt,* ed. W. K. Simpson, 188, "But I lived, and while I existed the barbarians were as though in the walls of a fortress; my troops broke open. . . . I caused the Delta to smite them"; M. Lichtheim, *Ancient Egyptian Literature* I, 104, "But as I live and shall be what I am, when the bowmen were a sealed wall, I breached their

strongholds, I made Lower Egypt attack them"; Ward, *op. cit.*, 30, "But as I live and as I shall exist! These foreigners were like a sealed wall which opened [immediately] when I pro[ceeded] against it. I caused the Delta to strike them."

121 P. 88-90, "A mooring-post has been driven in the district which I made of the limits of *Ḥbrw* at the Ways-of-Horus, peopled with citizen, filled with the choicest people of the whole land to oppose (the foreigners) with them"; cf. Ward, *op. cit.*, 28f.

122 See below p. 95f.

123 In particular Admonitions 2,1ff.; 5, 10; 6, 7ff.

124 The confinement of fighting to the area of Abydos (P. 73 f.) suggests that the turmoil mentioned by Neferyt occurred after Merikare^{c}, i.e., after the close of the Heracleopolitan rule.

125 The possibility of a revolutionary movement following the Old Kingdom was expressed first by Spiegel, *Soziale und Weltanschauliche Reformbewegungen im alten Ägypten*, 1950, but he found little following. Any attempts to alter socioeconomic conditions should be seen, not as ideologically inspired, but rather as direct reactions to prevailing physical conditions, intertwined with changes in the control of power.

126 Merikare^{c} P. 86f., "what was ruled by one is in the hands of ten" might refer to the same situation, although the passage is usually interpreted differently.

127 It seems that Menthuhotep II had, at least in his earlier years, a much closer relation with his followers than had existed in the late Sixth Dynasty. However, after he became lord of all Egypt, the attitude seems to have changed. This is indicated also by the various changes in the royal name, which reflect an increasing emphasis on the king's elevated power. His first nomen, "He who will sustain the wish of the Two Lands," reflects a political program of serving the wishes of the inhabitants; his second nomen, "Possessor of the White Crown," has a quite different stance, one that is maintained in the third nomen, *Nb-ḥpt-R*^{c} "Possessor of the direction of Re^{c}," with its claim of divine direction in his actions.

128 It was especially Winlock, *The Rise and Fall of the Middle Kingdom in Thebes*, 1947, 53ff., who saw the reign of Neb-tawy-Re^{c}--Menthuhotep IV as a period of civil war, which, however, was considerably mellowed by Hayes, *The Middle Kingdom* (CAH), 34, who sees the transition of power to Amenemhet I in less violent forms. The seeming mention of a "first jubilee" of this king in Hammamat no. 110 is puzzling, because no other text of this king contains a reference to it.

129 This is quite different from Admonitions 4, 2ff., "Great and small say 'I wish I might die!' Little children say 'he ought never to have caused me to live!'" and 2, 12, "Men go to them (scil. the crocodiles) of their own accord." An entirely different aspect of the eschatology is discussed in Merikare^{c} P. 53-57.

130 L. 23.

131 For the objections against her being of Nubian extraction, see below p. 129.

132 Daressy, ASAE 5, 1904, 124, published the inscription, which remained largely unrecognized. V. Beckerath, *Untersuchungen zur politischen Geschichte der Zweiten Zwischenzeit Ägyptens*, Äg.Forsch., 23, does not list this king.

133 *Livre des rois* II, 6.

134 *Ein Wechsel im Horusnamen Amenemhet I.*, ZAS 50, 1912, 119-20; cf. also Omlin, *Amenemhet I. und Sesostris I.*, 22f. All general histories disregard this inscription.

135 It is difficult to render *wḥm* idiomatically. Literally "to repeat," it is also used in the sense "to carry out," as in *wḥm m3ᶜt* "to perform truth"; cf. Goedicke, *Königliche Dokumente aus dem Alten Reich*, 181. This allows rendering the name *wḥm-mswt* as "the one who will carry out the creation," i.e., will act in accordance with the divine plan. It is noteworthy that Merikareᶜ P. 131ff. reflects quite clearly the idea of a divine plan for the creation.

136 The claims of Menthuhotep II in his Gebelein inscription presumably are only traditional. That military action was needed against the Libyans is shown by the campaign conducted by Sesostris in which Sinuhe participated.

137 Newberry, Beni Hasan I, pl. XLIVff.; Sethe, Urk.VII 11ff.; cf. Omlin, *op. cit.*, 28ff.; Hayes, *op. cit.*, 35f.

138 Cf. Sinuhe B, 272-73, "as the 'Green One' (*W3ḏyt*) is placed on your summit, may those with bad intentions be separated from you!"

139 P. 48f. "Beware of punishing wrongfully. Do not kill, it does not serve you. Punish with beatings, with detention, thus will the land be well-rendered" (translation of M. Lichtheim).

140 Ptahhotep 588f., "A son who hears is a follower of Horus, it goes well with him when he has heard."

141 Pap. An. VI, 51ff.

142 Sinuhe B, 73ff., "Send to him! Let him know your name as one who inquires from afar concerning his majesty! He will not fail to do good to a land that will be loyal to him" (translation follows M. Lichtheim).

COMMENTARY

I. THE ROYAL COUNCIL AND THE KING'S REQUEST

I|1 It happened, when the majesty of King Snofru, the blessed, was benevolent king in this entire country:[a]

On one |2 among those days it happened that the administrative council of the Residence entered the Palace to discuss business[b] |3 and that they went forth, when they had discussed business as well as their daily obligations.[c]

And then his majesty said to a nobleman |4 on duty: 'Rush and bring me back the administrative council of the Residence, which has left here after discussing the business on this day!'[d]

And they were promptly ushered in |5 at once.[e]

And then they were prostrate before his majesty, l.p.h., again and then his majesty, l.p.h., said to them:[f]

|6 'Fellows, see, I have summoned you that you seek for me a son of yours who is an experienced one,
a brother of yours in excellence,
|7 a friend of yours whom good fortune favored,
(one) who can tell me some true words and choice |8 opinions,
which should extend the view of my majesty for hearing them!'[g]

a) The frame-story opens with the same words as the "Story of Neferkareʿ and the General Sisene,"[1] establishing an important idiomatic link. The literary renaissance in the early Ramesside Period brings a return of the formulation in the Dedicatory Inscription of Ramesses II, l. 21,[2] but it occurs also in Urk.IV 26,12, which belongs in the literary tradition of the "Königsnovelle."[3] The construction has a forerunner in Urk.I 184,12,[4] which has a setting comparable to the "Königsnovelle."

Nswt mnḫ "benevolent king," see Gunn, JEA 12, 1926, 250f.; Scharff, ZÄS 77, 1942, 18; Gardiner, JEA 32, 1946, 74; Posener, *Littérature et politique*, 32; E. Blumenthal, *Untersuchungen zur Rolle des Königs im Mittleren Reich*, Akad. Wiss. Leipzig Abh. 61.1, 1970, 74; Wildung, *Die Rolle ägyptischer Könige I*, MÄS 17, 114; see also Sinuhe B 44 in reference to the predecessor of Sesostris I and in particular Kagemni (Pap. Prisse 2, 8) in reference to Snofru as *nswt mnḫ m t3 pn r ḏr.f*. The latter appears to have been the model for the occurrence here.[5] The possibility of a direct literary influence would explain the stress on Snofru as "benevolent king" *m t3 r ḏr.f* "in the entire country." There is no a priori reason for such an emphasis, so that one should consider the later passage, ll. 57-58, which describes the savior *ʾImny* as king only of the South until he will take the double crown (ll. 59-60), thus emulating the significance of Snofru.

For Snofru's resurgence in the late Old Kingdom and again at the beginning of the Twelfth Dynasty see Wildung, *op. cit.*, 105ff., and Posener, *op. cit.*, 34. The regard for Snofru as the model of a good Egyptian king is derived from, or at least strongly influenced by, his concern for law. This particular attitude is reflected by his prenomen *Snfrw* "he who makes proper" or "he who will make proper" and his Horus-name *nb-m3ʿt* "lord/master of law." We are probably right in recognizing him as the first major lawgiver of ancient Egypt, who might be reflected in the name Sasychis mentioned by Diodorus Siculus I 94 as a prominent lawgiver.[6] See also below, p. 104.

b) *Wʿ m nn hrw ḫpr* **recurs in Pap.** Westcar 9,21; *Dedicatory Inscription* (Inscription dédicatoire), 26; Kuban-Stela 8; see Westendorf, ZÄS 79, 1954, 65ff.

Ḳnbt nt Ḫnw "administration of the Residence" denotes here the highest administrative body; cf. *ḳnbt nt pr-nswt* in Hatnub Gr. 14,8 and *ḳnbt nt Ḫnw* in Beni Hasan I, pl. XV; the latter reflects the terminology of the time the text was composed; cf. S. Gabra, *Les Conseils de fonctionnaires dans l'Egypte pharaonique*, 18ff.

 is, of course, a New Kingdom adaptation; the Berlin Leather Roll I 3[7] makes it likely that *stp-s3* was used here originally.

The activity of the "court-council" is described as *nḏ-ḫrt*, while the Berlin Leather Roll I 2-4 is more specific, giving *nḏ-r*, *wḏ-mdt ḫft sḏm st* and *swnt-ḥr* "greeting, deciding according to hearing it and instructing," which comprise the council's activities. *Nḏ-ḫrt* is generally rendered "to greet,"[8] which would reduce the king's meeting with his administrative council to a kind of *levée* in the style of the *roi*

soleil. *Nḏ-ḫrt* is literally "to question affairs" with the implication of mutual questioning, i.e., "to discuss" them,[9] in which sense the term is also used below in l. 55. In other words, the *ḳnbt* met with the king to discuss the affairs of the country as a daily practice. This daily administrative council is repeatedly mentioned in the inscriptions[10] and has its parallel in the administrative procedures headed by the vizier.[11]

c) The contents of the meeting remain undisclosed, as they apparently are irrelevant to the concern of the text. The next specification describes the departure of the councilors. In the usual rendering[12] the references to the arrival and departure of the officials remain meaningless as an introduction to the text. However, when *nḏ-ḫrt* is taken as "to discuss business," a specific meaning of the introduction emerges. It is only after attending to the necessary business of ruling the country that Snofru, as a conscientious ruler, turns to other matters. Snofru is thus portrayed as a serious ruler, who places the welfare of the country before his personal interests.

In the second occurrence either *nḏ.sn ḫrt* has past meaning, as in Late Egyptian (cf. Erman, *Neuägyptische Grammatik*² §284), or *nḏ.n.sn ḫrt* in DeM 1183 is the original version. Thus it is to be understood that the "discussing of business" was completed at the time of departure by the members of the council.

Mi nt-ᶜ.sn nt rᶜnb is generally taken as an adverbial qualification of the entire clause. If the concern were the description of a daily practice, it would require a wording **mi rᶜnb* "like every day" and not a comparison with *nt-ᶜ*. The latter denotes "what belongs to the books" or "what belongs to the activity," i.e., fixed "routine" or "duty"; for *nt-ᶜ nt rᶜ nb* cf. Westcar 3,3; Urk.IV 700,7-8; Berlin 1204,12 (Schäfer, *Die Mysterien des Osiris*, Untersuchungen 4, 61). As the "discussion of business" could be held only "according to" (*ḫft*) prescribed regulations and not "like" them, *mi* has to be seen here as having additive meaning; for this use, see Wb.II 38; Gardiner, *Egyptian Grammar*³ §170.3. In short, at the administrative council meeting, not only new business but also the daily duties were discussed.

d) The introduction twice uses the construction infinitive + *pw* + *ꜣir.n.sn*, which has a much more general character than the *ḏd.ꜣin ḥm.f* following it. The serenity and formality of the king's counseling are juxtaposed with the dynamic construction derived from the spoken language describing the ruler's personal action outside the formalities of ruling the country.

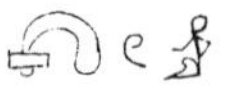 is generally rendered "seal-bearer," "chancellor," "Siegler," or "treasurer."[13] The man seems to act primarily as "courtier," i.e., as a member of the royal retinue rather than as a member of the administrative body or the holder of a specific administrative function. This makes it doubtful whether the man is to be envisaged as a "treasurer" or, for that matter, holder of a particular office. The man does not seem a common servant in the king's household, but rather a follower of distinction. This seems to result from the *nty r gs.f*, which is more than a specification of the man's whereabouts when the king called on him. A specific connotation transpires clearly from Peasant B 1,43, *srw ntyw r gs.f* "the jurors who were on duty," Shipwrecked Sailor, *mk wi r gs.k* "and I am with you," and Medinet Habu I 22,2 *srw smrw nty r gs.f* "officials and courtiers on duty"; cf. *op. cit.*, 310. Consequently, I propose taking the specification here as "nobleman who was on duty" to attend the king.

For the enforced imperative with *ỉzỉ*, see Gardiner, *op. cit.*, §337; it recurs in Peasant R 47; Westcar 8, 9; Sinuhe B 73; 274; Shipwrecked Sailor 13; Kuban Stela 11 and appears to be a colloquial expression; cf. Grapow, *Anreden* III, 24.

ꜥ3 "here" denotes the point of departure.[14] As Posener, *op. cit.*, 148, already pointed out, the wording *ḥr nḏ ḫrt m hrw pn* in O DeM 1184 is superior to *r nḏ ḫrt* in Ermitage 4. *M hrw pn* qualifies *ḫrt* and not *nḏ*, as seems commonly assumed, and should thus be rendered "business (*ḫrt*) on this day," i.e., what had to be done that day was the topic of deliberation.[15]

e) According to ll. 11f. *sṯ3.ỉn.tw n.f ḥr-ꜥ* should be read here, as pointed out by Gardiner, JEA 1, 1914, 102, note 3, and supported by Kuban Stela 12. For *sṯ3* "to usher in" persons to the king, cf. Sinuhe B 264; Westcar 8,10; Bersheh II, pl. XXI; BM 572; Wb.IV 353,1.

f) Ermitage 5 employs here and below (ll. 8 and 12) the spelling *m-b3ḥ*  *ḥm.f;* the ostraca offer no parallel to this idiosyncracy. This extended form[16] of the compound preposition is not otherwise attested in the Middle Kingdom and might be an interpolation of the New Kingdom copyist. The expression seems to convey a particular nuance by anticipating an action rather than specifying a mere location; cf. in particular Loret, *Inscription d'Ahmes* 9; Merikareꜥ P. 62; 124. The specification is significant for the understanding of the etiquette prevailing at the king's audience. It conforms with the description in Sinuhe B 253; cf. also

Urk.I 41,15 and H. Müller-Feldmann, MDIK 7, 1937, 95f., verifying that even high and esteemed officials had to prostrate themselves when appearing before the king.

g) *Rḥw* "fellows," "comrades" as jovial address to the officials, see Gunn, JEA 12, 1926, 251.[17] The term is frequently used during the Old Kingdom for "fellow workmen"; cf. Montet, *Scènes de la vie privée*, 205; Erman, *Reden, Rufe und Lieder auf Grabbildern des alten Reiches*, ABAW 1918, 15, 22f.; 39; cf. also Grapow, *Anreden* II, 34f., who considers *rḥw* as an enticing address.

For *ᶜš* "to summon," cf. Sinuhe B 248; Shipwrecked Sailor, 170; *Inscription dédicatoire* 40; Urk.IV 1072,16.

Dᶜr "to seek and establish," cf. Peasant B 2,93; Ptahhotep 463; Crum, Studies 44; CT V 269b; Urk.IV 57, 15. The king's request has three aspects and in this respect anticipates the later (11. 10-11) threefold qualification of Neferyt, who should thus be recognized as meeting all aspects. As a result the following juxtapositions can be set up:

s3.ṯn m s33	--*nḏs pw ḳn[n] g3b.f*
sn.ṯn m iḳr	--*sš pw iḳr n ḏbᶜw.f*
ḫnms.ṯn wd sp nfr	--*špss pw ᶜ3 n.f ḫt*

The common translation of the first element, "seek out for me a son of yours who is wise"[18] has to be questioned for two reasons. The quality of "wisdom" is not to be expected with young people, nor would there be the postulated parallelism between features found among those related to the courtiers and those found also with Neferyt. The rendering "wise one" can thus be ruled out for its incompatibility with youth, and the nature of the term can be established from the parallel applied to Neferyt. That in his case youthfulness is implied can be inferred from the use of *nḏs* in reference to Neferyt, which seems to have in this case more physiological than social significance.[19] The quality denoted as *s33* concerning the "son" corresponds to *ḳn n g3b*. The expression occurs also for Senmut (Urk.IV 414,17), where it is continued by *šms-nswt ḥr ḫ3st rsyt mḥtyt i3b(t) imn(t) - wᶜb ḥᶜw r imwt-pḏty dd n.f nwb n ḫswt* "royal follower in the foreign countries south, north, east and west--pure of limbs in between (military campaigns)--an archer to whom the gold of valor was given." There can be no doubt that *ḳn n gb(3).f* denotes here military prowess, as is common for *ḳn* "valiant." *Gb3* is a rare word for "arm"; cf. Wb.V 63,4; CT II 239a. It is used as a synonym to *ḫpš*, e.g., BM 1628; cf. also Polotsky, *Zu den Inschriften der 11. Dynastie*, Untersuchungen XI, §73.

In view of the qualification of *s33* as *m g3b* "by arm's strength," a rendering "wise one" is of course untenable, and the meaning of *s33* should be connected with physical action. I thus propose rendering it "experience" and "experienced one," with the specific connotation of military experience. This rendering suits the other occurrences of the term: Pyr. 854b denotes the king as *s33* "experienced one."[20] Merikareᶜ P. 33, . . . *pw n srw s33 <.f?>* "a [store-house] is it for the officials what he experienced";[21] Merikareᶜ, P. 54, *ḳsn pw srḫy m s33w* "it is difficult when the accuser is an experienced one" and Merikareᶜ P. 115-116, *s33.f m pr.f m-ẖnw-ẖt* "he is experienced when he comes forth from the *ẖt*"; similarly Urk. IV 969,16. Also indicative is Ptahhotep 523, where *s33* is parallel to *mnḫ*, while Ptahhotep 401 uses *s33* in parallelism with *šsp* "model." See further *Memphite Theology* (Shabakastone), 59, where *s33* is parallel to *gm* "to find out"; and Hatnub Gr. 24,2 *ink z3-z nḫt s33* "I was the son of a man, strong (i.e., successful) and experienced"; see also Janssen, *De traditioneele egyptische Autobiografie vóór het Nieuwe Rijk I Ar,*[22] especially the parallelism between *s33* and *sbḳ* "smart." *S3i* "to have experience," particularly in a military sense, improves also the understanding of Sinuhe B 48 *nb s3t pw* "a possessor of experience" in reference to Sesostris I and the similar passage in Siut I 182 *rḫ ḫnty ḫprt nb s3it* "who knows the limits of history, a possessor of experience."

The parallelism between the king's inquiry to his counsellors and the qualifications of Neferyt is most clearly demonstrated in the second stage, which has *ỉḳr* as key word in both cases. *ᵓIḳr*, used nominally, occurs also in Shipwrecked Sailor 186.[23] *Sš ỉḳr* is a recurrent expression from the Sixth Dynasty (Urk.I 186,16) on, in reference to an accomplished writer; see Janssen, *loc. cit.* I G, 30-33.

The third qualification in both contexts concerns material success. This is clear in the description of Neferyt as *špss pw ᶜ3 n.f ḫt*. *Špss* "wealthy man," Wb.IV 452,16; cf. also Urk.I 79,10; Urk.VII 48,11. Accordingly, *wd sp nfr* has to have a more material connotation than "who has done a noble deed";[24] furthermore, *wdi* is not attested with the meaning "to do, to accomplish." *Sp nfr* is listed in Wb.II 255,1-2 as "gute Tat, gutes Schicksal, Glück." Sinuhe B 160, where *sp nfr* denotes "good luck,"[25] corroborates this rendering, as does Ptahhotep 520-521, *ỉr ḫpr sp nfr m-ᶜ wnn m ḥry-tp* "when good luck happens through someone who is a superior";[26] similarly also Urk.IV 446,7 and *Inscription dédicatoire*, 67, *m33 spw.f nfrw* "to see your good fortunes/deed." Of particular interest is Urk.IV 920,14, *wdt r sp nfr* "which is placed to good fortune."[27] Accordingly, *sp nfr* has to be taken as "good fortune" in Neferyt, with *wd* as passive participle or perfective relative form,[28] and to be rendered "whom good fortune placed," with the connotation of material success.

Despite the spelling 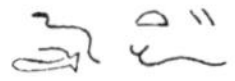, this should not be taken as a "verbal adjective" (*sḏm.ty.fy*), for lack of an antecedent qualified by it.[29] This makes it necessary to view it as a *sḏm.t.f*-form introducing a new sentence. The unusual spelling has a parallel in  in Ptahhotep 267 and is connected with the Late-Egyptian practice of writing  for the form indicator.[30] Its use here is determined by the desire to emphasize the subject. For the prospective use of the *sḏm.t.f*, see also Westendorf, *Grammatik der medizinischen Texte*, §269, 1 a.

Mdt nfrt is rendered "fine words" (M. Lichtheim, Faulkner, Wilson, Lefèbvre, Erman, Gardiner) and "vollendete Worte" (Helck). It occurs also in Ptahhotep 58, *dg3 mdt nfrt r w3ḏ* "a *mdt nfrt* is more hidden than greenstone" and Peasant B 1,318, *n rdỉ.n.k n.ỉ ḏb3w n mdt nfrt prrt m r3 n Rᶜ ḏs.f* "you can't give compensation for the *mdt nfrt* which comes forth from Reᶜ's own mouth." The latter suggests a meaning "proper saying" or "true words" and apparently has a more weighty connotation than "fine words."

Ṯsw stpw occurs similarly in Pap. Lansing 14, 10.[31] From the latter it cannot be taken as "select of speeches" in the sense of pronouncement, but rather as "selective of opinions" or "decisions."[32] The juxtaposition *mdt--ṯsw* occurs also in Khakheperreᶜ-seneb 1,[33] probably with the same progress between *mdt* "matter" and *ṯsw* "opinion," which is completed there by *ḫnw* "sayings."

Ḏ3y ḥr is generally rendered "to entertain" (M. Lichtheim, Faulkner, Wilson, Erman, Helck) or "to find diversion" (Lefèbvre, Gardiner), reflected also by Wb.V 514,10,12. Occurrences quoted are Amenemope 23,16, where *ḏ3 ḥr* appears to be erroneous for *sḏ3-ḥr* as in Amenemope 27,8[34] and Urk.IV 976,13, *ḏ3t-ḥr m sb3 r stt m wsḫt nt pr-ᶜ3* (with infinitival *ḏ3t-ḥr*) "supervising during the instructing to shoot in the Pharaoh's court."[35] Similar compounds are *ḏ3 m3ᶜ r* "to pay heed to," lit. "to extend the temple to"[36] and *ḏ3 ỉb r* in CT I 176i "to extend the heart to." Accordingly, I consider *ḏ3 ḥr* to mean literally "to turn the face," in the sense "to influence" or "to form an opinion or outlook." Such a rendering agrees with the serious and benevolent attitude ascribed to Snofru rather than the egocentric diversion attributed to Khufu in Papyrus Westcar.

II. THE COURTIERS' ANSWER

And then they prostrated before his majesty again and II9 then they said
vis-à-vis his majesty:
'There is a renowned lector priest of Bastet, O Sovereign, our
Lord,
Neferyt 10 is his name:
a citizen is he, valiant with his arm,
a writer is he, excellent with his fingers,
a wealthy one is he, who has greater wealth 11 than any peer
of his.
May he be permitted to see his majesty!'[h]

h) The king's request is followed by another prostration of the courtiers, apparently as a sign of their acceptance or consent; cf. H. Müller-Feldmann, *Darstellungen von Gebärden auf Denkmälern des Alten Reiches*, MDIK 7, 1937, 95f. Wb.I 343,7 does not list the adverbial *m-wḥm-ꜥ* "again" prior to the New Kingdom.

For *ḏd ḫft*, cf. Sinuhe R 67, B 75, B 266; Wb.V 620,8. The idiom indicates a formal relationship similar to *ḏd ḫr*.[37]

It is generally assumed that Neferyt bears a title *ẖry ḥbt ꜥ3t*[38] rendered "Great Lector-priest," but no such title is attested.[39] In the other occurrences (ll. 14, 16) *ẖry-ḥbt* has no qualification and is also undetermined in Pap. Ermitage.[40] This indicates that the later occurrences of *ẖry-ḥbt* introducing the name of Neferyt are intended as title, while the first instance spelled with determinative and qualifying *ꜥ3* describes Neferyt by his profession and renown.[41] That *ẖry-ḥbt ꜥ3* in its first occurrence is not a "title" but a profession is substantiated by the absence of an adjoined mention of a personal name. Thus *ẖry-ḥbt* should be read "a lector-priest" as in CT I 251h. For *ꜥ3* "important, renowned," see Wb.I 161,19. Cult affiliations of lector-priests are attested in the Old Kingdom as *ẖry-ḥbt n ỉt* and in the Middle Kingdom in connection with specific cults; e.g., Cairo 20387.

For the address *ỉty nb.n* cf. Grapow, Anreden II 46.[42] For the reading of the name see above p. 8.

The description of Neferyt's qualities was discussed by Derchain, GM 3, 1972, 9ff., who concluded that Neferyt was an upstart ("Emporkömmling,) who had made his career by his own diligence. Against extensive inferences drawn therefrom, Westendorf, GM 4, 1973, 41ff., preferred a more matter-of-fact interpretation, rendering the idiom *ḳn n g3b.f* as "active" ("tatkräftig"). As discussed above (note g), the tripartite qualification of Neferyt parallels the triple request of Snofru to his courtiers. Whereas Snofru inquired about three different possible candidates, Neferyt unites all three and thus meets all possible requirements, namely, military or practical experience, education and refinement of style, and material success in the form of wealth. There is, however, no discernible indication that he is described as an upstart in a derogatory sense, although it has to be noted that any indication of a traditional background is lacking. Neferyt is portrayed primarily as an individual whose position is the reflection of his own doings.

The final supplication of the courtiers to the king contains a gap that defies restoration. The optatival particle *ḥw* is usually combined with the particle *3* followed by the predicate.[43] Helck reads , but this disagrees with the traces and also does not fill the gap, nor does his translation "Dieser möge gebracht werden, dass (ihn) S.M. sehe" satisfy.[44] Nor can the rendering "would that he might be permitted to see his majesty!"[45] satisfy, as such a meaning would require a construction **ḥw rdt m33.f ḥm.f* in view of Peasant B 1, 36f.

III. INTRODUCTION OF NEFERYT

Then said his majesty, l.p.h.: 'Hasten and bring him to me!'
And he was [12] introduced to him at once.
Then he was prostrate before his majesty, l.p.h.
Then said his majesty, l.p.h.: 'Come, now, Neferyt, [13] my friend!
May you tell me some true words and choice opinions, which could extend the view of my majesty for [14] hearing them!'[i]

i) The fetching of Neferyt is treated marginally and repeats almost verbatim the recall of the courtiers in ll. 4-5; a similar episode receives detailed attention in Pap. Westcar 7, 9.

For the friendly address to Neferyt by Snofru see Gunn, JEA 12, 1926, 250, and Posener, *Littérature et politique*, 31. For the imperative *mi* "come!" with the enforcing particle *m* cf. Gardiner, *Egyptian Grammar*[3] §250; Edel, *Altägyptische Grammatik*, §6;5; James, *The Ḥeḳanakhte Papers*, 25, 130; W. Guglielmi, *Reden, Rufen und Lieder auf altägyptischen Darstellungen*, TAB 1, 137f.

IV. NEFERYT'S REPLY

Then said the lector-priest Neferyt: 'Something that happened or something that is bound to happen, O Soverign, l.p.h., [my] lord?'[j]

j) *Ḫprt* is commonly used in reference to the "past," i.e., something that happened;[46] for *ḫprt* "history" ("Geschehenes"), cf. Urk.VII 34,10; Merikare^{c}, P. 137; Sinuhe B 35; Shipwrecked Sailor, 142. For the partitive use of *m* see James, *The Ḥeḳanakhte Papers*, 104; Goedicke, *Die Geschichte des Schiffbrüchigen*, 57.

Ḫpr.ty.fy used nominally "that which is indeed happening" as a term for future[47] occurs also in Ptahhotep 275, *nn sprt.n.f nbt ḥs.s m ḫpr.ty.sn* "not all that he has asked for is what is to arrive"; Urk.IV 96,16, *mr.ti k3.k pw ḫpr.ty.sn* "that what your ka wishes is what actually happens"; Urk.IV 370,1, *ḏd.sn n.s ḫpr.ty.sy* "and they said to her what is actually going to happen." The connotation of the expression is less prospective than factitive.[48]

V. THE KING'S CHARGE

15 Then said his majesty, l.p.h.: 'Something that is happening! It is (still) today and the passing of it already happens!'[k]

k) Although the general drift of the king's observation is fairly clear, the exact rendering as well as its grammatical structure has not been convincingly explained.[49] Barta[50] in discussing the passage reads *mjn ỉs ḫprt sw3t ḥr.f*. He takes *min* as subject of a nominal clause and the participial *ḫprt* as predicate with *sw3t* in apposition to *ḫprt*. His readings **ḫprt* or *sw3t* are, however, unsupported by the text, and his structuring is improbable. This concerns especially his view of *swt* as an enclitic particle, which has no justification. Instead, the king's initial request should be identified as *m ḫpr.ty.fy*. The ensuing explanation has two parts, one a nominal, the other a verbal clause. The first is *swt min* "it is a today," the second *ỉs ḫpr sw3 ḥr.f* "and already happens the passing of it." The passage can be compared with Sinuhe B 189, *ỉw min ỉs š3ʿ.n.k tnỉ* "it is today that you began aging" and Peasant B 1,180-1, *ỉw min 3 ḫsf.n.ỉ 3dw* "it is today that I repelled the aggressor." However, different from these two passages, *swt min* is here a nominal clause with *min* as predicate "it is a today"; for *swt*, see Gardiner, *Egyptain Grammar*[3] §64; Sethe, *Der Nominalsatz im Ägyptischen*, §59; Deir Rifeh pl. VII, 35. *Ḫpr* is a perfective *sḏm.f* whose subject is the infinitival *sw3 ḥr.f* "passing at it," with *min* as antecedent of *ḥr.f*.[51] For *sw3* of the passing of time, see Wb.IV 61 B.

VI. THE KING WRITES DOWN NEFERYT'S PRONOUNCEMENTS

And then he stretched out his hand to a case [16] of writing equipment and then he took for him a scroll and palette.

And then he was putting in writing what the lector-priest [17] Neferyt said:[1]

1) The description of the king's actions seems intentionally circumscript to emphasize the remarkable personal actions of the ruler as a symptom of Snofru's joviality or as a special honor for the wise man.

For *ḏwn* cf. Ptahhotep 139; Rifeh, pl. XVI, 5; Hatnub, Inschr. X 5-6. The common assumption here is a genitival construction **hn n ẖtr-ʿ* "the box holding the writing materials" (Gardiner), "a box of writing equipment" (M. Lichtheim), or "Schreibkasten" (Helck). P. Berlin 3038[52] specifies a *hnw ẖry-ʿ* as the place of discovery of ancient writings. On the other hand, *hn n* "box for" is mentioned in Pap. Abusir pl. XXI. In the Old Kingdom there are rare early instances of writing utensils (*ẖrt-ʿ*) made of wood.[53] During most of the Old Kingdom they were made of soft material, presumably leather.[54] In Junker, Giza IV, Tf. IX, S. 71, *ẖry-(t)-ʿ* and *hn* are listed as two separate entries. The oval writing pack occurs only in the friezes depicting objects[55] but not in other scenes.[56] A wooden box seems to be used instead, which can also serve as a table.

Šd, used here reflexively, implies selectiveness; cf. Shipwrecked Sailor, 54. *Šfd* and *gsti* are mentioned together in Peasant B 1, 305.

Whereas earlier translators[57] took *ḏdt.n ẖry-ḥb(t) Nfrti* as heading of the following, Posener[58] has demonstrated it to be the object of *ỉrt m sš* "to put into writing" (Wb.I 109,17). The construction *wn.ỉn.f ḥr* + infinitive has the meaning of beginning a continuous occupation in the past. Other occurrences are Urk.IV 4,14-15;[59] 4,2; Urk.I 127, 7-9; 139,9; Peasant B 1, 24,42; see Edel, *Altägyptische Grammatik,* §931;

Gardiner, *Egyptian Grammar*[3] §470; Lefèbvre, *Grammaire*[2] §665.

VII. THE KING'S TRANSCRIPT: IDENTIFICATION OF NEFERYT

A knowledgeable one of the East is he,
One belonging to Bastet is he when she appears,
A child of the Heliopolitan district is he.[m]
III He, indeed, 18 is concerned about what is happening in the land,
he, indeed, is bringing to mind the condition of the East,[n]
that the Asiatics migrate forcefully,
19 that they diminish the measures of what is on the harvest
tax and that they take the assignment on the plowing.[o]

m) The king's transcript of Neferyt's sayings opens with a statement about Neferyt concerning his qualifications--his professional, religious, and legal background. It is to be understood as the king's opinion of Neferyt and is thus an integral part of the royal writing. It is structured in three sections, each with its own grammatical construction, the first being a nominal clause, the second a *ỉw.f sḏm.f* construction, and the third a *sḏm.f*. The first group especially makes it improbable that these passages should be taken as subsidiary clauses following the mention of Neferyt.[60] Instead the three *pw*-clauses should be regarded as independent atemporal statements about Neferyt.

Pap. Ermitage 17 has *rḫ ḫt pw n ʾI3b(t)*, whereas O DeM 1186 gives instead *rḫ ḫt pn [ỉ3b]t*, presumably by conflation of *pw + n*. The position of *pw* makes it clear that *rḫ ḫt* is a compound term. The indirect genitive attached to it, however, qualifies rather the object of the learnedness than the learned one himself. As in Merikareʿ, P. 115, *rḫ ḫt pw n ỉdbwy* "a learned one of the Two Banks," the statement should be taken as concerning, not Neferyt's origin, but rather the area of his knowledge; *rḫ-ḫt* has here less the quality of "sage" or "wisdom" than that of empirical knowledge.[61] That *rḫ ḫt pw n ʾI3bt* does not concern the origin of Neferyt is corroborated by the subsequent specifications of his professional and administrative affiliation, which are specific to the point that Neferyt's connection with *ỉ3bt* "East" is one of knowledge rather than origin. *ʾI3bt* "East" seems intentionally vague and is not congruent with the administrative term "East."[62] It denotes here the entire eastern fringe of the Delta, including in particular the Wadi Tumilat.

The affiliation with Bastet *(ny-sw)* concerns Neferyt's connection with the cult of Bastet as stated in l. 9, "there is a renowned lector-priest of Bastet." *Ny-sw* is apparently used here as an expression of professional or cult affiliation. It is common in the formulation of personal names,[63] but less so otherwise; cf., however, the parallel *ny-wỉ Rᶜ* "I am one belonging to Reᶜ" in Pap. Ebers 1,7. The expression has its forerunner in the use of *ny* + royal name to indicate professional affiliation.[64]

B3stt m wbn.s has found differing interpretations[65] and is now generally rendered "Bastet in her East" (M. Lichtheim), following the discussion by Posener, RdE 5, 1946, 255, in which the passage is compared to Pap. An. II 1,4-5 = Pap. An. IV 6,4-5. The latter enumerates the sanctuaries at the four sides of the Ramesside Delta-residence, or the quarters of it. In *ḫpr ᶜstrtỉ m p3y.f wbn* "Astarte exists at its orient," *p3y.f wbn* refers to the "orient" (Wb. I 294,8)[66] of the Residence. Applying this to the specification *ny-sw B3stt m wbn.s* in Neferyt l. 17, the latter could only be rendered "in its orient" with *ʾI3bt* "East" as antecedent of *wbn.s.*[67] However, this interpretation has several shortcomings. Most important is the lack of an attestation of *wbn* in this usage prior to the Eighteenth Dynasty. It would further entail that the eastern part of the East was a separate region and that the cult of Bastet was at its easternmost edge. It would seem beyond doubt that the mention of Bastet here has to be affiliated with the town of Bubastis, which is certainly not the easternmost point of the Delta. The connection of Neferyt with Bastet is a priestly one, as indicated in l. 9. I thus consider it necessary to take *wbn*, not as a geographical allusion, but as concerning the appearing of the deity in religious ceremonies, for which *wbn* is attested in the Middle Kingdom.[68]

For *ms pw n*, which recurs in l. 59, cf. Pyr. 482-483a, where the pedigree of the deceased is specified. In parallelism, *ms pw n* should be seen here as a legal specification of Neferyt's place of registration. Specifications of personal registration are found in a number of funerary ostraca from the Old Kingdom,[69] and the practice of registration is mentioned in the Dashur-decree (Urk.I 211,7-8; 212,18).[70] As the specification concerns only the legal registration of Neferyt at Heliopolis, there is hardly a basis for assuming that, at the time, the Bubastite and Heliopolitan districts belonged together, as Helck[71] proposes.

n) Already Gardiner, JEA I, 1914, 105, connected the two clauses beginning with *ꞽw.f* with the preceding and saw therein part of the introduction of Neferyt's sayings, a veiw shared by Posener.[72] Gardiner, *Egyptian Grammar*[3] §463 and Lefèbvre, *Grammaire*[2] §323f., point out a temporal concomitant use of the form.[73] Its use with pronominal subject is limited to Middle Kingdom literary texts: Sinuhe B 96;[74] Peasant B 1, 216; 261;[75] Shipwrecked Sailor 17-18;[76] Suicidal 21; 69; 80.[77] In view of the parallels, a habitual connotation can be postulated here as well, i.e., that Neferyt is continuously concerned about the situation in the East and that his statements about this subject are only a reflection or part thereof. The formulation in Pap. Ermitage is clearly better than O DeM 1186 for retaining the preposition *ḥr*. For *mḥ ḥr*, cf. Suicidal 32, 68, 78; Sinuhe B 199. 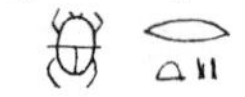 has been emended by Gardiner and Posener into *ḫpr.ty.sy* and consequently rendered prospectively.[78] However, as Helck, *loc, cit.*, 18, pointed out,[79] it should rather be read *ḫprt* "what is happening," i.e., the reference is contemporary with the account of Neferyt, which was inspired by the prevailing situation. Neferyt is thus not prophesying, but reporting prevailing conditions.

Sḫ3 "call to mind" as in Sinuhe B 222; Peasant B 1,21; 189; Shipwrecked Sailor, 128; Ptahhotep 16; 424. 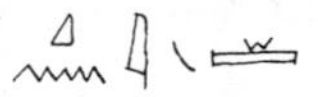 has been emended since Gardiner[80] into *ḳi n* "the form of" and rendered "condition" or "state" of the East; cf. Wb.V 16,8.

o) *Ḫp*, as intransitive verb, usually means "to travel," "to go" (Wb.III 258), from which developed the special meaning "to die." This basic meaning does not suit the context. Among the translations[81] Faulkner's literal rendering "travel in their power" comes closest to the intended meaning, i.e., the Asiatics are traveling forcefully, with the implication of undesired infiltration and roaming in the cultivation area. The verb apparently has here the rarely attested nuance "to move into,"[82] which might have led to the development of *ḫpp* "alien," "imported." The situation is akin to that described in Merikareᶜ P. 92-93 and 96-97 and should be compared with the famous immigration of bedouin into the Wadi Tumilat in Pap. An. VI 51ff.[83] The people are described here as *ᶜ3mw*, as in Merikareʿ, and they are mentioned as early as Urk.I 134,13, 16. The term is more likely an ethnic than a political term and appears to refer to Semites[84] in general rather than to a specific group of them. Consequently, it remains uncertain where to locate the people described here as intruders. The possibility that they were not mere bedouin but Palestinians who sought refuge in Egypt from adverse economic conditions in Palestine, as in the Joseph Story,[85] has considerable weight in view of l. 33 (see below, p.92). It would provide a wider perspective to the economic troubles that beset the Near East around 2000 B.C. and are reflected in numerous references to famine in Egypt and a decline of the physical culture in Palestine.[86]

M ḫpš.sn is an application of the common idiom *ỉr m ḫpš;* see Polotsky, *Zu den Inschriften der 11. Dynastie,* Unters. XI, §73; Janssen, *op. cit.* II F, 164-175; Fischer, Kush 9, 1961, 48. The particular connotation of doing something by one's own efforts, without any legal or traditional claim, applies here as well. It should be understood here as implying that the movements of the Asiatics were based on their strength rather than on rights or traditions.

O DeM 1187 has  for  in the Pap. Ermitage. The former probably is an extended orthographic error by assimilation to *thm,* Wb. V 531, 9, "to drive someone away." *Sh(3)* clearly is transitive with *ỉbw/ỉb* as object.[87] Wb.IV 205,19 renders it "(die Herzen) in Furcht versetzen o.ä." with the present instance as the only occurrence. Faulkner, *Concise Dictionary,* 237, gives for it "to terrorize," while Piankoff, *Le "coeur" dans les textes égyptiens* 120, lists it as "offenser le coeur." The word probably is identical with the transitive , which Gardiner, JEA 16, 1930, 22, translated "to confound." The term appears to be a key word in the Wisdom of Amenemope, where it occurs as both intransitive and transitive.[88]

The passage has never received a detailed discussion and is generally rendered "frightening those about to harvest and seizing cattle from the plough."[89] Despite the uniformity of the interpretations, they remain unsatisfying for several reasons. That the two clauses introduced by *sh.sn* and by *nḥm.sn* are parallel can be considered certain. Both are perfective *sḏm.f,* which has no circumstantial meaning. While in the second clause *ḥr* is considered as introducing an infinitive, such an interpretation cannot be made for *šmw*. There is no verb *šmw* "to harvest," nor can the assumed construction **ntyw ḥr šmw* be rendered "those about to harvest." *Ḥr* + infinitive implies involvement in an activity and not an intention toward an activity.[90] If people engaged in a specific occupation were to be denoted here, the text certainly omitted any indication of people whatsoever. Furthermore, although the relative construction **nty + ḥr +* infinitive occurs in Late Egyptian,[91] attestations of it in classical Egyptian are lacking.[92] A relative construction of the presumed type is meaningful only if defined either by a demonstrative or by subordination. Definition in a genitival construction is possible only in the case of a coherence between *regens* and *rectum*, that is, the relative expression has to be cognate to the element with which it is in genitival relation.

There are semantic considerations concerning the meaning of *šmw*, which denotes the harvest as tax-base rather than the reaped products themselves. The apparent structural parallelism between the two clauses is not retained in the proposed renderings and requires further discussion.

Finally, the significance of the two clauses in the story has to be considered. They are part of the summarizing introduction ascribed to the king, in which the subsequent deliberations of Neferyt are anticipated. They certainly concern more than temporary inconvenience experienced by harvesters or an occasional case of cattle rustling. It would also seem a rather superficial attitude on the part of the king that his interests in the welfare of the East were limited to such ephemeral events, which would not be in line with the statesmanship otherwise attributed to Snofru.

These considerations make an entirely new approach to the section necessary. Paleographically, the transcription 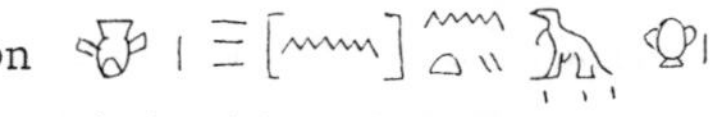  by Golenischchef, maintained uncritically, is open to question. The restoration is without doubt too long, and there are traces that do not suit the transcription of an indirect genitive.[93] They fit best a reading  ; see Möller, *Hieratische Paläographie* I LXII, and also l. 7. The sign preceding it differs widely from all other occurrences of or  in the text (ll. 3, 7, 23, 31, 36, etc.), with the possible exception of l. 13. As *ntyw ḥr šmw* "those which are on the harvest-tax" has to be basically in accordance with the object of *sh(3).sn*, the meaning of the expression can be presumed to fall within the realm of taxation. Needless to say, this prerequisite is not met by the traditional reading *ỉb/ỉbw* "hearts." The hieratic sign clearly shows a container, but it is slightly different from the specific form of *ib* as occurring in l. 20. Thus, it should be taken as the paleographically almost identical sign  , used here as the abbreviated form of *hnw;* see Möller, *loc. cit.* I, 506. *Sh(3)* does not require any special meaning, as proposed Wb.IV 205,19 "(die Herzen) in Furcht versetzen o. ä." and Faulkner, *Concise Dictionary,* 236, "to terrorize" but can be taken in the attested meaning "to lessen," as used especially in the Wisdom of Amenemope 19,2.

The parallel clause states the next and integrated consequence of the invasion by the Asiatics. The usual translation would restrict their impact to a limited situation. It seems unlikely that the taking or requisitioning of a yoke of cattle from plowing is really an outstanding event, especially as there would be no adverse impact on any people. Thus the formulation as contained in O DeM 1187, which gives  instead of  , appears to be the superior one. *Ḥtrw* has to be recognized as the term for "levy," "tax."[94] Consequently, *sk3* should not be taken as infinitive, but rather as the attested administrative term for "harvest," Wb.IV 316,10. By rendering in this fashion, the parallelism between the two clauses emerges clearly. *Šmw* and *sk3* are as parallel as *hnw ntyw ḥr* and *ḥtrw*. The two passages are complementary and concern the two steps of the taxation system: the first is the tax estimate based on the projected harvest, the second the actual tax collection after the completed harvest.[95] This process is reflected in the terminology. *Ḥtrw,* lit. "assignment", i.e., "what is tied on," denotes the tax estimate at the time of the ploughing *(sk3),* whereas the collected tax after the harvest is *šmw*.

Summing up the introductory lines assigned to King Snofru as his *résumé* or delineation of the concerns of Neferyt, which he is unfolding in the following, they concern the possibility of forceful, or at least undesired, intrusion by Asiatics into the eastern Delta. The focal point in the king's consideration is the fiscal consequences for the central administration, in the form of decreased tax revenue because of the impact of the intruders. The statesmanship displayed agrees with the picture of King Snofru in the opening lines as a concerned ruler.

VIII. NEFERYT'S OPENING STATEMENT

[20] He says: 'May my heart stir that you bemoan this land!
Begin yourself with it, do not oppress it!
See, he who could speak for it [21] was expelled;
furthermore, the official was cast down.[p]
Begin yourself there <in> the land!
[IV] Do not weary of what is in front of you,
        [22] but stand up against that which is before you.
See, officials in the governance of the land are no longer;
        what is to be done, is no longer done.[q]
May a day begin with reorganizing, [23] as the land is entirely lost,
        without that a remainder exists,
        without that the black of a nail remains from its dues.'[r]

p) It is only with the introductory *d̲d.f* that the transcription of Neferyt's sayings begins. There can be no doubt that it is an independent statement signifying the outset of the speech; see Grapow, *Anreden* IV, 84ff.

Since Gardiner's first rendering the opening words of Neferyt's discourse have been considered as an address to his own heart.[96] This universally held view not only leads to lexicographical inconsistencies but even more seriously interrupts the stylistic concept as well. As the opening words are usually taken, Neferyt talks to himself, with the heart as his interlocutor.[97] This interpretation disregards entirely the frame-story of the text, which portrays the situation as a dialogue between King Snofru and Neferyt. Although Neferyt is the principal speaker, it is illogical to assume that the introductory narrative is at this point completely disregarded. After all, Neferyt is not merely musing about problems, but is admonishing King Snofru. The concept of a dialogue is maintained throughout the text, as demonstrated by several instances (ll. 35, 38, 44, 47,

54-55) in which the deliberations are interrupted by direct address to the listening king. It can thus be presumed that Neferyt's opening words are directed to King Snofru, whose inquiry he answers in what follows. For the grammatical understanding of the passage this means that *ḫws ỉb.ỉ* is not an imperative, but a hortative *sḏm.f* on which *rm.k t3 pn* and [*r*]*myt.k* [*n*] *t3* [*pn*], respectively, depend.[98] As Posener emphasized, *ḫws* has the basic meaning "to pound" (into a recipient), and it is primarily used as a construction term derived from the *pisé* technique and its extension for gravel-filled walls, i.e., pounding the material into a form. We have here a metaphorical use[99] applied to the squeezing out of tears by the speaker's "heart," i.e., his "mind" or "will."[100] *ʾIb.ỉ* is, of course, the subject of *ḫws*, while *rmyt.k* or *rm.k* is object; for *rm n*, as O DeM 1187 is most probably to be restored, see Wb.II 417,8.

T3 pn refers throughout the text to the eastern Delta and the Wadi Tumilat in particular, as Erman, *loc. cit.*, 153, note 5, already pointed out, and not to Egypt as a whole. It is that particular area specified in l. 18; see above p. 70.

Since Gardiner's inaugural translation, *ᶜš3ᶜ* has been taken as a *sḏmw.n.f* relative form qualifying *t3 pn* and rendered "this land, from which you have sprung."[101] We have no information that King Snofru, who should be considered as the addressee of Neferyt's discourse, came from the eastern Delta.[102] Furthermore, *ᶜš3ᶜ* has the specific meaning of beginning an activity and not of mere existence.[103] From the structural analysis of the section, as displayed below, it results that *š3ᶜ n.k* cannot qualify *t3 pn*. A *sḏm.n.f*-form expressing relative past has no convincing place in an admonition, so that *š3ᶜ n.k* should rather be taken as an imperative followed by a reflexive dative; cf. Gardiner, *op. cit.*, §337.2. *Š3ᶜm* is not "to begin in something," but a well-attested idiom "to begin with something."[104] The antecedent of *ỉm.f* is *rmw.k* "your bemoaning."

For the understanding of ll. 20-22 an extensive structural analysis is necessary. The commonly held opinion about this section was first expressed by Gardiner[105] and has received only limited reconsideration since. However, a comprehensive survey reveals a balanced structure in parallel units:

š3ᶜ.n.k ỉm.f gr m ỉwḥ mk wn ḏd.tỉ r.f m stryt mk rf wn sr m ptḫ

š3ᶜ.n.k ỉm <*m*> *t3 m wrḏ mk st ḫft ḥr.k ᶜḥᶜ.k r ntt m b3ḥ.k mk rf wn srw m sḫrw nyw t3*

It is immediately clear that *š3 .n.k* is the key word in both lines. Consequently, it cannot be a relative form qualifying something that precedes it but has to be recognized as an independent form. It introduces here two courses of action to be pursued once the initiative is taken.

From the parallelism it becomes possible to resolve the meaning of  , which heretofore has been a particular problem.[106] As *m wrḏ* is indisputably a negated imperative,[107] *m iwḥ* has to be recognized as parallel to it and thus the same construction. This implies in turn that  cannot be the word for "silence," as commonly assumed, but only the adverb *gr* "also"; for it, see Gardiner, *Egyptian Grammar*[3] §205.1; Lefèbvre, *Grammaire*[2] §542; Westendorf, *Grammatik der medizinischen Texte,* §386; Merikareᶜ P. 127; Ptahhotep 412, 603; Louvre C 14, 12; James, *The Ḥeḳanakhte Papers,* 19f., 42. It is used here to indicate that Neferyt is bemoaning the land and expects the king to join him once he learns about its condition.

Although Neferyt expects to move the king to tears, he does not desire him to overreact. *ʾIwḥ* "to moisten," Wb.I 57,1-8,[108] makes little sense here. It is to be understood as either "to weep" (Wb.I 57,13), attested only from Ptolemaic temples, or "to oppress"; cf. JEA 22, 1936, 135; Siut IV 34. The word possibly is identical with the obscure designation *ỉwḥw;* cf. Junker, *Gîza* V, 11; Goyon, *Nouvelles inscriptions rupestres,* 58.

For the construction with *mk* see M. Lichtheim, *On the Iterative Use of the Particle mk,* JNES 30, 1971, 69ff. Gunn, *Studies in Egyptian Syntax,* 29, takes *ḏd.ti* as prospective passive participle, rendering it, "See, there is something that may be said about him," followed by Barta, *ibid.,* "Siehe das was über es (d.h. das Land) gesagt werden wird, ist ein Schreckliches"; cf. also Ptahhotep 153 L 1. *R.f,* as Barta maintains, refers to *t3,* with *ḏd r* having an accusatory connotation.[109] *Ḏd.ti* is object of *ỉwḥ*. *Stryt,* though seemingly a *hapax legomenon,* is probably the infinitive of *stri* "to reject," Wb.IV 344,9; cf. also below l. 36. The second *mk* is a mere continuation, *rf* stressing the consequential aspect. *Wn* introduces a pseudo-verbal clause with past meaning; cf. Gardiner, *op. cit.,* §326.

The second *mk* continues *ỉwḥ* and is basically parallel to the previous *mk*-clause. *Rf* acts here in the sense of "furthermore," so that *wn sr m ptẖ* has to be recognized as the nuclear sentence depending on *m iwḥ*. Reading and interpretation vary widely.[110] 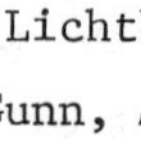 can not be taken to mean "great man," "great one," or "(hostile) chief," but in view of the parallel 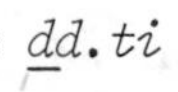 can only be the singular *sr* "official,"[111] taken up subsequently in the plural. *Ptḫ* is generally considered as a transitive verb with *t3* as its object. However, a pseudoverbal construction of this type should rather be construed with the preposition *ḥr* than with *m*, as found here. The latter suits better a construction with an intransitive verb as which *ptḫ* has to be recognized. *Ptḫ* as intransitive is well attested in the Middle Kingdom with the meaning "to be cast down"; see Wb.I 566,2; Admonitions 8,14; Peasant B 1,197. In Admonitions 8,14 . . . *sn ptḫ m snḏ n mwt* "their . . . are cast down through fear of death," we find the particular connotation of despondency, which applies here as well. *Sr* "official" in this context might be an oblique reference to Neferyt himself, whose worried outlook could arouse the king's ire. Thus he pleads for patience by the king and for seeing the good in the situation once the king takes action.

q) It is widely assumed that *t3* is misplaced and should be connected with *ptḫ*, and *š3ᶜ n.k ỉm* is considered to the preceding *š3ᶜ n.k ỉm.f*, both being taken as relative forms. However, as pointed out above, *š3ᶜ n.k* has to be taken as an imperative, closing the first section of the admonition. I thus propose reading *š3ᶜ n.k (ỉ)m t3* "begin yourself in the land," possibly "with the land"; the faulty *ỉm* could be attributed to a scribal error influenced by the parallel.

There is a fine differentiation between *ḫft-ḥr.k* and *m-b3ḥ.k*. The first has the connotation of actuality, the second that of retrospect; for *m-b3ḥ* with the connotation "previous," see Gardiner, *Egyptian Grammar*[3] §205.2. The meaning of the passage seems to be that Neferyt encourages the king not to be overwhelmed by the prevailing situation, but rather to tackle it; for *ᶜḥᶜ r*, see in particular Peasant B 1,202; 293.

The two available versions differ, as O DeM 1188 has a negative *nn wn rf*, which seems better than the affirmative formulation of Pap. Ermitage.[112] 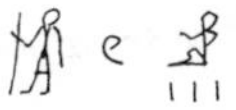 should be taken as an abbreviated writing for *srw* "officials," in parallelism with the singular *sr* in the preceding passage. Neferyt's point is that there are no longer officials governing the eastern fringe of the Delta, but that this should not influence the king against reorganizing the broken-down administration. For *sḫrw nyw t3* "governance of the land," see Faulkner, *Concise Dictionary*, 242; Spiegel, *Soziale Reformbewegungen im alten Ägypten*, 83.

It is curious that Pap. Ermitage is suddenly better than O DeM 1188, which otherwise is superior. *ʾIryt* "deed" (Wb.I 112,7; Westcar 4,11; 6,16) is probably erroneous for  "that which is to be done" as in Westcar 12,2, which would make better sense than the customary rendering. If *ỉryt* is taken as a nominally used perfective passive participle "what was done," the passage should be rendered "what was done is no longer done."

r) *Š3*^{c} *R*^{c} *m grg* has as variant *š3*^{c} *n.ỉ R*^{c} *m grg* in O DeM 1188, with the latter being preferable. The now customary rendering "Re^{c} should begin to recreate" (M. Lichtheim) was introduced by Erman, *Literatur der alten Ägypter,* 154, as "Re möge (wieder) zu gründen anfangen" and supported by Blackman, JEA 10, 1924, 198. Posener, *Littérature et politique,* 150, considers O DeM 1188 decisive and renders "(ce qui a été fait est comme ce qui n'a jamais été fait), de sort que Rê peut recommencer la création," while Barta, MDIK 27, 1971, 37, follows Wilson, rendering "Re muss mit der Schöpfung (erneut) beginnen." None of the translations fully takes into account the wording of either version. Pap. Ermitage is clearly *š3*^{c} *hrw m grg,* while O DeM 1188 has *š3*^{c} *n.ỉ R*^{c} *m grg.* It is difficult to decide which is the original version, although Pap. Ermitage appears to be the more likely. In either case, I propose to take it as a hortative interjection and render the former "may a day begin with setting (the land) in order" and the latter "may Re begin for me with setting (the land) in order." *Š3*^{c} *m* + infinitive is the usual construction; see Wb.IV 407,4. For *grg* "to set in order," in particular "to reorganize," see Vandier, *Mo*^{c}*alla* 165; Urk.VII 12,12; Koptus XII,3; Admonitions 5,4; Merikare^{c} P. 49. *Grg* as a transitive verb would require a direct object, which is omitted because of the proximity of *t3.*

3ḳ is attested in regard to the ruinous state of a land; cf. Wb.I 21,13; Medinet Habu 27,16.[113] For the adverbial *r 3w* cf. Gardiner, *Egyptian Grammar*^{3} §100.3; Lacau, BIFAO 30, 1931, 891. *Ḏ3t* "rest," see also Simpson, *Papyrus Reisner* I, 50. It should be read *nn ḫpr ḏ3t,* parallel to the following *nn zp.* The metaphor "black of a nail" for a miniscule quantity occurs only here, but cf. Wb.V 124,11 and Grapow, *Die bildlichen Ausdrücke des Aegyptischen,* 45. *Š3t* "dues," cf. Wb.IV 403,9; Gardiner, *The Wilbour Papyrus* II, 57; Faulkner, *Concise Dictionary,* 261. Barta, *loc. cit.,* certainly is right in connecting the suffix *.f* with *t3.* The concern of the section is that the assigned dues are no longer forthcoming, because there are no longer officials concerned with the affairs of the easternmost part of the Delta, with the result that the previously established order has collapsed.

IX. THE MISERY OF THE EAST BECAUSE OF THE DROUGHT

V24 'While this land is destroyed, none cares about it.
No one speaks and no one sheds a tear:
"Wherewith shall this land exist?"[s]
The sun is covered 25 and does never shine, so that people can see--
one can not live as long as clouds are always covering who is being red (i.e., the sun).
Every face is numb 26 for lack of it.[t]
While I shall say what is before me,
I cannot foretell something that has not yet come.'[u]

s) *Ḥḏ* is taken as passive *sḏm.f* by Westendorf[114] and rendered "vernichtet ist dies Land."[115] The passage has close parallels in *ḥḏ bw nfr* "success has perished" Peasant B 1,197, *ḥḏ šmt m grḥ zb m hrw* "perished is the going by night and the travel by day" Peasant B 1,202, *ḥḏ rk n mn* "perished is the time of suffering" Merikareʿ P. 142, *ḥḏ nwb* "gold is perished" Admonitions 3,8, *ḥḏ sprt* "perished are beans" Admonitions 3,11, *ḥḏ ỉrt h3b.tw ḥr.s* "perished is the doing for which one sent" Admonitions 10,2. They share the intransitive meaning of *ḥḏ*.

Nn + nominally used participle is synchronistic; see Satzinger, *Die negativen Konstruktionen im Alt- und Mittelägyptischen*, MÄS 12, §50.[116] *Ir rmw* was identified by Posener, *Littérature et politique*, 151, with Wb.II 417,12 "to make a weeping," as in Siut XIX 24, which has been generally accepted and which is superior to Wilson's "there is no eye that weeps." The three negated clauses trace a development from "concern" *(mḥ)*[117] to "saying"[118] to "bemoaning." The particular concern is formulated as a rhetorical question: *wnn t3 pn m m-ʿ*, while O DeM 1074 seems to have *mi m-ʿ* as alternative interrogative.[119] The first poses the question as "wherewith will this land be?" the other as "how will this land be?" As *wnn m* means "to be something,"[120] the question can also be rendered "What will this land be?" or better "With what will this land be/exist?" concerning the wherewithal of continued existence in the face of adverse conditions.[121]

t) It appears that we have two sentences, each comprising three elements differently arranged:[122] a pseudoverbal clause (*ỉtn ḥbs* and *ḥr nb ỉd*), a negated clause (*nn psḏ.f* and *nn ᶜnḫ.tw*), and a dependent imperfective *sḏm.f*-clause (*m33 rḫyt* and *ḥbs šnᶜ. . .*). *Ḥbs* "to cover" in reference to the sun disk is parallel in concept to *ḥbs ḥr* "to cover the face"; for a possible metaphorical use, cf. M. Lichtheim, *Studies in Honor of John A. Wilson*, SAOC 35, 65f. *Ḥbs* occurs again in l. 25 below with *šnᶜ* "clouds" as subject.

For *nn ᶜnḫ.tw* with prospective meaning, see below ll. 41-43; for the negatival construction, see Gunn, *Studies in Egyptian Syntax*, 159; Satzinger, *op. cit.*, §§57ff. The passage is rendered "one cannot live when clouds conceal" (M. Lichtheim).[123] There is general awareness that *ḥbs* as a transitive verb requires the mention of an object, which has led to various emendations. However, such a step is unwarranted; the object, though universally overlooked, is actually mentioned. 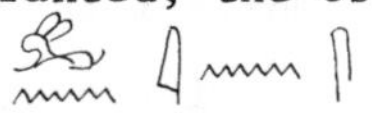 should be taken *wn ỉns*, i.e., "he who is being red." The accepted interpretation as auxiliary *wn.ỉn* + noun + Old Perfective[124] not only requires the deletion of *s*[125] but also produces a sentence unbefitting the context.[126] For *wn* + Old Perfective, see Gardiner, *Egyptian Grammar*³ §396.2. *ʾIns* "red" conveys the particular nuance of "blood color"; see Alliot, RdE 10, 1955, 4f.; Schenkel, ZÄS 88, 1963, 140. It applies here to the red sun on a hazy day.[127] *ʾId* "to be numb" is an extension of the normal application of the term to the sense of hearing, as pointed out by M. Lichtheim.[128] *N g3w* "for lack of," also Suicidal 64; cf. Gardiner, *Egyptian Grammar*³ §178.

u) *ʾIw.ỉ r ḏd* is unconnected with the preceding. As a direct address to the listening king, it interrupts Neferyt's deliberation and brings a renewed assertion of the limits of his pronouncements. They consist primarily of the disclaimer of "prophetic" talents and the definition of his sayings as concerning prospects innate in prevailing situations.

ʾIw.ỉ r ḏd is circumstantial, while *n sr.n.ỉ* is the main clause. Despite the spelling  in Pap. Ermitage and O DeM 1074, it should be read *ntt ḫft-ḥr.ỉ*. The passage is connected with *st ḫft-ḥr.k* in the preceding *rubrum* in 1. 21 and denotes in both instances what is in the offing. *N sr.n.ỉ* has, as is usual with this construction, the connotation of inability.[129] *Sr* has here, as Faulkner ("I will never foretell what is not to come") puts it, the meaning "to pronounce" (Wb.IV 190 III)[130] rather than "to prophesy" because of the construction. *Ntt* as object requires the translation "that which is," i.e., a fact; cf. Wb.II 354,1. In view of Peasant B 1,271, *ỉm w3w n ntt n ỉỉt* "do not worry about something before (it) has come," it should be considered a defective *sḏm.t.f*-form; similarly also Shipwrecked Sailor 30, *ḏʿ n ỉỉ.t* "a storm before (it) has come"; for the construction, see Satzinger, *op. cit.*, §40.3, and Gardiner, *Egyptian Grammar*[3] §486. When taken in this fashion, Neferyt's statement stresses the fact that he cannot predict the future, but that he only says what he anticipates.

X. EFFECTS OF THE DROUGHT ON THE EAST

VI 11 The watercourses of the arable land are empty:
One can [27] cross the water on foot,
and one will seek water for the ships to sail it.[v]
Its course has become riparian land:
The riparian land [28] will silt up the water-place until what is in the water-place will be riparian land.[w]
The south wind will ward off the north wind, so that heaven consists of [29] only one wind.[x]
The migratory birds will breed in the marsh of the Delta,
after they made a nest near [30] people (i.e., Egyptians),
after the weakened people had let them come near.[y]

v) *ʾItrw nyw Kmt* recurs in l. 35f. but is otherwise unattested. A rendering "river of Egypt" as a reference to the Nile might seem obvious.[131] This would expand Neferyt's frame of concern to all of Egypt or at least to the entire Delta. However, even in the following the concern of the discourse remains restricted to the eastern Delta, including the Wadi Tumilat, so that an application of the indication to an extended geographical area is improbable. It would thus seem preferable not to take *Kmt* here geopolitically, i.e., as denoting Egypt, but rather in its basic sense of "black land," i.e., "arable land."[132] *ʾItrw*, here, clearly a plural, should be taken as "navigable watercourses," whether natural (i.e., branches of the Nile) or artificial.[133] When considering *ỉtrw nyw Kmt* as "(navigable) watercourses of the arable land" the meaning of its two occurrences becomes clear. As major water arteries they are mentioned here to emphasize the arid condition of the country. When they become empty, the water level must be extremely low, just as the approach of wild animals (l. 35f.) to the watercourses serves as a picture for general disarray. Although a drought is opaquely implied, it seems that the emptiness of the big watercourses is also attributed to an administrative breakdown. For *šw* "to be empty" of watercourses, cf. Wb.IV 426,8.[134]

For *ḏ3 ḥr rdwy*, cf. Wb.V 513,5; also Peasant B 1,199. The possibility of fording does not necessarily mean that the watercourses were completely dry, but only that the water level was very low. This is corroborated by *tw r ḥḥi mw n ᶜḥᶜw* "one will search for water of/for the ships," i.e., navigable water.[135] For the absolute use of *tw*, also below ll. 34, 39, 48, cf. Ptahhotep 82; Gardiner, *Egyptian Grammar*³ §333; Lefèbvre, *Grammaire*² §670.

w) *W3t.f* in Pap. Ermitage is paralleled by 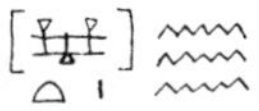 in O Petrie 38, 1. Both are correct as the suffix in *w3t.f* refers to the previously mentioned *mw* "water." The word *w3t* "road" has an extended use in regard to water.[136] Wb.I 247,1 renders it "Fahrstrasse eines Schiffes", but the occurrence here should literally be rendered "the road of water," i.e., its channel. As such, the term denotes the entire width normally filled with water.

Wḏb should be seen here as "riparian land," as in Pyr. 1392b and Urk.IV 118,10, rather than as "riverbank"; cf. Wb.I 409,3; Gardiner, *Ancient Egyptian Onomastica* I, 49*, where it is listed among hydrographic terms. From the prevailing context it can be deduced that *wḏb* denotes arable land along water that does not require artificial irrigation but is moist naturally. The picture given here is that the water in what formerly were channels has sunk so low that they are now moist ground. The sentence states the already prevailing condition and is continued by the description of further prospects.[137] The conceptual progress has been disregarded in former translations.[138] The prospects, previously formulated as *tw r ḥḥi* "one will seek," are continued in two clauses with *iw* + noun + *r* + infinitive. The same construction has to be seen following *w3t.f ḫpr.ti m wḏb*. On the basis of a parallelism it can be posed that *ỉw wḏb* is followed by *r* + infinitive. This makes it necessary to recognize 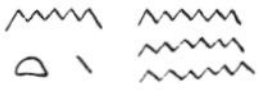 as an infinitive.

The word 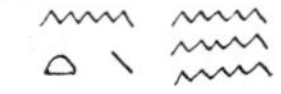 occurs in Merikareᶜ P. 125-126 in *mint ḏb3.ti m*  "a watercourse can be blocked by silt."[139] The word, which probably is a compound,[140] is apparently used here as a verb meaning "to silt up." The meaning of the passage appears to be that the riparian land encroaches on the remaining places having water, so that they, too, silt up and thus become riparian land. *St-mw* should be taken literally as "water-place" ("Wasserstelle") and not as an abstract, as Helck proposes.

x) Pap. Ermitage has 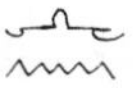 *pt m ṯ3w* 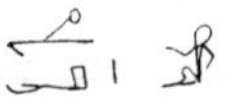 , while O Petrie reads *ỉw pt m ṯ3w wʿ*. Since Gardiner's inaugural translation[141] the latter has been considered erroneous, and the negative formulation has been considered the correct one. However, the possibilities of a negated nominal clause with adverbial predicate are very restricted and do not include a sentence with nominal subject, which is what occurs here.[142] It is thus necessary to accept *ỉw pt m ṯ3w wʿ* "as the sky consists of a single wind" as the original version. The south wind, bringing hot air, is dreaded in Egypt, especially when prevailing unabated[143] so that the cooling north wind cannot bring any respite or refreshment; cf. Pyr. 554e *ỉwt mḥty m-ḫt rsw* "as the north wind comes after the south wind." For *ỉw pt m ṯ3w wʿ*, see Pap. Leiden 350 vs. 5,11 *ỉw t3 pt m rsw nḫt* "the sky consists of strong south wind."

y) *3pdw*, though indicated as plural, is subsequently treated as singular. Although the term is used generically for "birds," its original meaning appears to have been "duck," as pointed out by Faulkner, JEA 38, 1952, 128. As designation of wild fowl, the term is used in Shipwrecked Sailor, 51; 85; Caminos, *Literary Fragments in the Hieratic Script* 12; 38. Ducks, of course, are migratory in Egypt.[144] The primary meaning of the passage here is that the migratory birds that usually come to the eastern part of the Delta will instead move into the central Delta, as already suggested by Erman.

Ḏrḏr, as first pointed out by Gardiner, *Notes on the Story of Sinuhe*, 75, connotes both "foreign" and "hostile," as does the Latin *hostis;* this twofold meaning applies also in Suicidal, 117; cf. Goedicke, *The Report about the Dispute of a Man with His* Ba, 166. For *msỉ* of the reproduction of birds cf. Wb.II 137,7; Edel, NGAW 1961, 8, 233f., where also *t3-mḥw* is listed as "roosting area"; cf. also Edel, NGAW 1963, 4, 128f. For *ẖ3t* "marsh," cf. Sinuhe R 66; B 226; Gardiner, *Notes on the Story of Sinuhe*, 87; Caminos, *op. cit.*, pl. 8,2,9.

ʾIrỉ sš "to make a nest," Wb.III 484,16. O Petrie has 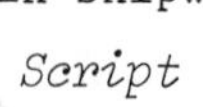
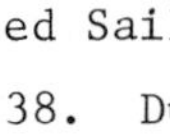 , which could be read *rmṯ niwtyw* "townsmen," i.e., people living in closed settlements; cf. Siut IV 18; Merikareʿ P. 105; Ashmolean Ostracon vs. 30; Caminos, *op. cit.*, 8. *Stkn*, clearly a causative of *tkn* "to approach," might best be rendered "to let approach," as held by Wb.IV 345,9; the same meaning occurs possibly also Caminos, *op. cit.*, pl. 3 B 3,5.

Sw refers to *3pd* and should not be deleted, as Helck, *op. cit.*, 26, proposes.  has been considered since Gardiner as the adverbial *n g3w*[145] with various implicit emendations.[146] However, such a rendering would require a specification of the want in some form. Because of its absence,  cannot be adverbial but can only qualify *rmṯ*. This requires reading it *ng(3)w* and identifying it with *ngw* "loss," Urk.IV 1344,16, and *ng3w* "to be impoverished," quoted Wb.II 349,7-8, attested only in the Nineteenth Dynasty.[147]

The prospect envisaged by Neferyt, sometimes described as puzzling,[148] has already been suspected by Gardiner to be an allegorical reference to foreigners.[149] As it seems unlikely that Neferyt would be particularly concerned about the effect of the drought on migratory birds, the allegorical meaning appears most probable. From the metaphorical use of migratory birds for foreigners, it is unlikely that they are envisaged as "foreign invaders"; rather, as foreigners, they share with the birds the habit of seasonal migration. We know that bedouin, at least from Ramesside times,[150] were admitted into the Wadi Tumilat to help them survive the summer. When taken this way, the passage expresses the possibility that the migratory people, who usually came to the eastern part of the Delta, would move on to the central Delta and become a burden to the impoverished population there.

This passage, however, does not work with a single allegory, but rather consists of a double entendre comprising the three parallel clauses. The second meaning is attained by using homophones to the words actually occurring. Thus the section can also be read:

> The turning away will rebuff the place of loyalty until he
> who is in the place of loyalty will turn away.
> The South-spirit will suppress the North-spirit, although
> heaven shall not consist of a single spirit,
> The foreign migrant will give birth in the marshland of the
> Delta after he made a dwelling near townspeople, as
> the impoverished people let him come near.

In this punning, *wḏb* "riparian land" is equated with *wḏb* "turn away." *Mw* in *st-mw* I take in the well-attested metaphorical sense of loyalty; see Grapow, *Die bildlichen Ausdrücke des Aegyptischen*, 50f. The first line thus concerns the prospect that continued neglect of the eastern Delta will discourage those who are still loyal to the king of Egypt and instigate them to turn away, too.

The second passage I connect directly with the preceding one and see therein a reflection of the impact of the Eleventh Dynasty on the North. Judging from the archaeological evidence, the Theban rulers of the Eleventh Dynasty had no interest in the welfare of the North after they subdued the Heracleopolitan rule.[151] I thus take *rsw* "south wind" either as a metaphor for "southern spirit" or as a double entendre for *rs(y)w* "Southerners," as in Urk.IV 1278,17; 1298,5. The point seems to be that in a balanced political situation in the country there should be harmony between South and North, and not an exclusive domination by one.

In the third passage the pun is apparently contained in *3pd*. Besides denoting "duck" it has a homophone in the verb *3pd* "to rush forward," Wb. I 9,12; Urk.IV 1291,5. As "those who rush forward" it is a conceivable reference to immigrants, but it could also be a slur on the Eleventh Dynasty Upper Egyptians.

XI. THE COLLAPSE OF FISHING AND HUNTING

VII,11 'Finished is the carrying off by those aiming for good fortune:
Those of the exotic lakes, they [31] used to be in possession
of gutting knives which shone from fish and fowl.[z]
All success has gone away and is eliminated [32] in the land of misfortune
by those aiming for food
and the bedouin roaming the land.'[aa]

z) Like Section V, this part of the discourse begins with *ḥḏ* and is concerned with the collapse of a specific aspect of the previous order. This occupies the first part of the section, and the second describes anticipated aggravations resulting from the breakdown. In this juxtaposition the section follows the pattern introduced in l. 26 (see above p. 81), in which Neferyt specifies his sayings as anticipations of possible developments. These concern possibilities of warfare and difficulties in organizing a defense. The first part of the section can a priori be presumed to state the prevailing conditions that will make future actions impossible. The graveness of the prospects envisaged makes one wonder about the generally held view that the beginning of this section expresses only regret about the loss of fish ponds.

The heading of the section should be recognized as *ḥḏ nḥm nf3 n bw-nfr*. Pap. Ermitage has , which is generally preferred to *nḥm* and considered to be the enclitic particle *ḥm*.[152] None of the other headings uses a particle to convey special stress, however, as there seems no reason to warrant such an emphasis. Thus the reading *nḥm* is preferable and should be taken as an infinitive used nominally. The *rubrum bw-nfr* in O DeM 1074,7 is a correction,[153] so that the verse-point preceding it is meaningless. It would seem apparent that the object of *nḥm* should be recognized as *nf3 n bw-nfr* and that *nf3* is the plural demonstrative, as is generally accepted.[154] However, *nf3* as demonstrative would either refer to some otherwise undefined term or be the late form of the demonstrative.[155] A word  occurs twice in the Middle Kingdom literary texts. In Admonitions 5,12f. (which has a parallel in 4,5)  "Forsooth, those have perished, who were seen yesterday",[156] the context speaks of travel and conditions on the roads due to general insecurity. Thus, what was seen in the past and has now disappeared are the travelers. From this it can be concluded that *nf3* is used here in reference to persons and not to things. Suicidal 34, *ỉr nf3 r t3* "as for those to the ground" is a general reference to burial; cf. Goedicke, *op. cit.*, 112.

Another occurrence is assumed in Sinuhe, Ashmolean vs. 33, where B 228 has instead  *nf*. The latter can not be demonstrative[157] but should be seen as a defective writing for 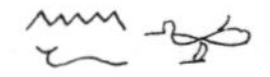 "wrong," as Gardiner[158] already presumed. The passage thus reads "my name was not heard in/from the mouth of the bailiff, except 'wrong one!'--when my limbs quivered and my legs were running away."

It is as a reference to people that *nf3* should be taken in *nf3 n bw-nfr*. This allows for a genitival or datival link between *nf3* and *bw-nfr;* the first requires reading "those of," the second "those for." Of these possibilities the latter appears superior, especially in view of the recurrence of the construction below in l. 32 and the juxtaposition there with the indubitable genitival *n3 n* immediately following. *Bw-nfr* "good fortune" is used as in Pap. Millingen 1,11 and with the connotation of material success as in Pap. Westcar 6,15; 11,20; cf. also Wb.II 354,26-27. *Nf3 n bw-nfr* as "those for good fortune" appears to denote people aiming for material success outside of agriculture, apparently by fishing and hunting. This is corroborated by the use of *nḥm,* which is identical to *nḥm* "take away," "carry off" concerning food, as in Sinuhe B 104;[159] cf. also Peasant B 1,11; 28.

N3 n šw-ḳʿḥ begins a new sentence that specifies *nf3 n bw-nfr*. *N3 n* is not a plural demonstrative, as is universally assumed,[160] but is rather the possessive prefix "those of", i.e., the people of an area; see Wb.II 199,5.[161] *Šw-ḳʿḥw* has been considered by Gardiner, *op. cit.*, note 15, as a "special phrase for fish-ponds," which has been generally accepted.[162] The term occurs also in the Kuban-Stela l. 30, *sṯ(?) rmw m šw ḳʿḥw nyw ẖ3t ỉdḥw* "spearing fish in the *šw-ḳ3ḥw* of the Delta-marsh"; further Book of Gates VIII and Edfu I 214. *Ḳʿḥ* occurs also in Caminos,

Literary Fragments in the Hieratic Script, pl. II B 1,7, but there is no discernible connection there with fishing or fish. Although the passage in the Kuban-Stela links the term with fishing, the designation itself contains no reference to fish or their pursuit, as Wb.V 20,13 suggests, seeing in it a designation of the inland lakes near the Delta coast. *Ḳꜥḥ* is clearly used to qualify *šw* "lakes" and thus should be recognized as adjectival. Such a use has been discussed by Grdseloff, ASAE 48, 1948, 508, who established its meaning as "rare," "unaccustomed," possibly better as "exotic." Applying this meaning to *šw-ḳꜥḥw* in Neferyt 1. 30, the term should be rendered as "exotic lakes,"[163] and it appears to be a reference to the lakes on the Quantara depression of the Isthmus of Suez, in particular Lake Ballah and Lake Timsah. *N3 n šw ḳꜥḥw* "those of the exotic lakes" denotes those entrepreneurs (*nf3 n bw-nfr*) who went to the lakes east of the Wadi Tumilat for fishing and hunting.

As *n3 n šw ḳꜥḥw* clearly is the subject of the sentence,   has to be recognized as Old Perfective, third person plural;[164] for the form, cf. Gardiner, *Egyptian Grammar*[3] §309; Lefèbvre, *op. cit.*, §336. While Pap. Ermitage has *wnyw ẖr wgsw* (), O Petrie has *wnyw ẖr wgs*, which is generally preferred.[165] This interpretation is acceptable if *wbnw* is taken as the object of *wgs* "to gut," "to slit open," Wb.I 377, 12ff.; cf. also Montet, *Scènes de la vie privée*, 41; Caminos, *op. cit.*, 18f. As object of *wgs*,  cannot be taken to mean "shine" or "overflow," but has to be a noun and as such should be equated with *wbnw* "wound."[166] The wording of O Petrie 38 can thus be rendered "those of the distant lakes, they were cutting wounds at the bottom of fish and fowl," which makes some sense, although it is not particularly satisfying. The main objection is the unnecessary emphasis on a detail that should have been obvious to everybody. I thus prefer the version as contained in Pap. Ermitage and render it "those of the distant lakes, they were carrying gutting-knives shining from fish and fowl." *Wn ẖr*, lit. "to be under" is the idiom "to be in possession of."[167] *Wgsw* has to be recognized, because of its determination by , as denoting the kind of knife used for gutting. In view of the qualification *wbnw* "shining,"[168] those knives have to be pictured as made of copper. Corroboration is supplied by Caminos, *loc. cit.*, pl. VI C 3,10 *wgs.k m ḥsmn* "you can gut with bronze," verifying that the gutting was done with metal tools.[169]

aa) *Bw-nfr* has the same material meaning here as above, referring to success in hunting and fishing. The collapse of physical conditions due to the prevailing drought eliminated the possibility of pursuing "good chance," *Rwi* "to go away" (into a far distance) is used metaphorically, as below in l. 45 and in the Story of the Herdsman 20,[170] and applies here also to the disappearance of the waters in which fishing and bird-hunting used to be plentiful.

Ptḫ is generally separated from the preceding and considered a separate syntactical unit,[171] as would seem supported by the verse-point preceding it in O DeM 1074. This interpretation requires the deletion of *m* before *t3* in Pap. Ermitage[172] and cannot explain the formulation *ptḫ t3*  in O Petrie 38. In all renderings except that of Barta, *ptḫ* is taken as a *sḏm.f*, which does not state a resulting condition, as most translations assume the meaning of the passage to be. In Pap. Ermitage *ptḫ* has to be recognized as Old Perfective,[173] used parallel to *rww*, i.e., qualifying *bw-nfr*. For *ptḫ* "to go to the ground," "to collapse," here possibly with a literal physical connotation, cf. Peasant B 1,197; Admonitions 8,14; CT I 249d (transitive); and above, l. 21.

T3 n ḳsnt "land of misery" describes the eastern Delta; for *ḳsnt* "misery" with the specific connotation of "famine," see Vandier, *La famine dans l'Egypte ancienne*, 61ff. The preposition *m-ꜥ* can be taken here to qualify *ḳsnt*, i.e., introducing the cause of the misery, or to concern *t3 n ḳsnt* "land of misery" treated as an integrated unit and thus stating those in whose possession the land is.[174]

Nf3y n, as above in l. 30 (see p. 88), denotes people in search of or aiming for something. Whereas previously it was "bounty" (*bw-nfr*), here it is *ḏf3w* "food"; cf. Wb.V 569,15.[175]

Sṯyw ẖtyw t3 "the bedouin roaming the land" is either parallel to *nf3 n ḏf3w* or appositional. *Sṯyw* denotes here specifically the bedouin who had taken refuge in the eastern Delta and does not refer to Asiatics, i.e., people settled in Palestine; the latter are denoted *ꜥ3mw* and are mentioned in the next sentence. In Sinuhe B 17 and 25 this specific meaning of *Sṯyw* is clear, as Sinuhe is at the time in the Wadi Tumilat and not on Asiatic soil proper.[176]

XII. ATTACKS BY ASIATICS

'And as strife 33| will develop for the East and the Asiatics will descend
to Egypt,[ab]
one will lack a fortification and assistance.[ac]
The garrison will not hear,
34| when one will scale the ladder by night
when one will enter the fortification,
when one will surprise the drowsy one.'[ad]
35| "You can be at rest, because I am watchful!"[ae]

ab) The structure of Section VII is identical with that of the preceding. After describing conditions, Neferyt points out prospects he anticipates, as he had promised earlier (l. 26; see above p. 81). The two clauses *ỉw* + noun + *r* + infinitive should thus be taken as prospective circumstantial clauses. *Ḫrwy* "enemies," "war," cf. Peasant B 1,282, *ỉw snm.k r sḫpr ḫrwy.k* "your greed(?) will bring about enemies of yours"; cf. also Sinuhe B 54f., *n ṯs.n ḫrwyw.f skw* "not can his enemies close ranks"; Merikareʿ P. 68, *ỉw mr wšš ḫt ḫrwy;* Fischer, *Inscriptions from the Coptite Nome,* 113.

For *ḥr ỉ3btt* "in the East," cf. Wb.III 131,29; *ḥr* can also be taken to introduce the reason for strife. *ʾI3btt* "East," as above in l. 18, should be taken as referring to Egypt's eastern fringe; see above p. 70. The juxtaposition with *Kmt* shows that *ʾI3btt* does not denote an area administratively integrated into Egypt. This agrees with the absence of an "East-nome" (i.e., the fourteenth nome of Lower Egypt), despite the insistence of Fischer[177] on its existence. *ʾI3btt* is, as previously held by Otto and Helck,[178] a geographical and not a specific administrative term.[179] The differentiation between "East" and Egypt proper is an important feature in our text (see above p. 10) and provides proof that the final incorporation of the "East" into Egypt was initiated by Amenemhet I[180] and completed by Sesostris I.[181]

ᶜ3mw denotes people from Asia proper; cf. Merikareᶜ P. 91; 97; Sinuhe B 265; B 141; JEA 4, 1918, pl. 9,1.7; Hammamat nos. 17,6; 43,7; Hatnub Gr. 16,6; 24,14; *Ḫw-Sbk* (Manchester 3306). The term *ᶜ3m (n) ḥry-šᶜ* appears to have a different meaning in the Old Kingdom. Urk.I 101,9 is ambiguous in its geographical implication, but Urk.I 134,13-15 makes it quite certain that *ᶜ3m* and *ḫ3st ᶜ3m* were located at the Red Sea, because a ship destined for Punt was made there.[182]

H3 appears to have here the hostile connotation "to attack," as common for the transitive *h3*, Wb.II 475,1ff.; Sethe, *Übersetzung und Kommentar zu den altägyptischen Pyramidentexten* I, 128. As a mere geographical specification *h3 r Kmt* occurs in Peasant R 7; cf. also Admonitions 3,1.

ac) Following the anticipated events is a description of what effect they will have. As they concern Asiatics, they are of particular interest, reflecting their belligerent intrusion into the Nile Delta proper. The particularly disastrous aspects, which Neferyt foresees in the event of an attack by Asiatics, are described as *g3w.tw ḫnrt ky-r-gs*.[183] As there is only one verb (*g3w*) and its form is clearly an impersonal *sḏm.tw*, the verb obviously has two objects. Despite the simplicity of the passage, it has found diverse renderings.[184] *G3w* "to be lacking," Wb.V 152,2; Cairo 20539 I 8; Polotsky, *Zu den Inschriften der 11. Dynastie*, §64a; Vandier, Mo alla 173.

Ḫnrt "fortress," possibly with the connotation "frontier-fortification." The reading, though corroborated for the Middle Kingdom, would be an anachronism for the Old Kingdom, where the frontier fortifications are denoted as *rtḥ* (Junker, Gîza III 174) and *ỉtḥ* (Moᶜalla insc. no. 6; Siut III 18; Hatnub Gr. 20,13 with a variant in Gr. 25,7, where *ḫnrt* is used instead of *ỉtḥ*). For *ḫnrt* "fortress" see also Louvre C 1; Hatnub Gr. 23,4. It refers here to the border fortification attested first in the late Old Kingdom.[185] They can be identified with the fortifications built by the Heracleopolitan kings (Merikareᶜ P. 102) and reactivated by Amenemhet I.[186]

Ky-r-gs, with *ky-r-gs.f* as variant in O Petrie 38,10, has found some ingenious interpretations (see above note 184). Syntactically, it can only be an object of *g3w* and is thus parallel to *ḫnrt*. The syntactical position also reveals that it is an idiomatically used compound.

This idiom occurs twice in the Eloquent Peasant B 1,44, *smwn sḫty.f pw ỉww n ky-r-gs.f* and B 1, 45-46 *mk ỉrrt.sn pw r sḫtyw.sn ỉww n ktḫt-r-gs.sn*. Wb.V 195,16, following Vogelsang,[187] renders the idiom "zu einem anderen kommen statt zu ihm," which makes little sense.[188] The literal meaning "another at the/his side" requires, rather, understanding the idiom as describing an "assistant" or "assistance," The occurrence in Peasant B 1,44 should thus be read "presumably, his peasant is it, who came for assistance".[189] While in the Eloquent Peasant the idiom occurs in juridical context, the occurrence in the "Prophecy" has a military setting; the meaning, however, remains the same.

ad) In *nn sḏm mwnf* we have an independent clause, which is followed by three dependent circumstantial clauses. *Mwnf* is best taken as "garrison,"[190] as in Urk.IV 730,17, although "protector (of a place)" as held Wb.II 55,7-9, is an equally valid and ultimately identical rendering. For *tw* + *r* + infinitive, see above 1. 27.

Tw r ỉsḳ m3ḳt m grḥ describes the first stage in the storming of a fortified place and is contrasted here with the unattentive garrison.[191] In view of the parallelism, the impersonal *tw* has to be taken to refer to enemies in the three passages. *ʾIsḳ* is listed Wb.I 133,6-11 as intransitive "to linger" and as transitive "to hinder"; neither meaning leads to a satisfactory understanding of the passage. According to the determinative, *ỉsḳ* is a verb of motion, and I conjecture its meaning as "to storm," lit. "to jump up" or "to jump from" the ladder into the besieged city.[192] This rendering is supported by the use of *ỉsḳ* in Sinuhe G 15[193] parallel to *ỉwd* "to separate from."[194] The same meaning prevails in *Mntw-wsr* 12[195] *n ỉsḳ.ỉ s m mḫnt* "I did not make a man jump from the/my ferryboat." *ʾIsḳ* is possibly identical with *sḳ* in Hammamat no. 7 in a military context[196] and might be related with *ḳ3s* "rope-ladder," Wb.V 13,17. *M3ḳt* "ladder," Wb.II 33,6; its use in storming a fortified place is indicated by the determinative of *sṯp* "to storm" in Urk.I 149,2.[197] *M grḥ* "by night," referring to nighttime in general, as in Urk.IV 959,15; Pyr. 132a.

ʿḳ with direct object "to penetrate a place," Wb.I 231,12. O Petrie 38 has *ʿḳ r ḫnrt*.

Snbt has been conjectured by Gardiner[198] to mean "to banish" (sleep), which has been universally maintained.[199] There can be no doubt that the sentence is construed as *tw* + *r* + infinitive and is parallel to the two preceding sentences, as S. Herrmann rightly emphasized. The impersonal construction is used in describing the last phase in the conquest of a fortified place by night. Being descriptive, the occasionally presumed occurrence of a suffix first person can be ruled out.  should thus be taken as a determinative of a compound expression *ḳdd-m-ỉrty*, i.e., one with "sleep in the eyes," a "drowsy one."[200] In view of this meaning, *snbt* can best be interpreted as "to surprise."[201] The word is probably identical with *znb* "to overstep" (a boundary), Wb.III 458,8; Sinuhe R 141, as already envisaged by Gardiner.

ae) The closing sentence of the section is completely different in structure from what precedes it. Most significant is the reference to a first and a second person singular, neither being mentioned in the remainder of the section. The introduction of otherwise unnamed persons makes it virtually impossible to connect this sentence with the foregoing, as has been universally maintained.[202] Even the assumption of a quotation is untenable, because neither does it have an introduction nor would the people involved be identified.

The text is preserved in O DeM 1074,11 as *sḏr.ti ḥr ỉw.ỉ rs.n.ỉ*, while Pap. Ermitage 35 is generally read *sḏr.kwi ḥr ỉw.ỉ rs.kwi*.[203] However, the hieratic original has  *ḥr ỉw.ỉ rs.kwi* (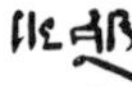), which provides a reading quite close to that of O DeM 1074, the difference being that the latter has an Old Perfective followed by *ỉw.f sḏm.n.f*, the former a *sḏm.f* followed by *ỉw.f* + Old Perfective. As the construction *ỉw.f sḏm.n.f* seems highly problematic,[204] the wording *sḏr.k ḥr ỉw.ỉ rs.kwi* "you can go to rest because I am watchful!" is preferable. For *sḏr* "to go to rest," cf. Pap. Mill. 1,12; Sinuhe B 293; Herdsman 9.[205] The use of *ḥr* as a conjunction occurs also in Peasant B 1,12; B 2,125; cf. also Gardiner, *Egyptian Grammar*^{3} §165.11; Lefèbvre, *op. cit.*, §735, 2.

The isolated passage obviously is a direct speech and is not part of the things Neferyt anticipates. As at the end of Section V (l. 26), the account is interrupted here by an address of Neferyt to his listener. The aim is to give reassurance that the situation is not desperate yet, as long as Neferyt keeps a watchful eye on it.[206] The interruption also serves to mark the completion of a thought and the turning to another prospect anticipated by Neferyt. While the intrusion of foreigners has thus far been anticipated as a prospect, Section VIII pictures the country as devasted and occupied as the result of a foreign attack, which leads to internal strife. This topic is continued beyond Section VIII, and its details are discussed in Sections IX and X.

XIII. THE EAST IN FOREIGN HANDS

VIII, 36 'The wild game (i.e., the desert dwellers) will drink water from the watercourses 36 of the arable land, while they are pleased about their riparian land,

as those to chase away 37 their coming are lacking.[af]

When this land will be seized and recovered, is an event not known--

as what will be is hidden.[ag]

Do not say: 38 "Who can listen because of deafness, as the prospect is mute?"[ah]

I present to you the land in passing a sickness,

39 as that which should not happen happened:[ai]

One will take up the weapons of warfare, and

the life of the land is in 40 revellion.'[aj]

af) *ʿwt-ḫ3st* "wild game" as in Sinuhe B 89; the term is common in the Old Kingdom; cf. Montet, *Scènes de la vie privée*, 86ff.; Davies and Gardiner, *The Tomb of Amenemhet*, pl. IX. In view of the metaphorical use of *ʿwt* for people in the Middle Kingdom,[207] *ʿwt ḫ3st* is likely to denote here "foreigners," as in the Demotic Chronicle V 15.[208]

All versions except Pap. Ermitage have *swr mw ḥr itrw*, which would seem the better wording, although *swr* + *ḥr* is attested otherwise in the Eighteenth Dynasty; cf. Wb.III 428,14. *ʾItrw nyw Kmt* "(navigable) watercourses of the arable land" occurred before in l. 26 and is discussed there (see above p. 82). The mention here has a different connotation, serving as a symbol for the depth of the penetration into the center of the agricultural land.

Ḳbb.sn ḥr wḏb.sn might seem at a first glance obvious and has consistently been rendered "(they) take their ease on their sand-banks."[209] Only Helck remarked on the use of *.sn* after *wḏb*, explaining it as a reference to *ʿwt-ḫ3st*. This point, though beyond doubt, produces the curious situation that arable land shall be in possession of the game of the desert. The metaphorical use of *ʿwt-ḫ3st* has already been pointed out and finds its corroboration in the particularities of the situation described. *Ḳbb*, too, has a more specific meaning here than "to be cool"[210] and is rather to be understood in the sense "to be idle"; for this meaning, see Merikareʿ P. 68;[211] in regard to the tilling of fields, see Ḥeḳanakhte I 26; II vs. 4.[212]

It seems better to read *ng3* as "to lack" than as an adverbial **n g3w* "for lack of," as is generally done.[213] The verse-point in O DeM 1074 and O Vandier indicates that *ng3* is the verbal predicate of a sentence.  is the causative of *twr* "to chase away," as held by Helck and Barta; cf. also Wb.IV 344,9; the word occurs also in l. 21 and in Hammamat no. 191,4. The reading of the object of *st(w)r* is uncertain. It is preserved only in Pap. Ermitage, and Golenishcheff left it untranscribed; Helck gives for it , which Barta proposed to change to *š3st*. The traces at the end of l. 36 do not resemble *š3* () as it occurs in ll. 20-22, and the reading is thus to be rejected. On the other hand, O Vandier clearly has 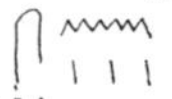 at the end, which is also a possible reading in O DeM 1074,12.[214] The signs making up the object of *st(w)r* are thus best read  or 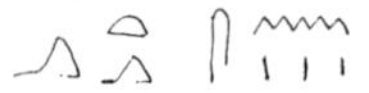 "their coming."[215] The complaint concerns the inability to ward off the arrival, rather than an expulsion afterwards.

ag) *ʾIw t3 pn r ỉṯt ỉnt*[216] is either a circumstantial or a temporal clause, and *nn rḫ bsw* is the main clause. *ʾIṯi-ỉni* constitute antonyms in Egyptian and, when paired together, are used as an idiom for wavering.[217] This idiomatic use has been applied in the present passage as a description of the commotion in the country.[218] The idiomatic use of *ỉṯi-ỉni* is well established, but its application in this instance seems inappropriate--especially since a literal rendering remains meaningless, the object of "taking" and "bringing" being undefinable. A more literal rendering "this land will be taken and brought back" thus seems in place here, indicating the loss and recovery of the area with which Neferyt is concerned. For *ỉṯi* with *t3* as its object, see Wb.I 90, 18,6; Sinuhe B 178; cf. also Urk.IV 2020,20 for the idiom in a military context.

Nn rḫ bsw is used in O Vandier; Pap. Ermitage has *n rḫ bsw*, which requires a passive rendering "the event is not known."[219]

Bsw is extremely difficult to render satisfactorily. Faulkner,

Concise Dictionary, 84, translates it "result, consequence," derived from *bsi* "to flow forth." The latter probably is identical with *bs* "to introduce," despite Gardiner's[220] emphasis on differentiating them. The seemingly opposite direction in the two renderings results from the different "Lokalvorstellung"[221] and dynamic aspect of Egyptian. Our passage has a parallel in Pap. Leiden I 350 IV,9[222] *nn rḫ bs.f* "there is none who knows his advent" (i.e., Amun's as the first principle). It is in this sense that *bsw* appears to be used here, referring to the advent of the political events in the area concerned, namely its loss as well as its political recovery.

Since Gardiner's initial study[223] *ḫpr.ty.fy* has been thought to qualify *bsw*. As *bsw* itself denotes a future event, a qualification by a prospective *ḫpr.ty.fy* would be pleonastic. Furthermore, *ỉmn* would be a predicate without a subject, because the proposed construction **ỉmn m ḏd* is a grammatical impossibility. It is thus necessary to separate *ḫpr.ty.fy* from *bsw* and to connect it with the Old Perfective *ỉmn*. The verbal adjective used nominally to denote the future occurred in l. 14 (see above p. 64) and is here a direct continuation of *bsw*. What might seem a truism--namely, that the future is hidden--is significant in evaluating the character of our text and the mentality it reflects, as is discussed separately (see p. 81).[224]

The proposed sentence[225] *ỉmn m ḏd* is grammatically impossible, as *ỉmn* clearly is a verb and thus cannot be predicate in a nominal clause with adverbial predicate. In order to overcome this fact, Barta, *op. cit.*, 40, emended the text to *ỉmnt m ḏd ptr sḏm* and translated it "Verborgenes ist im Sagen, Sehen und Hören." However, such a sentence would have to be construed with the *m* of identity, which entails a different meaning than that proposed. The recurrent assumption of an idiom **ỉmn m* "to be hidden from" is not supported by any other example. "To hide from" is construed with the preposition *r* (Wb.I 83,14), whereas the idiom using *m* means "to hide in" (Wb.I 83,15).

ah) *M ḏd* is a negated imperative, as in l. 21, and marks here a return from the description of anticipated events to addressing the listener, i.e., the king. Consequently,  has to be recognized as conveying a direct speech. The use of first- and second-person pronouns in the next sentence corroborates that we have here a direct address by the speaker, Neferyt, to the addressee, the king.

Ptr is not a particle, as has been proposed, because this occurs only in Late Egyptian. To connect it with *ptr* "to see" would necessitate that it be an imperative, because of the lack of any ending. This makes it necessary to understand  as the interrogative *ptr* despite the determinative .[226] As *sḏm* is not construed with the preposition *ḥr*, the question consists only of *ptr sḏm*. I take *sḏm* as a participle, as in Pap. Hearst 11,13.[227] *Ḥr* introduces the reason or circumstance that makes listening impossible; for this use, cf. Gardiner, *Egyptian Grammar*[3] §165.7; Edel, *Altägyptische Grammatik*, §765d. *ʾId* "to be deaf," here as noun or nominally used infinitive; cf. Gardiner, *op. cit.*, §298.

The question is followed by *ỉw sḏm.f*, which is either merely continuing or circumstantial. Only Pap. Ermitage preserves this sentence, and its reading apparently is not correct. *Gr* is obviously verbal predicate, which makes it necessary to recognize 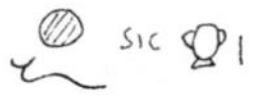 as the compound noun *ḫf*[*t*]-*ḥr*, Wb.III 275 A. Literally "who is *à face*," it denotes the person who is faced and thus can be rendered "partner" in a dialogue.[228] *Gr* is used here literally as "to be silent," and the proverb should be understood to have as its moral the impossibility of becoming knowledgeable when the prospects or the partner is unknown.[229]

ai) *Di.ỉ n.k* continues the admonition *m ḏd*, which was interrupted by the quote of the expected reply. *Di* as metaphor for "presenting an argument," cf. Wb.II 465; V 468 D. *Zyn mny* was explained by Gardiner[230] as a jingle comparable to "topsy-turvy," which has been generally accepted.[231] Although this rendering would seem to suit the context, it lacks a philological base. Literally, *t3 m sny mny* can only be rendered "passing through a malady," as taken in Wb.III 455,20-22.[232] The particular nuance conveyed by the idiom is not so much that of distress as of passing a stage of extreme danger that could lead to the gravest consequences but that still has room for recovery.

Tmt ḫpr ḫpr.ti[233] "what shall not happen has happened"; for the construction, cf. Satzinger, *op. cit.*, §64; Gardiner, *Egyptian Grammar*[3] §397,1. The Old Perfective *ḫpr.ti* indicates it as an accomplished fact. The almost parenthetical character of the passage makes it a qualification or description of *mn*, namely the state of sickness the country is passing through.[234]

aj) *Iw r šsp*, as in ll. 34-35, is a circumstantial clause describing how the "sickness" is apt to manifest itself. *Šsp* "to take up arms," Amenemhet (Mill. II,4); Wb.IV 530,7; Merikareʿ P. 106-107 *ḫʿw nyw ʿḥ3* "fighting utensils," Wb.III 243,15; the New Kingdom construction of the term is datival.

The syntactical connection of *ꜥnḫ t3* with the preceding is not entirely clear. It could be taken as a dependent clause, but in that case an introduction by *ỉw* could be expected. Previous sections ended with a concluding statement, and the same can be assumed here. The passage *ꜥnḫ t3 m sh3* is generally considered a verbal clause.[235] Though seemingly self-evident, this interpretation does not hold up under questioning. I am not aware that *ꜥnḫ* is used with *t3* "land" as its subject, as the use of *ꜥnḫ* appears to be restricted to animated beings, including plants. As a result the common interpretation of a verbal clause requires reconsideration. *Sh3* was discussed by Gardiner, *Admonitions of an Egyptian Sage,* 28f., leading him to a rendering "to be confused," "to go astray," while in our passage he rendered it "uproar" without attempting to reconcile the two meanings.[236] Wb.IV 206 gives for the nominal use "Aufruhr," "Ungesetzlichkeit." The word occurs as a verb in Merikare P. 106, *sh3/zh3 t3š.k r ꜥrsy* "your boundary against the South (side) will be attacked." As a transitive it is found also in Siut V 22-23 *ỉnk ꜥḳ3 bit šw m sh3 nb.f* "I was one straight of character, free of attacking his lord" and JEA 16, 1930, 22 *zh3 st* "attack them!" as well as Ptahhotep 476 *m wšb m sp n zh3* "do not reply with a case of attack!" This meaning also applies in Admonitions 2,11, *ỉw-ms sh3 dpt rsw ḫb3 miwt* "forsooth, the campaign[237] of Southerners will attack and towns will be destroyed"; similarly, Admonitions 12,12, *sh3 pw rdi.k ḫt t3 ḥnꜥ ḫrw ẖnnw* "An attack is it which you cause throughout the land together with the shouting of the lawbreakers."[238] The later use of the word corroborates the rendering "attack." LD III 128a,[239] *šsp.sn sh3 ẖnn* "they are beginning to attack and to break the law"; Pap. Leiden 345, rt. XXVII, 3[240] *pt m sh3* "heaven is under attack." It is this occurrence that parallels the construction in *ꜥnḫ-t3 m sh3*. This requires recognizing *ꜥnḫ-t3* as a compound term with a geographical connotation; *ꜥnḫ-t3* with this meaning is attested from the early Twelfth Dynasty at Bersheh,[241] in an epithet of Osiris as *nb ꜥnḫ-t3*. While the theological formulation "life of the land" would be an appropriate domain for Osiris's rule, such a general meaning "life of the land" would make sense in the given context as well, namely, that life itself is endangered in the area Neferyt is concerned with. However, one would like to see here a more specific meaning.

XIV. PROSPECTS OF WAR

IX,11 '(When) one will make arrows of copper,
one will request bread with [41] blood,
one will laugh at the outcry for pain,[ak]
one will not weep for a death,
one will not [42] spend a night hungry for a death.
(As) man's heart is concerned with himself,
one will not do the post mortem [43] presently,
(as) the mind has totally gone away from it:[al]
A man can sit down, that he bends [44] his back,
while one is slaying another.[am]
I can present to you a son as an enemy,
a brother as a foe, or
a man able [45] to slay his father.'[an]

ak) The section following the statement *ʿnḫ-t3 sh3* seems to describe internal strife rather than an attack by an external enemy. This makes me wonder whether *ʿnḫ-t3* has here really only a general meaning. It could be an opaque reference to Memphis or to the traditional kingship, as seems to underlie the designation *ʿnḫ-t3wy*. If the thesis of a reference to civil war is correct, a dualistic term like *ʿnḫ-t3wy* would be appropriate, and an attack on the traditional kingship in the country by a rival party could be clad in the choice of *ʿnḫ-t3*. The term appears first connected with Bastet in the Fifth Dynasty (Borchardt, *Das Grabdenkmal des Königs Sa3ḥureʿ* II, pl. 35); in the Middle Kingdom *ʿnḫ-t3wy* is used in connection with Ptaḥ[242] and Osiris.[243]

The opening *ỉw.tw r ỉrt* clause has virtual circumstantial force. *ʾIr ʿḥ3w* refers basically to the making of arrowheads, as in Pap. Sallier II 7,4 *ỉrw-ʿḥ3w* "the arrowhead maker."[244] The use of metal for arrowheads is attested since the beginning of the Eleventh Dynasty.[245] Its mention here seems to convey more than a reference to a new technological development. As already pointed out, the sentence mentioning the use of copper is a circumstantial clause, thus setting the frame for the subsequent account of the horrors of civil war. Consequently, the reference to the making of metal arrowheads appears to have the connotation of fighting in earnest.[246]

Dbḥ has here the much more forceful connotation "to demand" than the usual "to ask for," "to beg"; cf. Goedicke, *The Report about the Dispute of a Man with His* Ba, 139. *T3* has here the general connotation "food" rather than specifically "bread"; cf. Scharff, ZÄS 77, 1942, 16, and the common claim, "I gave bread to the hungry."[247] *M* introducing *znf* should be taken as instrumental, i.e., the means by which bread is acquired.[248]

The other dreadful prospect, when fighting will break out, has found differing interpretations.[249] The two available versions differ, as Pap. Ermitage has *sbṯ.tw m*  *n mr*, while Cairo 25224 has *sbṯ.tw.f m*  *n mr*, the latter being generally considered superior. The generally accepted view of the passage does not lead to a satisfying sense, because the laughter remains without motive. As it would seem improbable that the text relates an outbreak of senseless laughter, a different meaning can be expected here. *Zbṯ* as construed with the preposition *m* has the meaning "to laugh about"; see Wb.III 434,7.[250] Since "to laugh about laughter" makes very little sense indeed, I propose emending  into *sbḥ*. We have here apparently a conflation of *sbḥ* "outcry," which is attested in the spelling ,[251] with *zbṯ* "to laugh" mentioned just before it. *N mr* is, as Posener has already pointed out, parallel to *n mt* in the next sentence and thus requires datival rendering. *Mr* connotes here more than "illness" and might better be rendered "affliction," i.e., injury caused by fighting.[252] It continues the description of the perils of war that was opened by the reference to injury in the search of food.

al) *Rm n* has here the connotation "to shed a tear for" as in Suicidal 76,[253] rather than "to mourn", i.e., "to weep because of someone," which is expressed by *rm ḥr*, Wb.II 417,9.[254] *Mwt* should be taken as "a case of death" or "a dead one" rather than as "death" itself.[255] For the construction *nn rm.tw* and its future meaning, see Satzinger, *op. cit.*, §57.

By realizing that *rm n* does not have a funerary connotation, the significance of *nn sḏr.tw ḥḳr n mwt* becomes clear. It is generally considered a reference to ritual fasting as a part of mourning.[256] However, the use of *sḏr* specifies the activity as belonging to the night only, and under normal circumstances there is no eating during the night. Thus, the passage should be taken to state the height of outrage, i.e., that one would not even spend a night hungry, even for death. As the question of mourning is brought up later, the passage has to concern another aspect. It could be presumed to concern the aiding of a dying person, but the abstinence from food would seem insignificant for such an occasion. To spend a night doing something appears to be a metaphor for minimal effort, as in the recurrent phrase "I did not cause anybody to spend a night angry against me about something,"[257] or Urk.I 223,9 "I never spend a night with my seal away from me." In view of this use I am inclined to understand the meaning of the passage as juxtaposing a minimal effort, such as the most primary obligation to apply oneself, i.e., in the case of possible death. In other words, even if it entails death, people will not make the slightest effort. This interpretation is corroborated by the appositive clause *ỉb n s m-s3.f ḏs.f* "the heart of a man cares only for himself"; for the idiom *ỉb m-s3*, cf. Ḥeḳanakhte II rt. 2.[258]

Nn ỉr.tw s3mwt min contains two problems, one the exact meaning of *s3mwt*, the other the use of *min*. As for the first, there is general consensus that the word denotes some aspect of mourning.[259] Besides the present occurrence it is also attested CT I 380a; 382c; BD 50,3 and O BM 5634 vs. 15[260] as *s3mwt n s3.f* in a list of workmen. The word has no attested cognate and should be recognized as a compound *s3-mwt* "after death" (post mortem), describing possibly the initial phase following immediately after death. As the period of personal mourning, it precedes the official part when outsiders participate in the funeral service, so that the determinative  is very appropriate. The entry in O BM 5634 vs. 15 explains the worker's absence as "mourning for his son."

The second problem in the passage is the nature of *min*, which is commonly considered to mean "today."[261] As Lefèbvre[262] pointed out, the use of the future construction rules out the mention of "today," which would lead to an irreconcilable contradiction. In order to avoid it, I consider *min* with a more general connotation "at present," "presently"; cf. Admonitions 3,7; Suicidal 103ff.; 130ff. Although there remains an unresolved rest, the presumed meaning is lack of attention to the immediate obligation, so that self-concern overrides it.

am) For *stni*, see Posener, *op. cit.*, 152; also *m stni ỉb.k ḥr nṯr* "do not let your heart turn away from god."[263] The word is probably to be connected with *wstn* "to move freely," Wb.I 367.[264]

As in other sections, the account of anticipated events is followed by a summarizing observation pertinent to the subject. This section had dealt with man's innate cruelty during internecine fights. It can be presumed that this particular attitude is epitomized by the description of a bizarre case of man's ability to be cruel. The available translations do not satisfy this requirement,[265] but rather offer philologically ambiguous translations or resort to more or less extensive emendations or interpretations. Grammatically there can be no question that *ḥms z* is a perfective *sḏm.f*. Basically it is a statement of actuality, and there is no reason to make it prospective--especially in view of *r ḳᶜḥ.f s3.f*--because *r + sḏm.f* has by itself the connotation of intent. In order to convey the implicit stress on actuality, *ḥms z* is best rendered "a man can sit down."[266]

The purpose of this motion is specified as *r ḳᶜḥ.f s3.f*, clearly the construction *r* + perfective *sḏm.f*.[267] *Ḳᶜḥ*, lit. "to angle," "to bend in an angle,"[268] is apparently attested only here with *s3* "back" as its object. The usual idiom for "to bend the back," i.e., "to bow" is *ksi*; the choice of an unusual term is significant, especially in view of its basic meaning, so that *ḳᶜḥ s3* should be rendered as "to angle the back." Needless to say, this cannot mean "to turn one's back," as some translators proposed, especially not for the purpose of sitting down. Considering the latter, I take *r ḳᶜḥ.f s3.f* as describing the typical pose in which Egyptians squat to relieve their bowels. The reference to this base activity makes good sense in the passage dealing with man's unlimited ability to exercise cruelty toward his fellow men. What Neferyt apparently wishes to convey is the fact that man, even in the most inappropriate situations, can still exhibit his cruelty and lack of concern. The pseudoverbal clause might best be recognized as having circumstantial meaning. For *ky--ky*, cf. Gardiner, *op. cit.*, §98; Urk.VII 33,2.

an) The cruelty that man is able to exhibit is demonstrated by showing that even family ties do not stop it. The topic occurs in Admonitions 5,10; 13,3. The difference, if any, between *ḫrwy* and *ḫfty* is not fully clear; for the latter, cf. Zandee, *Death as an Enemy*, 217ff. Needless to say, the possibilities cited are the gravest conceivable offenses to Egyptian moral thought.

XV. FUTILITY OF ADMINISTRATIVE MEASURES

X, 11 'Every pronouncement is completed with "As loves me!",
but all success is gone away.[ao]
The land 46 perishes, as laws are decreed for it, which are annulled by crimes;
one will be scot-free in inquiries[ap]
as crimes are 47 something, which is as when it was never done.[aq]
One will take the very property of a man, which is given to a litigator.[ar]
I can show you a lord in worries, while an outcast is satisfied.[as]
48 The one who does not act will be paid for,
while the doer will be empty.[at]
One will give things in a case of serious crime in order to silence sentencing,
(while) one rejects 49 a sentence (about) an aggravated assult
and one says "don't kill him!"'[au]

ao) Section X, which follows the picturing of internecine fighting, has as its main theme the breakdown of law. Its structure is somewhat different from that of the preceding sections, as the discourses are divided by a direct address to the listener, after which the account of anticipated events continues.

The theme is introduced by juxtaposing prevalent assertions and reality. *R3-nb* "every mouth" might seem a global reference like *ḥr nb* and is possibly attested in the Eighteenth Dynasty,[269] although the instance is not ascertained. An alternative is to consider *r3* in an extended meaning "pronouncement," "statement," possibly with juridical connotation as in CT I 11f.; 19b; JEA 47, 1961, 6; ZÄS 59, 1924, 10, 33; cf. also Wb.II 391,23. "To fill the mouth with" (*mḥ r3 m*) appears to occur only in reference to food, as in Peasant B 1,10, 15; cf. also Pyr. 425a; JEA 19, 1933, 172. The literal meaning of the opening passage is generally accepted as "every mouth is full of 'love me'," although some have expressed doubts about the validity of such a rendering.[270] Features of the recent "love culture" might suit a verbatim translation, but the phenomenon is altogether too modern to be applied to ancient Egypt. The context that the passage introduces deals with lawgiving, and an appropriate reference to this theme can be expected in the opening. The passage *r3 nb mḥ m mr wi* is paralleled by *š3.tw r.f hpw* "one passes laws for it (the land)," so that *r3 nb* should have a meaning similar to *hpw* "laws." As already pointed out, the literal interpretation of *r3 nb* as "every mouth" lacks support, so that *r3* is better accepted here in its extended meaning "pronouncement".[271] Once the idiomatic use of *r3* as "pronouncement" is recognized, the posing of a similarly extended use of *mḥ* becomes a necessity. Literally "filled with," I consider it here to denote a feature of a document and thus understand it in the sense of "to contain" or "to be completed (i.e., concluded) with"; for this interpretation see the Demotic *mḥ (n) mtr* "to complete a document with witnesses."[272] *Mr wi* has always been considered a quotation; however, instead of taking it as a verbal statement, I see in it a reference to a specific legal or documentary formula used in pronouncements to establish the implicit legal force and the authority on which it is based. Just as *ᶜnḫ* "as lives," the opening word of the oath formula, is used to denote the oath as legal instrument, *mr wi* represents the opening words of the royal oath *mry wi Rᶜ* "as Reᶜ loves me," with the reference to Re omitted; see Wilson, JNES 7, 1948, 140.[273]

Bw-nfr nb rwi occurred above in l. 31 (see p. 87f.), referring to success in fishing and hunting. Although the context is slightly different here, the meaning is basically the same, referring to the successful application of pronouncements confirmed by a royal oath.

ap) *3kw t3* is a perfective *sḏm.f*, which could be taken as prospective. Barta, *op. cit.*, 42, proposes the gramatically untenable rendering "Das Land wird zugrunde gerichtet werden," while M. Lichtheim, *op. cit.*, 142, gives an equally impossible "The land is ruined." *3ḳ* "to perish" of land occurs also above in l. 23, with the connotation of legal breakdown, while in Medinet Habu I 27,16 a more physical meaning prevails. The latter applies also in Suicidal 74, *msw.f 3ḳ* "his children perish,"[274] while Suicidal 107, *ỉw sf 3ḳ* "gentleness perished," falls under the former; cf.

also Ptahhotep 12 *pḥty 3ḳ* "strength perishes"; Admonitions 6,3 *ỉt 3ḳ* "grain perished."

Š3.tw is, like the preceding *3ḳ*, a perfective *sḏm.f* and should be treated as continuation. *Š3* "to decree laws," Wb.IV 403,1; for the specific connotation of *š3*, cf. also Morenz, *Untersuchungen zur Rolle des Schicksals in der ägyptischen Religion*, Akad. Wiss. Leipzig Abh. 52,1, 15ff. *Hpw* "laws" is not an Old Kingdom term and appears with the Middle Kingdom for undefined reasons; cf. Peasant B 1,65; 274 Louvre C 1; Siut I 268; Cairo 20539 I 2; Urk.VII 2,12; but see also Ptahhotep 90. *R.f* refers to *t3* and is not a particle.[275] *Ḥdd* is an imperfective passive participle[276] qualifying *hpw*.[277] For *ḥd* "to infringe," "to destroy" an agreement, cf. Siut I 281; cf. also Peasant B 1,275; JNES 19, 1960, 261, l. 10. *M* is used instrumentally or causally and introduces the element by which the laws are destroyed. *ʾIryt* "deeds," "actions," Wb.I 113,7; cf. also Cairo 20539 I 11, where *ỉryt* has hostile connotation, as here.

Wš.tw is a perfective *sḏm.f* and is thus to be separated from the participial *ḥdd*.[278] The passage describes how the laws are destroyed by actions. Pap. Ermitage 46 and C 25224 have *wš.tw*, while O BM 5627 has *wšd*. The latter denotes "legal inquiry," Wb.I 375,13.[279] *Wš* can be expected to have a similar meaning. The term is used intransitively in documents to indicate "absence," "to be lost," "to be destroyed."[280] The juridical implication appears to be unattested elsewhere. There is, however, a clearly recognizable pun on the idiom *gm wš* "found lost,"[281] as *wš m gmyt* "lost in the finding." *Gmyt*, as nominally used participle, is an application of the use of *gm* "to investigate."[282] This rendering remains unsatisfactory because of the seeming lack of any connection with the context. The next passage *ỉryt m tmmt ỉr(w)*, especially, would be isolated. These shortcomings disappear when *wš* is taken transitively; see Gardiner-Sethe, *Letters to the Dead*, 22; CT I 162b. The object is most probably omitted, so it can be rendered "one will delete (them) in the investigations."

aq) *ʾIryt m tmmt ỉr* is very similar to ll. 46-47, except that the nominally used participle is here imperfective. The variants differ somewhat, and Helck, *Die Prophezeiung des Nfr.tj*, 40, restores the original wording as *ỉrt m tmmt ỉrw*.[283] *Iryt* has to be identical with the same word "what was done" earlier in the line and denote the acts of lawlessness committed, i.e., "crimes." The meaning of the passage is that crimes are handled as if they had never been done.[284]

ar) O BM 5627,3 makes it clear that *tw r nḥm* is to be seen here as the same construction as in ll. 27, 34, 39 above. Pap. Ermitage and Cairo 25224 have the impersonal *tw* but omit the preposition *r*.[285] *Nḥm* "to take away" property legally, as in Urk.I 13,6; 298,16;[286] Pyr. 411c. The confiscation of goods outside legal action is expressed by *ỉṯỉ* in the Old Kingdom; see Edel, *Untersuchungen zur Phraseologie der ägyptischen Inschriften,* §25. In the Middle Kingdom, *nḥm* is less defined in its use, cf. Sinuhe B 104; Peasant B 1,11, 23, 28, 233; Petrie, Koptus 8, 6; the present occurrence apparently has a juridical connotation and denotes a "confiscation." *Ḫt-s* is treated as a compound and as a masculine word,[287] as indicated by the perfective passive participle *rdw*. Lefèbvre *op. cit.,* 102, note 43, takes *rdw* as an Old Perfective. This would presuppose an unattested nonenclitic use of the particle *rf* or some other introduction of the Old Perfective. The use of the particle *rf* to emphasize the object is noteworthy; cf. Gardiner, *op. cit.,* §252.3c.[288] *Ḫt-s* "property of a man" appears to have the specific legal connotation of "inherited estate" rather than temporarily acquired possessions. For *ỉḫt* as "inherited estate," cf. Urk.I 2,17; 72,1; 305,5; Pap. Berlin 9010,8;[289] Siut I 288; Ḥeḳanakhte I 2,3. See also Bakir, *Slavery in Pharaonic Egypt* 11; Goedicke, *Private Rechtsinschriften aus dem Alten Reich,* 200; *idem, Königliche Dokumente aus dem Alten Reich,* 116; Mrsich, *Untersuchungen zur Hausurkunde des Alten Reiches,* MÄS 13, 27ff. For the construction *nty m rwty,* see *nty m mr.f* "who is in his pyramid" Suicidal 42; cf. also *ntt m ib* in Siut I 219; Pap. Berlin 3029 2,9.[290]

The full meaning of the passage has not been recognized in previous translations.[291] It is not a mere juxtaposition of economic change by taking from one and giving to another. The absence of a specified agency, at least in regard to the distribution of property, makes such an interpretation highly improbable. When taking *ḫt-s* as a compound, *rdw* as passive participle qualifies *ḫt,* i.e., "the property . . . is given to one who is in the *rwt*." It is generally assumed that the recipient is an "outsider." *Rwty* "outsider" occurs immediately after, which makes it unlikely that the relative construction *nty rwt(y)* has the same meaning. Literally "who is in the *rwt(y)*," the term denotes a person who is in a place denoted as *rwty*. In view of the apparent semantic difference from the subsequent *rwty* "foreigner," I take  as spelling for *rwt--rwyt* "law-court."[292] *Nty m rwt* "who is in court" remains somewhat ambiguous, as it could be taken as a reference to someone accused in court; but a more likely interpretation is that it denotes a "litigator," i.e., a person pursuing litigation without just cause. The point Neferyt tries to convey is the complete disregard for social merits, culminating in the prospect that inherited property is not safe from criminal prosecution.

as) The disregard for tradition is continued with a direct address by Neferyt to his listener of the type found in ll. 38 and 44. In addition to contrasting the opposites in the social scale and the way they fare, the passage also utilizes rather extensive punning. *Nhpw* draws on its similarity with *hpw* "laws,"[293] which is a key word of this section. *Nhp* "to mourn"[294] is probably identical with *nhp* "to jump up," which has a number of idiomatic usages.[295] In view of the juxtaposition with *ḥtp* "to be satisfied," "to rest," a rendering "to worry," "to jump around" would seem best suited in this context. *Nb* is used here with its full social connotation of "lord," "master," principally the possessor of property. *Rwty* is obviously a pun on *nty m rwty*. It has to denote here a person, in view of the parallelism with *nb*, and also because of its connection with *ḥtp* "to be satisfied"; cf. Wb.II 189,8; Ḥeḳanakhte II 37.

Rwty "foreigner," cf. Hammamat no. 199,5, *wḏꜣ ʾib sꜣḳ sw r rwty* "well is the heart which rallies itself against a foreigner"; cf. also Admonitions 3,1, *pḏwt rwty ʾii.ti n Kmt* "alien foreigners have come to Egypt."[296] The particular connotation of *rwty* appears to be complete unfamiliarity on the side of the Egyptians. In other words, *rwty* denotes somebody beyond the perimeter of Egyptian geographical or social acquaintance. In its social application *rwty* is best understood as "outcast," with the connotation of one who should be outside or belongs outside. The idea promulgated is treated in detail in Admonitions 2,7ff.; 7,7ff.; cf. S. Herrmann, *op. cit.*, 12ff.; Posener, *op. cit.*, 43.

at) The remainder of the section deals with injustices in the legal process. As in the preceding sentence, there is an apparent juxtaposition between *tm-ʾirw* and *ʾirw*. Both are nominally used participles; for the construction of *tm ʾirw*, cf. Gardiner, *Egyptian Grammar*[3] §397.1; Satzinger, *Die negativen Konstruktionen im Alt- und Mittelägyptischen*, §64. *ʾIrr* "doer" has criminal connotation,[297] as in Peasant B 1,193; 218; Pyr. 298b; 326d; 414b; CT VI 181h; *ʾirw*, on the other hand, is attested as a term for "witness"; see Sethe, ZÄS 61, 1926, 67ff.; also Goedicke, ZÄS 101, 1974, 92f.; MIO 7, 1960, 304. The two verbs *mḥ* and *šw* require here a juridical meaning. For *šw*, see Wb.IV 426,18; Gardiner, *The Inscription of Mes, Untersuchungen*, 4, 96 (S 6). In contrast, *mḥ* requires identification with the use "to pay in full"; cf. Gardiner, ZÄS 43, 1906, 34; Černý, *Griffith Studies*, 54; *idem*, BIFAO 41, 1942, 114; Gardiner, JEA 22, 1936, 181; cf. also Simpson, *Pap. Reisner* I 35; Lefèbvre, *Inscriptions concernant les grands prêtres*, 66. Although the words in the passage are simple, their meaning nevertheless is difficult to grasp. The concern with the breakdown of law as the overriding theme of the section has been generally disregarded.[298] When it is taken into consideration, the contrasted cases become clearer: the one who did not act is paid for, while the evildoer will get off free. There remains an ambiguity concerning *tm-ỉrw*, which I suspect to be a technical term for the victim of a crime that can not be settled by property compensation. Consequently, I take *tm-ỉrw* as "one who cannot act (any longer)," i.e., somebody killed or maimed in juxtaposition with *ỉrw* "the (evil)doer" ("der Täter"), i.e., the one who committed the crime. While the latter goes free, the former is compensated materially instead of by legal prosecution.

au) The above rendering receives corroboration from the remaining sentences of this section, which detail the actions leading to the breakdown of law. The formulation follows the pattern *tw* + *r* + infinitive found first in l. 27. *Rdi ỉḫt*, lit. "to give things," is a well attested idiom "to pay." Occurrences are:[299] Dunham, *Naga ed Dêr Stelae*, no. 73; Lutz, *Egyptian Tomb Steles*, no. 34,5; Cairo 1627 *ỉnk ḏd nfr wḥm nfr rd ḫt n tp-nfr* "I was one who spoke properly, who carried out properly and who paid correctly";[300] BM 1164,2 *(ỉnk) ddi ḫt n nḫnw m ḏbʿ w.f ḏs.f* "(I was one) who paid (even) to children with his own fingers" as an expression for excessive consideration; JEA 4, 1918, pl. VIII 8-9 *ỉnk ḥḏ ḥr rdw ḫt m ỉšt nt ḏt(.ỉ)* "I was a cheerful one, who paid with the possessions of (my) estate"; MMA 12.184,4, *dd ḫt n nty n snw* "I paid to one without affliction"; Urk.VII 65,18 and Cairo 20539 I b 3, *dd.ỉ ḫt r st ỉryt* "I gave a thing according to its place."

O DeM 1187,1 appears to have here the best version with *ḥr* introducing *msḏd*, but the use of *m* in Pap. Ermitage also makes good sense. *Msḏd* is a technical juridical term denoting a major crime; the term has its origin in the condemnation formula *msḏd-nswt pw* in Urk.I 284,17; 285,18;[301] cf. also Deir Rifeh XVIII, 13; CT I 13d.

For *sgr r3 mdw* "to silence a mouth which speaks," cf. Urk.VII 54,14 *sgr ḳ3-ḫrw r tm.f mdw* "One who silenced the excited one until he did not talk" with juridical connotation, which also prevails in Abydos III pl. XXIX l. x + 4. The verb *mdw* does not seem to have juridical connotation in the early Middle Kingdom, to judge from Peasant B 1,21; Suicidal 66; and above l. 49, while the noun *mdw* is certainly used in such a fashion; cf. Goedicke, *Untersuchungen zur altägyptischen Rechtsprechung*, MIO 8, 1963, 359ff. The meaning of the passage *tw r rdt ḫt m msdd r sgr r3 mdw* "one will pay in a case of capital crime in order to silence a mouth that would speak"[302] concerns the practices of Egyptian jurisdiction. Whereas minor or civil cases were subject to arbitration and thus could be settled by material restitution, major or criminal cases had to be submitted to legal processing; see Goedicke, *op. cit.*, 366f.; *idem, Private Rechtsinschriften aus dem Alten Reich*, 213f.; Seidl, *Einführung in die Ägyptische Rechtsgeschichte bis zum Ende des Neuen Reiches*², Äg. Forsch. 10, 32ff.; Mrsich, *Untersuchungen zur Hausurkunde des Alten Reiches* §249, note 1096.

The inappropriate attempt to suppress the due process of law by making material restitution in a criminal case[303] is juxtaposed with the inappropriate leniency in the case of a criminal convicted for an act of violence.[304] The passage is preserved in two versions. Pap. Ermitage and Cairo 25224 have *wšb.tw*, while O DeM 1189 and O BM 5627 have *wšd.tw*. The latter occurred in the same text in l. 2. *Wšd* "to inquire legally" (Wb.I 375,13)[305] appears to have here the technical meaning of "legal reviewing." *Wšb* is found in the early Middle Kingdom literature intransitively "to answer someone" and transitively "to answer" something, almost in the sense "to rebuke"; for the latter, see Peasant B 1, 152; Suicidal 4; 55f; 85f.[306] *Ṯs* "sentence," especially also for the "legal sentence," "verdict," cf. Wb.V 403,11; Sinuhe B 184; 227;[307] Peasant B 2, 107.

Pap. Ermitage 49 quotes the verdict[308] as *ᶜ prw ẖr ḫt*, while O Gardiner 331 has *ḥr* introducing the case as *ᶜ prw* <*r*> *ḫt*. The pseudoverbal *ᶜ prw* is to be connected with the idiom *pr ᶜ* "to be violent," Wb.I 527,6,8; Peasant B 1,116, *ᶜ.k prw* "you were violent," while Sinuhe B 52 uses *pr-ᶜ* with positive connotation "active one"; see also Pap. Sallier II 10,1, *pr-ᶜ-ib* "impassioned."[309] See further Maystre, *Les déclarations d'innocence*, 90, concerning *pr-ᶜ* as a sin confessed in the Osirian judgment. *H̱r ḫt*, lit. "under a stick," has the connotation of "aggravated assault with a deadly weapon." *H̱r* can be taken as referring either to the assaulted one (who is "under the weapon") or to the assaulter who is bearing the weapon.[310] For *ḫt* "weapon," cf. Wb.III 340, 19; Merikareᶜ P. 2, 10.[311] The variant requires an emendation to *ᶜ pr*

<*r*> *ḥt* "a violence to a body."

Mdw.tw continues *wšb.tw* and introduces the objections to the sentence concerning an assailant. As the verdict is cited verbatim, the objection is also given in its full wording. *M sm3 sw* has to be recognized as negative imperative "do not kill him!"[312] It results that for aggravated assault the death penalty was obligatory.[313] The request "kill not!" here is diametrically opposed to that in Merikare^{c} P. 50; 139-140. In the breakdown of law there is excessive concern for the criminal, while the peace-loving citizen will have to worry about himself.

XVI. DEMAGOGUERY AND ITS POLITICAL EFFECTS

XI,11 'Slogans are for the mind/heart like fire (and)
50 not shall one endure a demagogue:[av]
While the land diminishes,
its administrators are numerous.
While it dries up,
its servants are rich.
While the grain is little,
51 the measure is great and
one measures it in overflow.'[aw]

av) The theme in Section XI[314] is not as pronounced as in other sections. There are two distinct features. One concerns the difficulties produced by a multitude of leaders and the administrative havoc they cause. The other, more extensive in its treatment, discusses meteorological afflictions to the country. The mention of anticipated events is headed by an adage, setting the tone for the later developments.

Ḫn n mdt is an idiom of the early Middle Kingdom literature and recurs in Peasant B 1,19; 37; Admonitions 12,7; see also Gunn, JEA 12, 1926, 282, note 4, who renders *ḫn n mdt* as "proverb." Posener[315] translated it "une tirade," reflecting a connotation of inflammatory rhetoric.[316] The overriding concern of the idiom seems to be a general acceptance that stifles the thinking mind. In the present context *ḫn n mdt* refers to the slogan or consensus with which the previous section closed.

Ḥr ỉb, as adverbial adjunct, qualifies the genitival expression *ḫn n mdt*. *ʾIb* seems to have here the meaning "mind" as center of thought, rather than "heart" as seat of emotions; for this meaning, see Peasant B 1,104 *n.k ỉmy ḥr ỉb.k* "what you have on your mind"; Khaᶜkheperreᶜ-seneb rt. 13 *snn.ỉ ḥr ỉb.ỉ* "I am distressed because of my mind"; cf. Kadish,

JEA 59, 1973, 78; see also Piankoff, *Le "coeur" dans les textes égyptiens*, 45ff.

Fire is used here as a metaphor for destruction against which there is no protection; cf. Grapow, *Die bildlichen Ausdrücke des Aegyptischen*, 49f.; see also Admonitions 7,1; 11,13; 12,2.

Wḫd in Pap. Ermitage 50 is unquestionably better than Golenischeff's reading 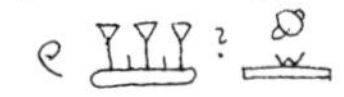 in Cairo 25224.[317] The verb is attested is Admonitions 10,12; Khaʿkheperreʿ-seneb rt. 13; 14; vs. 4;[318] further Ḥeḳanakhte II 5, 43;[319] Hatnub Gr. 20,17; 22,7,9;[320] Louvre C 167,9. The transitive verb consistently means "to endure," "to be patient with." The construction *nn + sḏm.n.f* is a rare one.[321] Its particular nuance is a generalized inability, i.e., "one can never do something." Clear examples are Ptahhotep 380-383, "who is serious the whole day, can never spend a pleasant moment" (*nn ỉr.n.f 3t nfr(t)*) and "who is the whole day frivolous, can never set up house" (*nn grg.n.f pr*), Suicidal 59f. *nn pr.n.k r ḥrw m3.k Rʿ* "you can never go forth above while you see daylight."[322] Merikareʿ P. 115 "never can a king, a lord of courtiers, act stupidly"; Ptahhotep 579 "as for a fool, who does not listen, he can never accomplish anything (*nn ỉr.n.f ḫt nbt*)"; Admonitions 14,12 "never can one find someone to stand up to their protection" (*nn gm.n.tw*); Siut III 22 "never can I be silent until I have beaten" (*nn gr.n.ỉ r*).

Wḫd being transitive,  has to be recognized as its object.[323] In view of  at the end, it can only be a verbal clause used as a noun.[324] *Pr* I take here in the sense "to attack," "to charge," as in Siut III 21; IV 14; Moʿalla II η 2; Wb.I 520,1. Pap. Ermitage has *pr.n r3*, which should best be considered a *sḏmw.n.f*-relative form, "one whose mouth attacked," while *pr m r3* in Cairo 25224 means "one who attacked with the mouth." Representing a descriptive designation of a "mouth-fighter" or "demagogue," the categorical refusal has its parallel in Merikare P. 27; 49.

aw) The application of the adage opening the section is cast in three balanced pairs of statements illustrating the economic breakdown following demagoguery. *ʿnḏ t3* denotes the diminishing of the economic resources, as in Admonitions 12,1 *ʿnḏ ỉdrw.f* "as his herds diminish";[325] for the transitive use of *ʿnḏ*, cf. also Vogelsang, *Kommentar zu den Klagen des Bauern*, 104. The perfective *sḏm.f* states here actualities, as recognized by previous translators.[326] *T3* seems to have here a geophysical rather than a political meaning, in the sense of a decrease in arable land, which is continued in the subsequent allusions to a drought.

Ḫrpw hardly has specific administrative significance; it is probably to be taken literally as "those who give directives," i.e., administrators,[327] rather than people wielding authority. Such a rendering is supported by Pap. Sallier II 9,1-2 *mk nn ỉ3t šw* <*m*> *ḫrpw wp* <-*ḥr*> *sš ntf ḫrp* "behold, there is no office free of administrators except the scribe; he is an administrator." That *ḫrpw* denotes administrators of limited power is also suggested by Admonitions 8,2-3, *mṯn* [*ḫr*]*pw ḫprw m nbw* "behold, administrators have become masters."

The reading 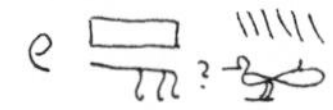 and 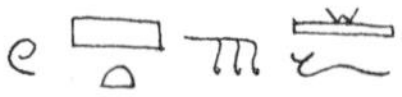 in O Gardiner 331, 2 is probably to be emended into the related *wšr.f*.[328] For *wšr* "waterless land" as a sign of drought, cf. Wb.I 374,11; Vandier, *La Famine*, 73; Gardiner, *The Wilbour Papyrus* II, 94. *Wš*<*r*>*.f* obviously is parallel to *ᶜnḏ t3* and requires the same rendering.[329] This parallelism applies equally to the second part of the sentence, where the first pair had *ḫrpw.f*. Consequently, a mention of people is necessarily presumed in the parallel, which supports the reading *b3kw.f* () in Pap. Ermitage 50 and O Gardiner 331.[330] *B3kw* "servants" denotes persons in a dependent position; cf. Bakir, *Slavery in Pharaonic Egypt*, CASAE 18, 15ff. In view of the implicit contrast, *ᶜ3* has to be recognized here as having the meaning "rich"; cf. BM 614,11,14;[331] Fischer, WZKM 57, 1961, 69-71, and especially the causative *sᶜ3* "to make rich," as in Merikareᶜ P. 42; cf. Kees, ZÄS 63, 1928, 76. The idea of wealthy servants is recurrent in Admonitions 7,7ff., particularly in 8,2.

Ktt "little," "trifling," Wb.V 147,8. *ᵓIt* as generic term for "grain" as food, cf. Ḥeḳanakhte I 5; Peasant R 4; Admonitions 10,4. *ᵓIpt* "grain-measure," Wb.I 67,6; though listed there only since Dynasty XVIII, the term occurs already in the Old Kingdom; cf. James, *The Mastaba of Khentika*, called Ikhekhi 0.44; *idem*, *The Ḥeḳanakhte Papers* VI, 12; VII, 4; p. 64f.; 68; Peasant B 1,294. For *ḫ3* "to measure (grain),"[332] cf. Ḥeḳanakhte II, 5; III, 6; VI, 12. *Wbn* "to overflow" of the grain measure, cf. Peasant B 1,294; Wb.I 294,12.

XVII. ANOTHER DROUGHT

'Re^{c} removed himself from men:

He shines and the daytime exists,
but one knows not that noon happened,
and one [52] is not able to calculate his shadow.
The face is not clear when one looks,
nor do [53] the eyes fill with water,
as he is in the sky like the moon.[ax]
(But) one who went astray, will return, when the heart is experienced,
and so [54] his rays will be from the face (of the sun) again in the previous fashion.'[ay]

ax) Cairo 25224 has *ỉw R^{c} ỉwd.f sw*, while Pap. Ermitage 51 has a lacuna sufficient to contain *ỉw*. For *ỉwd* with double object, see Wb.I 58,13; Admonitions 4,14; Sinuhe R 28. The notion of Re^{c}'s separation from men recurs as a topos in Merikare^{c} P. 124. However, in contrast to the theological interpretation given there, the passage here has a predominantly meteorological meaning, as becomes clear from the details given in the following.

Wbn.f opens a line of negative observations. The previous translations at this point do not adhere closely to the text.[333] O DeM 1261 has *wbn.f ỉw wn* , which clearly indicates that we have here two connected sentences. While *wnwt* is certain, the determination by ⊙| seems questionable. *Wnwt* "hour" is not determined in this fashion, and it is thus to be read *wnwt-hrw* "day-service," as is clear in Urk.IV 959,13. The abbreviated spelling ⊙| for *hrw* is common; e.g., CT I 254 d. *Wnwt* is probably used here in its extended meaning "time service" or "time observation," as reflected in the title *wnwty* "time watcher"; cf. Wb.I 317,9; Gardiner, *Ancient Egyptian Onomastica* I 62*.

What follows is a description of the difficulties of using a sundial, because the sun is not bright but only hazy. The description of the heat accompanying the drought resembles that of ll. 24-26.

Mtrt "noon," Wb.II 174,6; Pap. Sallier II 10,2, *ꜣir pr.k m ꜥt-sbꜣ ḫr smi.tw n.k mtrt* "When you leave from the school, since noon was announced for you. . . ." For *ṯnw* "number" in connection with time-concepts, cf. CT V 235b. The passage is the oldest reference to the measuring of time with a sundial; cf. Sloley, JEA 17, 1931, 170ff.; Borchardt, *Altägyptische Sonnenuhren*, ZÄS 48, 1911, 9-17.

NN bꜣḳ ḥr dgꜣ.tw[334] and the next clause, *ꜣiw nn ꜣibḥ ꜣirty m mw*, form a pair that is completed by the affirmative clause in l. 53, *wnn.f m pt mi ꜣiꜥḥ*, thus forming a contrasting pattern to what precedes, which consists of an affirmative *wbn.f wn wnwt-hrw* and two negative clauses, *nn rḫ.tw ḫpr mitrt* and *nn ṯn.tw šwt.f*. Gardiner, JEA 1, 1914, 104, rendered *bꜣḳ* with "to be dazzled" ("Not dazzled is the sight when he is beheld"),[335] which is followed by Wb.I 424,16, "das Gesicht wird geblendet(?) wenn die Sonne scheint" and Faulkner, *Concise Dictionary*, 78, "be dazzled of sight" (*ḥr*). This rendering disagrees with the basic meaning of *bꜣḳ*, which is "to be bright," "to be clear." There is no need to postulate any special use of *bꜣḳ* in this instance, as long as *ḥr* "face" is understood as reference to the "face" of the sun; see ZÄS 65, 1930, 75; cf. also the frequent epithets of Re composed with *ḥr*.[336] For *bꜣḳ* "to be clear" in reference to the sun cf. also Wb.I 424,15; for *dg* without an object, see Wb.V 497 A, Siut IV 19, although this use is otherwise unattested this early.

ꜣIw introducing a negated sentence seems to act as coordinator. Examples are few, but see Urk.I 11,14; Urk.IV 847,3; 38,11; cf. Satzinger, *op. cit.*, §49.

ꜣIbḥ "to be moist" construed with *m*, cf. Wb.I 64,7.[337] The passage proceeds logically from the previously mentioned observation of the sun and its physiological effects. The reason for this change is the topic of the next passage, *wnn.f m pt mi ꜣiꜥḥ* "he is always in the sky like the moon," describing the luminescence of the sun, diminished by the prevailing haze.

ay) *Nn thꜣ nw.f nyw ššꜣw* has caused considerable difficulty, especially in view of the affirmative clause following it. Gardiner, JEA 1, 1914, 104, rendered "his accustomed (?) season fails not, for in sooth his rays are in (men's) face after his former wise"; Erman, *op. cit.*,

156, "Und doch weicht sie nicht ab von ihrer vorgeschriebenen Zeit und ihre Strahlen stehen vor dem Antlitz in ihrer früheren Weise"; Lefèbvre, *op. cit.*, 103, "(Toutefois) sa révolution normale [ne sera pas] troublée, ses rayons seront devant le visage à la facon d'autrefois"; Wilson, *ibid.*, "His prescribed time does not fail. His rays are indeed in (men's) faces in his former way," suggesting that a negative might have dropped out in the second clause; Faulkner, *Literature*, 238, "(though) his accustomed times do [not] go astray, and his rays are in (men's) sight as on former occasions," explaining that "the sun performs its normal motions but sheds no more light than the moon." A different approach was introduced by Posener, *op. cit.*, 155f., who affiliated the two passages with the moon rather than with the sun, thus rendering "Son temps habituel ne se dérangera pas; les rayons (de la lune) s'offriront à la vue dans leur condition de jadis." This interpretation was followed by Helck[338] and M. Lichtheim,[339] while Barta, *op. cit.*, 43, renders "wie der Mond, dessen Zyklus (wörtl. dessen Zeit der Erfahrung) nicht übertreten wird" and interprets this as meaning that "die Sonne hat sich unnatürlicherweise dem Mondzyklus genauenstens . . . angepasst."

Against this interpretation a number of lexicographical, semantic, and conceptual arguments have to be brought forth. *Styw* "rays" is not used in regard to the moon, whose shine lacks the brilliance in *styw*. *Ḥr* is consistently singular in the variants, and in Pap. Ermitage and O Gardiner 331 it has *.f* as attached qualification. *Th3* is intransitive with *nw.f* as its subject. *ꜣIꜥḥ* was mentioned before as part of a comparison. If the continuation concerned the moon, it would require a relative construction, or the change of subject would have to be marked syntactically. As there is no previous concern with the moon, but only with the veiling of the sun in the prevailing heat, there is no apparent reason for questioning the moon's schedule. There was no previous mention of any impediment to the visibility of the moon, so a comparison with its former performance would be unwarranted.

There are serious doubts about the correctness of the restoration 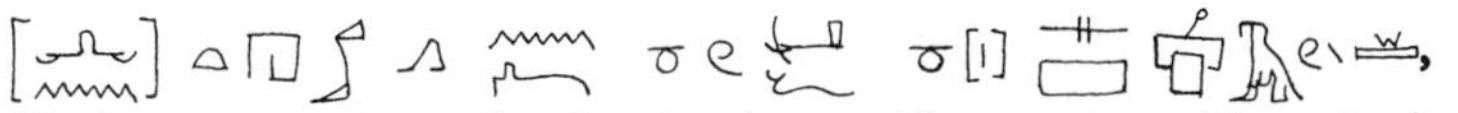, because of insufficient space at the beginning. The restoration is based on Cairo 25224 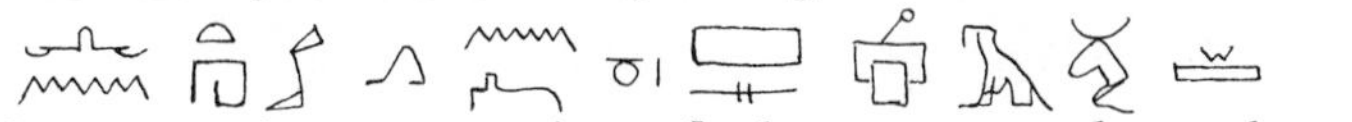, which appears to have a reinterpretation of the passage altogether, in view of the different writing of *nw*.[340] The latter obviously is the word for "time," which is attested in conjunction with *th3* in the idiom "to miss time";

see Wb.II 219,12; V 321,21; Cairo 20543. As *nw.f* can only be the object of *th3*, the latter has to be recognized as infinitive or as passive. The former would interrupt the context; the latter would constitute an unattested construction and would hardly make any sense here. The other point, of epigraphic concern, is the reading of  , which makes little sense after *nw.f* "time" and is totally out of context after . O DeM 1261 clearly has  .[341] The traces in Pap. Ermitage are  , which could suit a reading  as in l. 39, but also 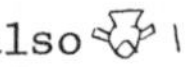 as in ll. 64 and 65. *ᵓIb šs3w* "the heart is experienced"[342] apparently is not paralleled as an idiom, but there is no conceivable obstacle to the formation. However, the major syntactical question remains--namely, how the passage is integrated with its context. As there are no clear indications that the sentence is directly intertwined with the preceding, it is necessary to conclude that the passage is a self-contained semantic unit. Only an adage or a proverb can satisfy such a context, and it is necessary to the passage in this way. Even so there remains the question of how to correlate the established trends with the extant wording. Taking the version in Pap. Ermitage affirmatively as *th3 nw.f ỉb šs3*, it is necessary to consider *nw.f* as *sḏm.f*. This step necessitates seeing *th3* as a noun placed in anticipatory position. *Th(w)* is attested since Peasant B 1, 237, further Urk.IV 1081,4; Amenemope 4,10; 5,12; Anii 6,11; Wb.V 320,24 gives for it "Frevler";[343] Peasant B 1,237, *ỉw mḥ.tw ỉb ỉm.k ỉw.k ḫpr.ti m thw* "one trusts in you, but you have become a *thw*" suggests a less derogatory meaning, "one who went astray." In the Middle Kingdom *thi* recurrently has the meaning "to disobey," which is an extension of "going astray"; cf. Goedicke, *The Report about the Dispute of a Man with his* Ba, 92. Such a rendering makes good sense in the adage under discussion, which I propose rendering "one who went astray--he will take care/return, when the heart has become experienced." The spelling  requires an identification of the word with *nwi* "to care for," "to assemble,"[344] although an affiliation with *nwy* "to return"[345] would make even better sense. The adage is close to the Second Parable of the *Ba* in the Suicidal (ll. 80-85).[346] *Thw* is, of course, an oblique reference to the sun, which is not shining as usual but has removed itself (*ỉwd*, l. 51) and is hiding behind haze. The adage conveys the idea of hope, because within reason there is always the prospect of a return to established order. As such, the adage bridges the description of adverse conditions in the country and the eventual return to normal.[347]

After the quotation of the adage, Neferyt's discourse continues and completes his description of meteorological phenomena with a prospect of the end of the adverse conditions. *Wnn ỉs* is the affirmative equivalent of the common *n ỉs;*[348] for the position of the particle *ỉs* between the verb and the nominal subject, cf. CT IV 84b. *Stwt.f* "his rays" refers, of course, to the sun, as does *ḥr* or *ḥr.f*, which denotes here the face of the sun, as in l. 52. *M ḥr* qualifies *stwt.f*, which is difficult to reflect faithfully in translation; "his rays from the face will be again" seems to be as close as one can get.

Pap. Ermitage and Cairo 25224 have *m zp*, while O Gardiner 331 and O DeM 1261 have *mỉ zp.f;* both are equally correct, one stressing the reappearance "in his fashion," the other "like his fashion." The plural *ỉmyw-ḥ3t* and its determination with 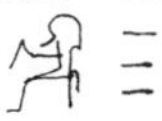 are erroneous, as the adjectival "which was before," i.e., "previous," is needed here qualifying *zp*. For *ỉmy-ḥ3t*, cf. Urk.IV 140,17; 766,6; for the genitival construction, as found in O DeM 1261, cf. Urk.IV 115,4. For *zp*, cf. Merikareʿ P. 26; Siut III 14; Urk.IV 140,17.

XVIII. SOCIAL UPHEAVAL FOR LACK OF LEADERSHIP

XII, 11 'I present to you the country in passing a sickness:

When a weakling is the master of action, one will [55] consult and consult.[az]

I present to you the lowly against the superior:

One who should be attentive has become self-concerned.[ba]

One lives from (the hope for the) Necropolis:

while [56] a wretch will make a stela,

the great one will worship, in order to exist (beyond).[bb]

The beggars will eat [57] offering cake,

while the servants abandon the heights.[bc]

The Heliopolitan district, the birthplace of every god, will no more be the burial ground.'[bd]

az) The section has a less clear topic than the previous one. It concentrates on social upheaval and contains only one point of political significance. The opening line is identical with l. 38 and seems to denote a specific situation. In the prior occurrence it was followed by a reference to the outbreak of fighting and civil strife, but the second occurrence of *sny-mny* is not followed by such a reference. The adverbial clause states the conditions or circumstances in the country; cf. Gardiner, *Egyptian Grammar*[3] §§215-216. *S3-ᶜ* recurs in Merikareᶜ P. 136, *ṯsw r ṯst m psḏ n s3-ᶜ* "commanders to raise the back of the *s3-ᶜ*"; Deir Rifeh pl. XIX, 19, *sšnn s3-ᶜ;* Urk.IV 1078,1, *ỉw nḥm.n.ỉ s3-ᶜ m-ᶜ nḫt-ᶜ* "I have rescued the *s3-ᶜ* from the strong armed"; Urk.IV 1079,5, *n sẖ.ỉ ḥr.ỉ r3-sy r s3-ᶜ* "I was not neglectful toward the *s3-ᶜ*"; Cairo 42155[349] *ḳn mi s3-ᶜ* "brave like a *s3-ᶜ*"; as an insult it occurs in Pap. Anastasi I 8,7; 9,3. *S3-ᶜ* is literally "weak of arm" and thus denotes a "weakling," i.e., someone unable to be effective; cf. Wb.IV 14,17; III 419,10-11; Faulkner,

Concise Dictionary, 209. The antonym is *nḫt-ᶜ* as demonstrated by Urk.IV 1078,1.[350] *Nb-ᶜ*, lit. "master of arm," appears to be unparalleled; I take ᶜ in this compound figuratively as "action," as in ᶜ *dw*, Moᶜalla II θ 3;[351] also Merikareᶜ P. 124; P. 136-37;[352] possibly also in Peasant B 1,276 and R 125. The idiom *pr-ᶜ* seems to be based on this extended meaning of ᶜ, so that it should be rendered "outgoing of action." *Nb-ᶜ* as "master of action" seems close to *nb-ḏrt* in Merikareᶜ P. 124[353] and as such has to be understood as a designation of the person holding and exerting authority.

Tw nḏ ḫrt requires the emendation of the preposition *r* and adheres to the recurrent pattern of an impersonal future, as in ll. 27, 34-35, etc. *Nḏ ḫrt* occurred previously in ll. 2-3,[354] where it denoted consultation as the central feature of the business of governing by the good king. Here, as the sole activity of a weak ruler, the connotation cannot have an equally positive meaning. I take *nḏ ḫrt nḏ-ḫrt* as a redoubled infinitive,[355] used to express the exclusiveness of the counseling and carrying the implication that the king's activity exhausted itself in endless consultations without ever reaching needed decisions. For the construction, cf. Sethe, *Das ägyptische Verbum II*, §§720ff.; Gardiner, *Egyptian Grammar*[3] §§298 Obs.; Edel, *Altägyptische Grammatik*, §§723-729.

ba) *Ḫry r ḥry* was rendered by Gardiner, JEA 1, 1914, 105, as "I show thee the undermost uppermost," followed by Erman, *op. cit.*, 156, "Ich zeige dir, wie das Untere nach oben gekehrt ist," which found universal acceptance, including Wb.III 392,11, "das Untere nach Oben gekehrt (von verwirrten Zuständen)." In view of the subsequent discussion of social upheaval, it would be more appropriate to take *ḫry* and *ḥry* as designations of persons according to their social standing. *Ḫry* "lowly (one)" is recurrent in the plural *ḫrw*, as in Peasant B 1,95; Merikareᶜ P. 96; Ḥeḳanakhte I 16; II 13,14 with the particular meaning of "dependents." *Ḥry* as term for a superior is common; cf. Wb.III 141f.; already in the Old Kingdom as *ḥry-pr* (cf. Junker, Gîza VI 80). For the prospective nature of the construction, cf. Gardiner, *Egyptian Grammar*[3] §163.4.

Pḫr.ti m-s3 pḫrw ḫt[356] has found varying interpretations. Lefèbvre, *op. cit.*, 103, gave for it "ce qui était tourné sur le dos est (maintenant) tourné (sur) le ventre (?)," followed by Barta, *loc. cit.*, 43, "das, was auf den Rücken gewendet sein sollte, ist bäuchlings gewendet worden," and M. Lichtheim, *loc. cit.*, "what was turned on the back turns the belly," interpreting it as "he who was easily overthrown now overthrows others"; Wilson, *loc. cit.*, has "turned about in proportion to the turning about of my belly"; Helck, *op. cit.*, 48, "folgend einer Umdrehung meines Körpers," with a reference to Urk.IV 971,11; Faulkner, *op. cit.*, 239, renders "men pursuing him who flees away," considering the literal meaning to be "men turn round after him who turns his body round." None yields a convincing meaning, nor do these renderings suit the context, except with extensive interpretation.

The grammatical structure of the passage was to a degree recognized by Barta.[357] *Pẖr.ti* is a nominally used *nisbe* derived from *pẖrt* "service,"[358] and the second *pẖr* is a perfective active participle. *Pẖr m s3* is a recurrent idiom; see Wb. I 546,17-18; Pyr. 670b; Urk.IV 971,11. Literally "to go behind," it is an expression for "to serve attentively." *Pẖr* in the sense "to be concerned with someone" is also construed with a direct object; see Wb.I 545,11. The particular wording was apparently chosen here for reasons of contrasting *s3* and *ẖt*. *Pẖr ẖt*, "to turn the body around,"[359] seems to be unparalleled in the particular nuance proposed here, although it seems necessary because of the juxtaposition implicit in the passage. *Pẖr ẖt* "to attend the body" I take as a figurative expression for "selfishness."

bb) *ᶜnḫ.tw m ẖrt-nṯr* "one lives in the necropolis" allows for several interpretations. It can be taken literally, i.e., that one settled in tombs. Such a rendering has little to support it, because there is no apparent reason for the mention of the necropolis. Another possibility is to take *ẖrt-nṯr* figuratively, i.e., that life is in a way as if one were dead.[360] However, neither interpretation explains the use of the term *ẖrt-nṯr*, which has a more specific connotation than "cemetery," i.e., an area where dead ones were buried. *H̱rt-nṯr* denotes the specific burial ground in which a ritual burial, the prerequisite for overcoming death, was performed; see Urk.I 305,6;[361] Merikareᶜ P. 70; cf. also Kees, *Totenglauben und Jenseitsvorstellungen*, 27. By extension *ẖrt-nṯr* denotes also the "netherworld" as "the domain of god," which has to be seen as the realm of Osiris; see Spiegel, *Die Götter von Abydos*, 16; Morenz, *Ägyptische Religion*, 217f. Once *ẖrt-nṯr* is recognized as denoting the ritual burial ground, a generic reference to "living in the cemetery" can no longer be maintained, because it is unlikely that a specific term, i.e., the ritual burial ground, the *terra sacra*, is used in a generalizing fashion or that the survival took place only in the restricted area of the "necropolis." Not every burial ground in the Old Kingdom had the qualification of being a *ẖrt-nṯr*, lit. "property of (the) god."[362] I propose taking *ʿnḫ m* in the well-attested meaning "to live from," Wb.I 194,5ff.[363] Rendering it "one will live from the necropolis," I take it as implying that the eschatological expectations had to substitute for the inadequacies of mundane existence. In other words, people lived by eternal hopes despite the prevailing conditions.

The expectations are matched by the prevailing social conditions, which favor the upstarts, enabling them to make appropriate funerary preparations while others have to struggle for mere survival.

ʾIri ʿḥʿ does not necessarily mean "to amass riches," as is generally assumed,[364] but can also have the sense "to set up memorials"; see Wb.I 221,12, where the idiom is listed for the New Kingdom, although it occurs already in the Middle Kingdom: see Cairo 20458; H. W. Müller, MDIK 4, 1933, 170; possibly also 20061. *Ḥwr* refers to the ethically, rather than the socially, inferior; cf. further note 307.

The second part of the passage is poorly preserved. Its restorations and interpretations vary widely among those who have attempted them. Helck, *loc. cit.*, restores in the lacuna "fight" and renders "ein Getümmel wird entstehen." A different view was proposed by Barta, *loc. cit.*, who expanded the frame of the passage to *iw ḥwrw r ỉrit ʿḥʿw wr r tri(?) r ḫpr ỉn šw3w wnm.sn t* "der Elende wird grossen Besitz erwerden, mehr also der Geachtete(?), bis es geschieht durch den Besitzlosen, dass (nur) sie Brot essen." Faulkner, *loc. cit.*, translates "while the great lady will [beg] to exist" and M. Lichtheim, *loc. cit.*, "the Great [will rob] to live." None of these fits into the prevailing context, with its eschatological concern. "The great one" for the Egyptians remained a model, even if he fell into dire straits, so that a criminal action could not be attributable to him. As for Faulkner's rendering, there is no previous mention of a "great lady," and such a person would not be a match for the *ḥwrw*. The restoration *r3-ḏ3w* would be difficult to fit into the available space, as Helck realized; furthermore, there is nothing in the context pointing to fighting, especially not to a "melee," which is the specific meaning of *r3-ḏ3w*.[365] The grammatical structure of Barta's restoration is untenable: "bis es geschieht durch die Besitzlosen, dass (nur) sie Brot essen" would be more simply worded in Egyptian as **r wnm.t šw3w t* "until the beggars eat bread."

The reading as established by Golenischeff requires an improvement in Pap. Ermitage by reading  instead of  ; for the hieratic writing of  by a mere dot see, e.g., 11. 50, 53.[366] The mention of *wr* "great one" produces the expected kind of parallelism. I thus restore the passage 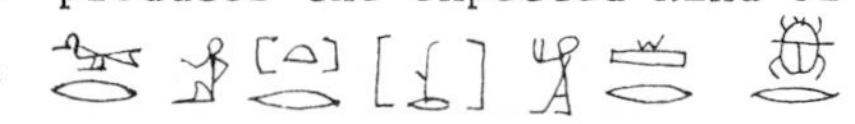 "the great one will worship/pray in order to exist (yonder)." Cairo 25224 apparently has *twr* instead of *tri*. For *tri* "to worship" religiously, see Merikare^{c} P. 112; 125 *tri nṯr* "to worship god"; Wb.V 318,5.[367] *Ḫpr* denoting eschatological existence or the transformation to an existence beyond death, cf. Suicidal 62.

bc) Different from Barta but in agreement with most translators,[368] I see here a participial statement. A different view was taken by Posener, *op. cit.*, 156, who read it *ỉn šw3.w.w wnm.śn t* "Ce sont les pauvres qui seront nourris," taking *sn* as a suffix pronoun rather than as part of *snw* "offering cake." Pap. Ermitage is otherwise consistent in spelling the suffix pronoun 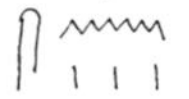 (11. 3, 5, 8, 9, 18, 19, 36, 60, 63, 67, 68), thus undercutting this ingenious suggestion. Furthermore, much of the section concerns funerary matters, so that a mention of *snw* "offering cake" suits the context very well. In  "offering cake,"  appears to serve as determinative; cf. CT I 263a; Wb.IV 155,11-12; Cairo 1622. *Šw3w* "beggar" occurs in Urk.I 77,16; 266, 10; Giza 7152; Pap. Millingen I 6; Sinuhe B 309; Admonitions 2,4,7.

 is in this form a *hapax*. Wb.I 470,1 lists it without a rendering. Helck, *loc. cit.*, suggests a meaning "die Diener sind oben auf" following Wilson, *loc. cit.*, "the servants jubilate" and Lefèbvre, *loc. cit.*, "les serviteurs seront exaltés." A serious attempt toward an understanding was made by Barta, *loc. cit.*, who envisaged a connection with *bḥ* "forced labor" and proposed reading it "zu gut für Dienerarbeit sein." His division of the strange term into two words is very appealing, especially since the determinative  at the end points to a noun rather than a verb. This noun, especially in view of the partly ideographic spelling, I suggest reading  *ḳ3w* "height"; a physical meaning[369] makes no sense in the given context, so a figurative use has to be presumed here. I am not aware of such a usage except as *ḳ3w pt* "the height of heaven" that the deceased reaches; see Pyr. 335a^{W} "lo, W. has reached the height of heaven"; similarly Pyr. 949b; CT I 16c, "how important is the monthly feast for the height of heaven"; CT IV 63s, "I am the lord of the height." *Bḥ* clearly is an Old Perfective; it can be deduced that *bḥ* cannot be a transitive verb, as it would have a passive notion in this form. I thus equate *bḥ* with  "to flee,"

"to abandon," despite the different aspirate;[370] the word occurs in Sinuhe B 63; Moʿalla II ζ 1 and VI β 1. *B3k* denotes here people who are under obligation to render services in the funerary cult; for *b3k*, see Lorton, *The Juridical Terminology of International Relations*, 90ff.; cf. also Bakir, *Slavery in Pharaonic Egypt*, CASAE 18, 17ff. *B3kw* denoting the servants of the house occurs also in Admonitions 4,14; Urk.I 47,4. The meaning of the passage, in my understanding, is that the servants of the house abandon their obligation to perform the funerary cult for their former master; cf. Kees, *Totenglauben und Jenseitsvorstellungen*, 253ff.

bd) The concluding passage of the section makes no sense in the form in which it appears, namely, as "gone from the earth is the nome of On, the birthplace of every god,"[371] because the disappearance of the Heliopolitan district is neither plausible nor suitable to this context with its dominating funerary concerns. Others have resorted to translations that are grammatically untenable.[372] The verse-point in O Gardiner 333 establishes *msḫnt nt nṯr nb* as a separate syntactical element, which has to be an appositive in view of the absense of a predicate. "Birthplace of every god" is, however, meaningless in reference to an undefined *t3* "land." In order to establish a role of *t3* "land" that allows the apposition, it is necessary to connect it with *ʿnḏ-ḥḳ3* "Heliopolis." Thus, I assume here a change in the word order, by which Heliopolis was placed in anticipation, and consider the grammatically correct word order to be **nn wn r t3 ʿnḏ-ḥḳ3*. The idiom *wn + r* is listed Wb.I 309,3 "sich befinden an etwas," so that I propose rendering literally, "there is no more existing for the land of the Heliopolitan district, the birthplace of every god." An alternative to this interpretation is to take *t3* here with the specific meaning "burial ground" (Wb.V 213 IV)[373] and *msḫnt nt nṯr nb* as qualifying *ʿnḏ-ḥḳ3* but separated from it for syntactical reasons. Such a reading has the advantage of not requiring any emendations and can be rendered "The Heliopolitan district, the birthplace of every god, will no more be the burial ground."

Msḫnt, specifically the "bearing stool," is a recurrent metaphor for the cemetery as the place where the dead ones are to be reborn; cf. Wb.I 8; CT III 274b. *Nṯr* denotes here, as usual, the ritually buried deceased; see Goedicke, *The Report about the Dispute of a Man with his* Ba, 28ff.; *idem*, *The Berlin Leather Roll*, (P. Berlin 3029), *Festschrift zum 150jährigen Bestehen des Berliner Ägyptischen Museums*, 99. The role of Heliopolis in the funerary administration during the Old Kingdom has not been investigated. The close link between kingship and the royal followers includes funerary care for those who rendered services for the king (e.g., Urk.I 99; 139). The administration and legal affiliation of the graves was apparently in Heliopolis, except in the Sixth Dynasty, when the funerary estate of the individual king played an important role. It is noteworthy in this context that the cemetery at Giza belonged administratively to Heliopolis; see Fischer, JNES 18, 1959, 132f. Without being able fully to pursue this problem here, I consider the mention of Heliopolis in the closing passage of Section XII as a statement that the funerary concepts of the Old Kingdom, which continued into the Heracleopolitan Period, were to cease, and be replaced by individual funerary preparations.

XIX. THE NEED THAT A KING COME TO HELP

XIII 11 It is such that a king 58 of the South shall come, Imeny, the triumphant, with his name,

a son of a woman of the Elephantine district,
59 a child is it of the Residence.[be]
He shall assume the white crown,
he shall wear the red crown,
60 he shall unite the double crown.[bf]
He shall appease the Two Lords with what they desire,
(namely) to change the course by 61 grasping the oar and by turning aside the tiller.[bg]

be) Section XIII is the base for considering the text a "prophecy," instigated by Golenischeff's inaugural translation "Dès que le roi, Améni de nom . . ., sera venu du Sud," which has basically been followed by all later translators, assuming that it prophesies a savior to end all trepidations. Most of the attested pseudoverbal constructions introduced by noun or pronoun followed by *pw* belong to the group of literary texts with which our composition is connected: Peasant R 1 opens, *s pw wn Ḫw-n-ʾInpw rn.f*, which requires a rendering "there was a man whose name was Khueninepu"; similarly Shipwrecked Sailor 89, *ỉnk pw h3.kwỉ r bi3* "it is I, who had embarked for the mine-country"; and Pap. Westcar 6,5 *nḫ3w pw n mfk3t m3t ḫr ḥr mw*""it is a pendant of true turquoise which has fallen into the water"; also Khaʿkheperreʿ-seneb vs. 1, *ỉnk pw ḥr nk3 m ḫprt* "it is I who is meditating about what happened." The very use of the demonstrative *pw* necessitates that the clause in which it serves as predicate, has present meaning. This eliminates the possibility of considering *nswt pw* to refer to a future event. The construction is principally that pointed out by Gardiner, *Egyptian Grammar*[3] §§325, 332 who compares the use of *pw* with French *c'est que*. This particular formulation is recurrent in medical texts to state the diagnosis of an ailment; see W. Westendorf, *Grammatik der medizinischen Texte* §§402, 404, 405; H. Grapow, *Von den medizinischen Texten* (Grundriss der Medizin der alten Ägypter II). J. H. Breasted, *The Edwin Smith Surgical Papyrus* 61f., it is in this specific technical sense that the construction with *pw* is used; i.e., the diagnosis of what is needed to overcome the situation in the eastern Delta.

As in the opening statement of the Eloquent Peasant, a person is introduced whose name is subsequently stated; *nswt pw r ꜣit* refers to an unknown king and requires a literal rendering, "it is that a king shall come." Thus the passage has to be recognized as an evaluation of the situation, requiring a king of the South to come to the rescue of the North, rather than as a prophecy. That *n rsy* "of the South" qualifies *nswt* has been discussed by Posener, *op. cit.*, 156, who pointed out the similar formulation in Urk.IV 5,16. Although he recognized the particular grammatical structure, he ultimately (p. 47) opted for a fairly free rendering, "Voici que surgira au Sud un roi." *Rsy* "South" as a geopolitical term appears in the late Sixth Dynasty (Urk.I 134,11) and subsequently in the term *tp-rsy*, denoting the seven southernmost districts of Upper Egypt,[374] which correspond to the base of the Eleventh Dynasty. Merikareᶜ P. 71 and P. 75 have *ᶜ rsy*, which appears to have the same political connotation as *rsy* here, namely the state in the South. *ꜣIi* with the connotation "to come in succour," see Peasant B 1, 67; Wb.I 37,15.

That *ꜣImny* is an oblique reference to Amenemhet I is beyond question.[375] At the same time *ꜣimny* can be interpreted as "the hidden one," which is of course a reflection of the anticipatory form in which the text is cast. The epithet *m3ᶜ-ḫrw* applied to the royal cartouche has been considered an interpolation from the time after the king's death.[376] As the text is preserved at this point in a single copy, it is impossible to corroborate this. *M3ᶜ-ḫrw* does occur in reference to the living king as "triumphant,"[377] so the assumption of an interpolation seems unnecessary; for *m3ᶜ-ḫrw*, see Anthes, *The Original Meaning of m3ᶜ-ḫrw*, JNES 13, 1954, 21ff.; Goedicke, *Königliche Dokumente aus dem Alten Reich*, 136.

The king's parents, both mother and father, are specified. Matrilineage is a phenomenon of the Theban Eleventh Dynasty; e.g., Intef the Great born of *ꜣIkw* (TPPI §14); *W3ḥ-ᶜnḫ*--Intef II born of *Nfrw* (TPPI §§15-

17; 20); *Nb-tp-nfr*--Intef III born of *Nfrw* (TPPI §20); Menthuhotep III--*Nb-t3wy-Rʿ* born of *ʾIm* (Hammamat no. 191).[378] A nonroyal imitator of this practice is Intef born of *Myt* (TPPI §§31-33); it continues in the Middle Kingdom for commoners but not for royalty, with a marked emphasis on the matrilineage.[379] The home registration of *ʾImny's* mother is given as *T3-Sti*, which denotes Nubia and the southernmost administrative district of Upper Egypt, i.e., from Elephantine to Gebel Silsila, although a subdivision into the region of Elephantine and of Kom Ombo existed in the First Intermediate Period.[380] Although *T3-Sti* can denote an integral part of Egypt, the occurrence here has repeatedly been interpreted as referring to Nubia, and the possibility of a Nubian ancestry of the Twelfth Dynasty has been conjectured.[381] It would be most unusual if this text, which can be labeled in modern terms as "nationalistic," portrayed the savior king as half foreign.[382] There can thus be no question that the home of Amenemhet I's mother should be seen as Elephantine. The emergence of Elephantine in the early Twelfth Dynasty after a period of insignificance is possibly to be connected with this.[383]

The legal home of the savior king is introduced as *ms pw*, as in 1. 17 (see above p. 69). The place of residence is given as  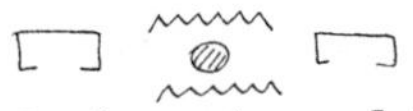 (Cairo 25224).[384] Read *H̱n-Nḫn*, it is considered a designation of Upper Egypt; Wb.III 372,15.[385] The term occurs also in Petrie, Abydos I 54,[386] in Siut III 28,[387] and in C. Nestmann-Peck, *Some Decorated Tombs of the First Intermediate Period at Naga ed-Der*, pl. II, p. 13f.[388] Although the occurrence in Cairo 25224 would seem to support a reading *H̱n-Nḫn*,[389] the examples of the First Intermediate Period do not necessitate such a reading. I would take  rather as a reading sign and read the whole word as *ẖnw* "Residence."[390] The term certainly can not refer to all of Upper Egypt in Siut III 28, where the political actuality of *tp-rsy*, i.e., Theban control of the South of Upper Egypt, is juxtaposed with , which refers to the political party with which the local rulers of Siut were affiliated. As it is unlikely that "the head of the South should listen to what Upper Egypt says," 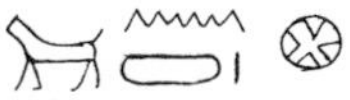 needs to be taken as reference to the political entity to which the "head of the South" (*tp-rsy*) was opposed at the time. The political situation is basically clear, and it is thus necessary to conclude that  refers to the Residence of the Tenth Dynasty, presumably Heracleopolis.[391] In two of the early attestations the term is used in reference to the districts controlled by the "Residence" as distinguished from another political center existing simultaneously, whereas Siut III 28 clearly is a reference to the residence of the Heracleopolitan kings of the Tenth Dynasty, in contrast to the Theban Eleventh Dynasty. Once *h̲nw* is recognized as denoting the Residence, the significance of the mention in Neferyt's prophecy still retains some ambiguity. It might be taken as a reference to the residence of the Eleventh Dynasty, but the consistency of the other use of the term could speak against such a view. It would be tempting to pose an affiliation of the Twelfth Dynasty with Heracleopolis. Neither the name of its founder, Amenemhet, nor the later traditions about this group of kings supports such a thesis. All epitomes of Manetho agree that the Twelfth Dynasty came from Diospolis, i.e., Thebes; and the name Amenemhet as well as certain religious features in the early Twelfth Dynasty corroborate this tradition, so it is necessary to take *h̲nw* here as reference to the residence of the Eleventh Dynasty kings, i.e., Thebes, and to conclude that Amenemhet was a legal resident there. This would agree with his position as vizier under the last Eleventh Dynasty king.

bf) The assumption of royal authority is stated in four parallel sentences. Despite their similarity,[392] legal differences prevail between the formulations used, perhaps reflecting particularities of the coronation. While *šsp* "to accept" in regard to the crown appears to express the bestowing of the office on its bearer,[393] *wṯs* seems to have a slightly different connotation,[394] reflecting the different roles of the two crowns. It appears that *šsp* is particularly connected with the white crown, and that *wṯs* is used for the red crown; so in particular Petrie, Koptus 8,8, *nn šsp.f ḥḏt nn wṯs.f dšrt* "he shall never receive the white crown and wear the red crown." The combining of the two crowns apparently is a separate legal act.[395] Although *sḫmty* is mentioned in Pyr. 805c and Sesostris Hymn IV,1, the physical combination of the two crowns can be established for the Third Dynasty; cf. Abubakr, *Untersuchungen über die altägyptischen Kronen,* 1937, 60ff.; Schäfer, OLZ 35, 1932, 697ff.

bg) *Nbwy* as the religious "Two Lords" of Egypt occurs also in Cairo 20539 I 3. *Sḥtp* "to placate" a deity, cf. Urk.VII 63,15; El Bersheh II, pl. XXI. There can be no question that Cairo 25224 has the correct wording with the imperfective *m mrrt*[*.sn*], as corroborated by Urk.VII 63,15.

The last words of the section have caused considerable difficulty. Gardiner, JEA 1, 1914, 105, rendered "the 'Surrounder of fields' in his grasp, the oar . . .," presuming that *pẖr-ỉḥ* is the name of some cult-object used in the rite of the king running with an oar in one hand. His view was followed by Wilson, *op. cit.*, 446, "The encircler-of-the-fields (will be) in his grasp, the oar. . . ." Lefèbvre, and Posener left it untranslated but considered it a reference to the ritual running as part of the coronation ceremony. A next step was taken by Helck, *Die Prophezeiung des Nfr.tj*, 51, who translated "Der Feldumkreiser ist in seiner Faust und das Ruder in Bewegung," seeing in it a reference to the  – object and the oar carried in the ceremonial running at the coronation; a similar view was taken by M. Lichtheim, *op. cit.*, 143, "With field-circler in his fist, oar in his grasp"; Faulkner, *op. cit.*, 239, gives "the land will be enclosed in his grasp, the oars swinging" as a reference to the occasion "when he is rowed on his royal progresses through the land." An entirely different rendering is offered by Barta, *op. cit.*, 44, "Der Acker wird umlaufen beim Fassen des Ruders und beim Bewegen . . ." without interpreting its meaning.

Principal grammatical and epigraphical observations have to be pointed out before tackling the semantic problems. *Ḫf*^{c} determined by  cannot be a noun but has to be recognized as the verb "to grasp." This applies equally to *nwd*, which obviously is parallel to *ḫf*^{c}. 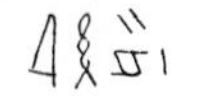 could not be accompanied by a diacritical stroke, because  is determinative, especially as the | is remarkably tall.[396] *Nwd* is determined by  and not by , so that the gap following it should contain one more word; judging from the diacritical stroke at its end, it can only be a noun.

In order to advance the understanding of the passage, its place in the context, as well as its structure, must be determined. It is generally assumed to stand unconnected at the end of the section; this would be different from the practice in the previous sections, which display an integrated composition. There can be no doubt that the last passage contains no reference to the king as subject, because in the foregoing he was introduced by the suffix third person. The seeming lack of continuity disappears when the passage is recognized as stating what the two divine lords of Egypt desire and what the king accomplishes. Consequently, the passage does not make reference to a rite in the royal coronation at all but concerns the king's ability to carry out the divine will.

The passage, which has an infinitive as its predicate,[397] has *pẖr ỉḥ* as its main part, to which two parallel constructions of *m* + infinitive + noun are subordinated. In other words, from *pẖr ỉḥ* depend *m ḫfꜥ wsr* and *m nwd*. . . . With the help of this structuring the reading and rendering become possible. The first task is to secure the reading, the second to restore the missing last word. The reading 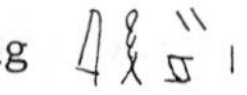 and its identification with *ꜥḥt* "farmland" is untenable. Instead, we have to read  ; for the hieratic form of  , whose discernible traces are  , see Möller, *Hieratische Paläographie* II, 374. The word  is identical with the Late Egyptian "to go somewhere" (Wb.I 120,10), whose imperative is used as an interjection.[398] The term applies in particular to navigation[399] and appears to have the meaning "to move to get somewhere," i.e., the course. *Pẖr*, either "to turn" or "to revolve," concerns here steering the course of history or altering the course of events after a long period of distress.

Ḫfꜥ "to grasp an object firmly," cf. Wb.III 272,5,7. *Wsr* "oar" is mentioned here primarily as a propellant, so the parallel statement should also mention an instrument for directing. This consideration leads to restoring *ḥpt* after *nwd;* for the word, cf. Wb.III 67; Boreaux, *op. cit.*, 447f.[400] *Nwd* "to vacillate," Wb.II 225,2,8-9; Peasant B 1,92; 99-100; 107; 262;[401] CT IV 72f.; V 64c; 392a. The later use of *nwd* in reference to the vacillations of life (Wb.II 205,7) helps the understanding here and suggests a rendering "to ply the rudder."

The desire of the two divine lords of Egypt, which the savior king will satisfy, is thus "to turn the course by grasping the oar and plying the rudder." The metaphor is derived from navigation, applied to the necessity to steer the country; see Grapow, *Die bildlichen Ausdrücke des Aegyptischen*, 153ff.; also Peasant B 1,267. In addition, the metaphor seems to contain a slur on Menthuhotep II, whose nomen *Nb-ḥpt-rꜥ* "lord of the steering rudder of Reꜥ" utilizes the nautical term.

XX. OUTLOOK TOWARD THE FUTURE

[XIV 11] 'Rejoice! O people of his time! A freeborn man [62] will be able to establish his name for eternity and everlastingness![bh]

Fall to disaster! O those contemplating treason [63] (even) after they abandoned their plans for fear of him.[bi]

The Asiatics will fall to his terror,
and the [64] Libyan will fall to his flame.'[bj]

bh) The invitation to the king to carry out the divine wish to alter the course of events will have its impact on Egypt's inhabitants, depending on their attitude. Indeed, as a message to future people, it is formulated as an imperative directed to those reacting positively and to those contemplating opposition.

Ršy is a plural imperative, as first recognized by Erman and generally accepted since. For *rš*, cf. also Shipwrecked Sailor 124;[402] Sinuhe B 70; Ptahhotep 557; Pap. Anast. III 5,3. *Rmṯ* has here the connotation of law-abiding citizen.[403] The cause for rejoicing is the return of order, in particular to society, enabling a man of free birth to make a career and to fill a place in an order, which will also bring eschatological benefits to him.

S3 n s was explained by Gardiner, *Admonitions of an Egyptian Sage*, 30, as "a man who was able to point to a well-to-do father, in opposition to the base-born slave," followed by Wb.III 406,1 and corroborated by Blackman, JEA 22, 1936, 104, who rendered the passage under discussion "A man of noble birth will make his name for ever and ever." Although it is clear that *s3-s* does not refer to the offspring of a slave, there is little reason to move to the opposite extreme and see in the term a reference to a social standing beyond free birth. Such a general meaning is borne out by other occurrences of the term, which all have *s3-s* and not the indirect genitive used here: Ptahhotep 493, *3ḫ bit nt s3-s n.f*, "the character of a man's son is significant/useful for him (the father)"; Admonitions 2,14, *ỉw-ms s3-s . . .* "forsooth, a man's son . . ." juxtaposed with *s3 ḥmt.f* "son of his maidservant"; Admonitions 4,1, *n tn.n.tw s3-s r ỉwty n.f sw* "a man's son can no (longer) be distinguished from one who has it not," *sw* referring to the side-lock of freeborn children; Merikareᶜ P. 61, *m tn s3-s r nds* "do not distinguish a man's son from a commoner";[404] Hatnub Gr. 24,2, *ỉnk s3-s ỉwty . . . f* "I was the son of a man who had no opponent," where the negative relative *iwty* qualifies *s* "man";[405] Petrie, Abydos III 29, *ỉr s3-s ỉrw st* "if the son of a man shall do it" his father is expected to take action; and Siut III 62, *ỉr ḥry-tp nb z3-z nb sᶜḥ nb nds nb* "as for any representative, any man's son, any noble and any commoner" with a distinct parallelism between *z3-z* and *nds*. As idiom for "freeborn" *s3-s* makes better sense here than as a man of superior social background, because the message seems to be a renewed opening of prospects for those willing to act.

ʾIri rn, lit. "to make a name" in the sense "to establish the reputation," cf. CT II 24e, but also with the meaning "to establish the nature" of something, comparable to Genesis 2:18-23, as in CT I 307e; II 6d; 7e; 23e.[406]

bi) The beneficial prospects for the loyal subjects of the savior king are matched by a dire threat to any opponents. *W3ww r dwt*, which in O Gardiner 331 is distinguished by a *rubrum*, is universally considered a nominally used participle and taken as parallel to *k3yw sbi* following it.[407] The result is an improbable construction, necessitating a prospective rendering of a *sdm.n.f* form.[408] The prevailing parallelism requires that *w3ww/w3yw* be taken as plural imperative, followed by a vocative. For *w3 r* with prerogative connotation, see Gardiner, *Admonitions of an Egyptian Sage*, 53; cf. also Siut IV 13; For *dwt* as the embodiment of all bad things, cf. Zandee, *Death as an Enemy*, 253; further Sinuhe B 273; Peasant B 1,59;[409] Wb.V 548,9. *K3 sbi* "to think of rebellion," Wb.IV 88,13; Medinet Habu 86,23; Urk.IV 140,5; Cairo 20539 I 10; Bersheh II 13,8,21; Cairo 20538 II c 19, (*nn ỉs n sbi* "there is no tomb for the traitor"); Neferhotep 22; Urk.I 281,10; cf. also Zandee, *op. cit.*, 296.

Sḫr.n.sn r3.sn is a relative past in the prospective setting; cf. Gardiner, *Egyptian Grammar*[3] §414.2. For *sḫr r3*, see Wb.IV 258,4; the idiom can be compared to "drop a matter."

bj) *Ḫr n šᶜt*, also Fakhry, *The Inscriptions of the Amethyst Quarries at Wadi el Hudi*, 14,12-14 (Sesostris I); ASAE 39, 1939, 187ff., pl. 25,4-5 (Sesostris I); Wb.IV 417,7; see also E. Blumenthal, *op. cit.*, 211f., who stresses the interchangeability of *šᶜt* and *nswt*<*nsrt*. It appears that both terms imply military action.[410]

The *Ṯmḥw* are not previously mentioned in the text, but see Sinuhe R 12-16.

XXI. RETURN TO ORDER

'Although the traitors belong to his wrath
and the discontented belong to 65 his might,
XV the Uraeus, which is on his brow, is pacifying for him the discontented.[bk]
66 One will (re) build the Fortification-of-the-Ruler, l.p.h.,
without allowing the Asiatics to descend 67 to Egypt.
They shall request water in the manner of supplication
68 in order to let their herds drink.[bl]
And order will come (back) to its place 69 and disorder will be cast away.
Rejoicing will be the one who observes 70 and he who will be serving the king.'[bm]

bk) *ʾIw sbiw nyw dndn.f*[411] is often taken as if it were datival with the verb *hr* omitted,[412] although there can be no doubt that it is used here genitivally; for the construction, see Edel, *Altägyptische Grammatik*, §366. *Nyw dndn.f* "ones belonging to his wrath" is the predicate to *sbiw*. The formulation is atemporal, describing an unmaterialized fact. The meaning of the passage is the potential punishing power of the king against traitors and discontented ones, which is not exercised because the king's spiritual authority makes the application of force unnecessary.

The symbol of the authority is the uraeus on the king's forehead; cf. Kees, ZÄS 65, 1930, 68; Moret, *Le rituel du culte divine journalier*, 232f.; Erman, *Hymnen an das Diadem der Pharaonen*, 7,1ff.

Shri "to make content," cf. Cairo 20539 I 2,3; Hammamat no. 114; Bersheh II 26; Wb.IV 208 A II. The datival *n.f* is correct in Cairo 25224 and O Gardiner 326.

bl) In the last section Neferyt returns to the particular problems of the eastern fringe of the Delta, the description of which had triggered his discourse, and describes the measures the savior king will take and what effect they will have. The fortification system "walls-of-the-ruler" (*ỉnbw-ḥḳ3*), well known from Sinuhe B 17 as the point where Sinuhe left Egypt, apparently was not the first installation of its type in the area but was preceded by an earlier fortification system. Reference was made to it above in l. 33 and in Merikare^{c} P. 100; see Scharff, *Der historische Abschnitt der Lehre für König Merikare^{c}*, 32; Posener, *op. cit.*, 24ff.; and below

All available versions agree on the formulation *nn* + infinitive; for the construction, cf. Satzinger, *op. cit.*, §61. The descent of Asiatics for arable land (*kmt*), also above in l. 33, describes a situation in which different conditions prevailed.

Dbḥ.sn is a main clause and should not be connected with the foregoing.[413] *Sš3* "to supplicate,"[414] also Shipwrecked Sailor 129;[415] Ptahhotep 431-32; Merikare^{c} P. 143, *m sš3 ỉwt.f min* "do not beg that he come today"; Urk.IV 2027, 17. The requested watering of the herds stays in contrast to the roaming of the desert flocks described in l. 35. The practice of allowing bedouin to water their flocks in the Wadi Tumilat is the topic of a model letter quoted Pap. Anast. VI 51-61; see Caminos, *Late Egyptian Miscellanies*, 293ff.; Giveon, *Les bédouins Shosou des documents égyptiens*, 131ff.

bm) The converse of the return of order and the expulsion of wrong is in Kha^{c}kheperre^{c}-seneb rt. 11, "justice has been expelled; wrong is in the council-chamber"; cf. Gardiner, *Admonitions of an Egyptian Sage*, 102; Kadish, JEA 59, 1973, 78; Morenz, *Altägyptische Religion*, 232. Cairo 25224, which has repeatedly proved to contain the better version, has the pseudo-verbal *ỉsft [dr].ti r rwty*, while Pap. Ermitage has *ỉsft dr sy r rwty*; for the latter, cf. Grapow, ZÄS 71, 1935, 52ff.; Westendorf, *Der Gebrauch des Passivs in der klassischen Literatur der Ägypter*, 72; Barta, *op. cit.*, 44f.

Ršy is a prospective *sḏm.f*, with two nominally used *sḏm.ty.fy* forms as its subjects. *Gmḥ* has the connotation of perceiving, rather than of mere visual perception, as in Deir Rifeh I, 6,[416] *m33.n(.ỉ) m-ḫt dg.n(.ỉ) nḥḥ gmḥ.n(.ỉ) ḏt* "I saw the hereafter, I looked at eternity, and I perceived everlastingness"; cf. also Hammamat no. 199,5 *gmḥ.n(.ỉ) ḥnty* "I perceived the ends." *Šms nswt* "to serve the king," WB.IV 483,17;

Urk.VII 62,6; Janssen, *Het traditioneele egyptische Autobiografie*, II F u; Sinuhe B 171.

XXII. NEFERYT WILL BE ACKNOWLEDGED

'The educated one will pour [71] water for me, when he realizes that what I said, happened.[bn]

Colophon.

It was completed by the scribe . . .

bn) The closing line contains an assurance that the learned one will honor Neferyt for his prophecy once he realizes that what was said has happened. *Rḫw-ḫt* "knowing one"[417] seems to have here a practical meaning "learned one," i.e., someone familiar with writing and with Neferyt's sayings.

Sti mw as a gesture of honor for a deceased, see Urk.I 75,10; 76,9;[418] Admonitions 7,5; BM 152,4; 1164,8; Qaw-Bowl III 4;[419] Urk.IV 27,1; 149,17, etc.[420] For *m33* "to realize," see Shipwrecked Sailor 28-29.[421] *Ḏdt.n.i͗* "what I have said" is treated as a masculine noun, thus the Old Perfective *ḫpr;* for *ḏdt.n.f* in the sense of "statement" cf. Blackman, JEA 19, 1933, 201.

The scribe's name is missing in the colophon.

NOTES TO THE COMMENTARY

1 See Posener, *Le conte de Neferkare et du général Sisene* (Recherches Littéraires, VI), RdE 11, 1957, 119-37.

2 See Gauthier, *La grande inscription dédicatoire d'Abydos*, Bibl. d'Et. 4, 3; cf. also J. D. Schmidt, *Ramesses II*, 22f.

3 See above p. 14f.

4 *Ḫpr swt skdwt m wi3y ᶜ3y . . . sk sw dy m st.f nfrt nt ḏt . . . nb n k3t ḥw 3 ỉr rḫ(.ỉ) ṯnwt nt . . . sk sw d[y m st.f nfrt nt ḏt] ḥr m k3t nt mḥ 5* "A journey happened in the Two Great Ships . . . (people), now that he was placed in his final place of eternity. [Then said his Majesty] to all the . . . of the work: I truly wish to know the number of . . . now that he was [placed in his final resting place.] ⌜The face⌝ consists of worked stone of 5 cubits, they said to his majesty."

5 The literary affinity leads to the question whether the Instruction of Kagemni is a prototype or whether the wisdom text, which is usually assigned to the Old Kingdom, might possibly have a closer relation with our text. Its poor state of preservation provides no sufficient base to investigate this possibility.

6 Kees, *RE sub Sesochris*, proposed the identification with *Nfr-k3-Skr*, the eighth king of the Second Dynasty, but the proposal of Berard, *Rev. des études grècques*, 50, 1937, 289, to see in Sasychis a mistake for Asychis, i.e., *Wsr-k3.f*, the first king of the Fifth Dynasty, has great appeal in view of the king's apparent concern for law as reflected by his Horus-name *ʾIrw-m3ᶜt* "the maker/doer of law." The difference between Sasychis and Asychis might be due to a conflation of Soris (Snofru) and Asychis (Userkaf). It could, however, also be theorized that Snofru is identical with Mnevis, whom Diodorus lists as the first to establish written laws in Egypt. A confusion between Σνευις and Μνευις is well within the limits of conceivable conflation. It would make much better sense than the usual identification of Mnevis with Menes; cf. Sethe, *Untersuchungen* III, 121; Seidl, *Einführung in die ägyptische Rechtsgeschichte bis zum Ende des Neuen Reiches*, Ägypt. Forsch. 10, 60.

7 See Goedicke, *The Berlin Leather Roll*, *Festschrift zum 150jährigen Bestehen des Berliner Ägyptischen Museums*, 1974, 90.

8 See in particular Posener, *loc. cit.*, 147, and E. Blumenthal, *op. cit.*, 331.

9 The epistological use of *nḏ ḫrt* in the sense of "to greet" is the same extension as found in current American usage of "how are you?" or "how do you do?" as greeting; cf. Bakir, *Egyptian Epistolography*, Bibl. d'Et. 48, 46f.; James, *The Ḥeḳanakhte Papers*, 127.

10 E.g., Urk.I 149,2-3, *sr ỉwt hrw n stp m nḏt-r3* "who announces the coming of the day of storming in the council"; Hatnub Gr. 29,5, *hrw n nḏt-r3* "day of council"; Urk.IV 342,11-12 (divine council); cf. also Urk.IV 649.

11 Cf. the Duties of the Vizier §4 = Urk.IV 1105,12-13; cf. Helck, *Zur Verwaltung des Mittleren und Neuen Reiches*, 31f.

12 See in particular Posener, *ibid.*, "(puis) ils sortirent afin de présenter leurs salutations, selon leur coutume de chaque jour." While he finds this meaning not particularly satisfying, he does not draw the necessary conclusion from the literal meaning of *nḏ ḫrt*, which he understands as "s'enquérir de la condition," although he emphasizes the extended use of the idiom. He assumes that the introduction of the text underwent redaction in what he calls "le style simple des contes populaires." There is nothing in the text that would make it a likely candidate for attracting general popularity, as the questions dealt with are not of general human concern but remain confined to a historical situation. Similarly, Gardiner, JEA 1, 1914, 101f., rendered "and they went forth again in order that they might perform their duty according to their daily observance," commenting that the officials were present to report to the king.

13 See Helck, *op. cit.*, 84f., for the administrative role of this official; cf. further Sauneron, BIFAO 51, 1952, 137ff.; Fischer, *Inscriptions from the Coptite Nome*, Analecta Orientalia 40, 126-29.

14 Cf. James, *The Ḥeḳanakhte Papers*, 109f.; Goedicke, *The Report of Wenamun*, 113; 176.

15 If *nḏ* were qualified, the adverbial adjunct would be *hrw pn* and not *m hrw pn*.

16 Wb. I 421, 7-10; cf. Gardiner, *Egyptian Grammar*[3] §178. In Pyr. 1189b the presumed occurrence of the term probably is wrong and is possibly better explained as *m3ḥw* or *ḏḥnw* "the rhythm indicator." Siut pl. XIX,18 is unclear, and Cairo 20542 has the word ʿ "portion."

17 I am not convinced that *rḥw* is used only to convey Snofru's joviality. It might have been selected as a typical Old Kingdom expression to convey authenticity, because the term falls into disuse after that period.

18 M. Lichtheim, *loc. cit.*, 140; similarly Helck, *Die Prophezeihung des Nfr.tj*, 8, "dass ihr mir einen Sohn von euch, der weise ist, suchen lässt" with the literal rendering "als einen Weisen." Faulkner, in *The Literature of Ancient Egypt*, ed. W. K. Simpson, 235, "a son of yours who is wise"; also Wilson, ANET 444; Lefèbvre, *Romans et contes*, 97, "que parmi vos fils vous m'en cherchiez un qui soit plein d'esprit"; Erman, *Die Literatur der Aegypter*, 152, "damit ihr mir einen Sohn von euch sucht, der verständig ist"; Gardiner, JEA 1, 1914, 102, "from your sons one who has understanding."

19 For *nḏs* "youth," see Wb.II 385,6. *Nḏs* is a common designation for subject, from the late Old Kingdom into the Middle Kingdom; see Fischer, *Dendera in the Third Millenium B.C.*, 87-88; Goedicke, *The Report about the Dispute of a Man with His* Ba, 131f.

20 A rendering "wise one," as Sethe, *Übersetzung und Kommentar zu den altägyptischen Pyramidentexten* IV, 117, proposes, and Faulkner, *Ancient Egyptian Pyramid Texts*, 152, maintains ("Wise One"), is not required by the context.

21 Or "a storehouse for the officials in the experience"; for the restoration *pr-šn*ᶜ cf. Williams, in *Essays in Honour of T. J. Meek*, 16.

22 Cf. also II, 49.

23 See Goedicke, *Die Geschichte des Schiffbrüchigen*, Äg. Abh. 30, 71.

24 M. Lichtheim, *loc. cit.*, 140; Helck, *loc. cit.*, 9, "der Vollendetes äussern kann"; Faulkner, *loc. cit.*, 235, "who has achieved some noble deed"; Wilson, *loc. cit.*, 444, "who has performed a good deed"; Lefèbvre, *loc. cit.*, 97, "un qui ait accompli (?) quelque haut fait"; Erman, *loc. cit.*, 152, "der Gutes getan (?) hat"; Gardiner, *loc. cit.*, 102, "who has achieved some noble deed."

25 Westendorf, in his discussion of the passage in *Festschrift für Siegfried Schott* 125ff., proposes a metaphorical meaning "death" as the "good event" but fails to convince with his argumentation. The passage *mi m-s3 pw ḫpr sp nfr* is rather to be rendered "Come! After this, good luck should occur!"

26 Cf. Žaba, *Les Maximes de Ptahhotep*, 100, "si une bonne action est faite par celui qui est un chef."

27 The passage concerns the abilities of Baky as wet-nurse, which brought good luck to the family.

28 For the identity of these explanations, see Edel, *Altägyptische Grammatik*, §600.

29 Having the characteristic of an adjective, the form cannot be separated from the term it qualifies. If it were here **ḏd.ty.fy*, it would have to qualify **sp nfr*; a connection with three antecedents, separated by various qualifying expressions, is even more unfeasible.

30 Cf. Erman, *Neuägyptische Grammatik*^{2} §442; Gardiner, *Egyptian Grammar*^{3} §409 and §387,2.

31 Cf. also Caminos, *Late Egyptian Miscellanies*, 421.

32 Wb.V 403,11; Sinuhe B 227.

33 Cf. Kadish, *British Museum Writing Board 5654: The Complaints of Kha-kheper-re*ᶜ*-senebu*, JEA 59, 1973, 77ff.

34 See I. Grumach, *Untersuchungen zur Lebenslehre des Amenope*, MÄS 23, 148.

35 Decker, *Die physische Leistung Pharaos* (Diss. Köln), 106, is certainly wrong in rendering "sich vergnügen beim Unterricht im Schiessen in der Halle Pharaos." *D3t-ḥr*, lit. "extending attention," has here the implication of supervision, while avoiding any mention of the inferior position of the royal prince during the training.

36 See Caminos, *Literary Fragments in the Hieratic Script*, 17.

37 Cf. Gardiner, *Notes on the Story of Sinuhe*, 32; Varille, Kêmi 4, 1931, 119ff.

38 For the reading *ẖry-ḥ(3)bt* "bearer of the feast ritual," see Edel, *Altägyptische Grammatik* §104. Sethe's reading of the title in ZÄS 70, 1934, 134, on the basis of Urk.I 189,10, which Gardiner, *Ancient Egyptian Onomastica* I, 55ff.* follows, was based on an error; cf. Schott, *Mythe und Mythenbildung*, 1, Anm. 6.

39 See Posener, *op. cit.*, 34; in Pap. Sallier IV 1,2, which he cites as a parallel, *ᶜ3 n W3st* should be separated from *ẖry-ḥbt*. *Ḫry-ḥbt* has as its qualifications *smsw*, *ḥry-tp*, and *ᶜš3*, but not *ᶜ3*.

40 Turin has in both instances a determinative, but its orthography is generally of poor quality.

41 It is the same distinction as found, e.g., between  and  "scribe" and "a scribe"; see also Edel, *Altägyptische Grammatik*, §54.

42 See also the occurrence in *Inscription dédicatoire*, 39.

43 Westcar 5,1; 9,23; cf. Gardiner, *Egyptian Grammar*³ §238.

44 Similarly M. Lichtheim, "May he be brought for your majesty to see!"

45 Wilson, similarly Faulkner, Lefèbvre, and Gardiner, rendered "would it [might be vouchsafed to] him to see thy (?) Majesty."

46 Posener, *op. cit.*, 31, note 2, considers it uncertain whether the reference is to the past or the present; cf. also Gunn, *loc. cit.*, 251; Barta, MDIK 27, 1971, 36.

47 Despite the insistence of Gunn, *Studies in Egyptian Syntax*, 41, the prospective nature of the form is not at all certain. The fact that it frequently occurs after *ỉr* has influenced the issue considerably.

48 What prospectivity it conveys is implicit in *ḫpr* itself because of its expressing transfigurative being. For the form cf. also Gunn, *op. cit.*, 40, note 1.

49 M. Lichtheim "As soon as today is here, it is passed over"; Helck ". . . denn das Heute ist bereits zu etwas geworden, was Vergangenheit ist"; Faulkner "Today has come into being and one has passed it by"; Wilson "If it has taken place today, pass it [by]"; Lefèbvre "si aujourd'hui même (quelque chose) est arrivé, passe par-dessus"; Erman "Ist heute etwas geschehen, so gehe an ihm vorüber"; Gardiner "Today (a thing) happens and is past (?)."

50 MDIK 27, 1971, 16 renders "denn (bereits) das Heute ist in der Tat das, was geschehen ist, es ist das, was an einem vorbeigegangen ist."

51 Cf. also the idiom *ỉri sw3* "to pass by," Wb.IV 61,21 = Siut III 1.

52 Cf. Luft, *Das Verhältnis zur Tradition in der frühen Ramessidenzeit*, *Forschungen und Berichte* 14, 1972, 62.

53 Petrie, *Medum* XIII; M. Murray, *Saqqara Mastabas* I 2. Junker, *Gîza* IV 71, considers the object depicted Gîza III Tf. V an "ovaler Holzbehälter."

54 Jequier, *Les frises d'objets*, MIFAO 47, 264f.; Montet, *Scènes de la vie privée*, 146. Cf. also the royal writing equipment *3ʿw n sš* mentioned Urk. I 42, 8.

55 Jequier, *ibid.*

56 L. Klebs, *Die Reliefs und Malereien des mittleren Reiches*, 51.

57 Gardiner, Erman, Lefèbvre, and Wilson.

58 *Littérature et politique*, 148f.; he is followed by Faulkner, M. Lichtheim, Helck, and Barta.

59 Cf. Goedicke, JARCE 11, 1974, 40f.

60 So M. Lichtheim "that wise man of the East . . ."; Faulkner, "he was a sage of the East . . .'" Helck "der ein Wissender des Ostdeltas war . . ."; Posener, *op. cit.*, 149 "ce savant de l'Est . . ."; Wilson "that wise man of the east . . ."; Lefèbvre "ce savant de l'est . . ."; Erman "der Gelehrte aus dem Osten . . ."; Gardiner "that wise man of the East. . . ." I do not know of a case in which a nominal clause is used as a qualifying appositive or as a virtual relative clause, as the previous translations presuppose.

61 Brunner, ZÄS 93, 1966, 33f., considers prophesying one of the arts of any "sage" (*rḫ-ḫt*) in Egypt. Neferyt makes projections on the basis of past experiences and does not claim to convey wisdom, with the possible exception of the last section of the text (11. 55ff.).

62 See Fischer, JNES 18, 1959, 129ff.; Gardiner *Ancient Egyptian Onomastica* II, 204*; Helck, *Die altägyptischen Gaue*, 187f.

63 Ranke, *Die ägyptischen Personennamen* II, 226; cf. also Edel, ZÄS 85, 1960, 79ff.

64 Urk.I 81,5; 80,14; 52,4,11,16; 53,4 cf. Goedicke, *Die Stellung des Königs im Alten Reich*, 82.

65 Helck "Bastet in ihrem Osten"; Faulkner "Bastet when she rises"; Posener, *op. cit.*, 149 "Bastit dans son orient"; Wilson "Bastet at her appearances"; Lefèbvre "Bastit à son orient"; Erman "der zu der Bastet gehört . . ."; Gardiner "Ubast at her rising."

66 Another occurrence of *wbn* in this form is Urk.IV 1973,4; 1984,12.

67 Posener, *ibid.*, considers *wbn* as replacement of *ỉ3btt*, which would leave the suffix, as occurring in O Turin, unaccounted for.

68 Wb.I 293,13; see in particular Cairo 20040.

69 See Goedicke, *Four Hieratic Ostraca of the Old Kingdom*, JEA 54, 1968, 23ff.; similar are the ostraca published by Zaki Saad, *Royal Excavations at Saqqara and Helwan (1941-1945)*, CASAE 3, 106; pls. XLIIf.

70 Cf. Goedicke, *Königliche Dokumente aus dem Alten Reich*, *Äg. Abh.* 14, 64; 240.

71 Die altägyptischen Gaue 183.

72 *Op. cit.*, 149 ". . . alors qu'il méditait sur ce qui devait arriver dans le pays et qu'il évoqait la condition de l'Est."

73 Edel, *Altägyptische Grammatik*, §885, leaves the question open because of insufficient material in Old Egyptian. Westendorf, *Grammatik der medizinischen Texte*, §232f, takes it as habitative.

74 Grapow, *Der stilistische Bau der Geschichte des Sinuhe*, 46, considers the form synonymous with the *sḏm.n.f*-form following it. However, there are distinct nuances between the different forms used in the section, which he disregards. Only *ỉw.ỉ dỉ.ỉ* seems to have truly habitual connotation, while the *sḏm.n.f* has here, as usual, a predominantly narrative meaning.

75 B 1,216 is important for its parallelism with the construction *ỉn* + noun + Old Perfective, which has general connotation. In B 1,261 *ỉw.k ỉr.k twtw n bw nb* "you do the same as everybody" clearly is generalizing.

76 *ʾIw r3 n s wḥm.f sw* is an adage; cf. Goedicke, *Die Geschichte des Schiffbrüchigen*, 11.

77 Cf. Goedicke, *The Report about the Dispute of a Man with His* Ba, 101.

78 Likewise Gunn, *Studies in Egyptian Syntax*, 40, note 1, followed by Lefèbvre, *Romans et contes*, 98, note 12.

79 He is followed by M. Lichtheim, *loc. cit.*, 144, note 1, but she takes it as past: "what had happened."

80 JEA 1, 1914, 103, note 2, quoting Pap. Sallier I 6,2 as parallel; cf. Caminos, *Late Egyptian Miscellanies*, 316. See also Barta, MDIK 27, 1971, 36.

81 Faulkner, in W. K. Simpson, ed., *The Literature of Ancient Egypt*, 236, note 6. Other translations are Gardiner "when the Asiatics approach in their might"; Erman "wenn die Asiaten kommen in ihrer Kraft (?)"; Lefèbvre and Posener "quand les Asiatiques feraient irruption avec leurs forces"; Wilson "when the Asiatics would move about with their strong arms"; Helck "indem die Asiaten in ihrer Macht kommen"; M. Lichtheim "with Asiatics roaming in their strength"; Barta "wenn die Asiaten herankommen in ihrer Kraft."

82 Wb.III 258,8; cf. Pyr. 888b.

83 See Caminos, *Late-Egyptian Miscellanies*, 293ff.

84 Despite the objections of Posener, *Princes et pays*, 42, the etymology עם "people" for *ᶜ3m* still seems the only convincing one. *3* probably serves as a vowel indicator and is thus insignificant.

85 Gen 41:54-42:2; 43:1-2.

86 Cf. de Vaux, *Palestine in the Early Bronze Age*, CAH I,2, 233ff.; Ward

Egypt and the East Mediterranean World 2200-1900 B.C., 19ff.; B. Bell, AJA 75, 1971, 1-26; see also 32ff.

87 Gardiner rendered "their hearts raged against those who are gathering in the harvest" and wrongly took *ỉb* as subject, which was not followed by other translators.

88 See I. Grumach, *Untersuchungen zur Lebenslehre des Amenope*, MÄS 23, 89; 92f.; 97; 102.

89 So M. Lichtheim. Others are: Helck ". . . und die Herzen derer, die bei der Ernte sind, beunruhigen und die für das Pflügen bestimmten Gespanne rauben"; Faulkner ". . . and terrorize those at the harvest, taking away their teams engaged in ploughing"; Wilson ". . . would disturb the hearts [of] those who are at the harvest and would take away the spans of cattle at the plowing"; Lefèbvre "qu'ils terrifieraient les coeurs (de) ceux qui sont à la moisson et qu'ils enlèveraient les attelages en train de labourer"; Erman "wenn sie die Herzen der Erntenden kränken und ihre Gespanne beim Pflügen rauben"; Gardiner "and their hearts rage against those who are gathering in the harvest, and they take away (their) kine from the ploughing."

90 Cf. Gardiner, *Egyptian Grammar*[3] §§319f.

91 Cf. Erman, *Neuägyptische Grammatik*[2] §842; Erman, ZÄS 44, 1907, 113.

92 A small number of examples is known from the Old Kingdom, basically in settings close to vernacular; see Edel, *Altägyptische Grammatik*, §§927; 1059.

93 O DeM 1187 is transcribed , but there are doubts concerning the presumed indirect genitive and the sign preceding it; cf. Posener, *Ostraca hiératiques littéraires de Deir el Médineh* (Doc. de Fouilles) II, pl. 36. The hieratic sign over *ntyw* is much too curved to be read , and the sign in front of it can only be read  (grain). The sign over *ntyw* I propose to read 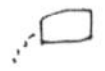; for the form see Möller, *Hieratische Paläographie* I, 685.

94 Wb.III 201; Simpson, *Papyrus Reisner* II 18; cf. also Helck, *Zur Verwaltung des Mittleren und Neuen Reiches*, 38.

95 For the bipartite process of taxation, cf. Berger, *A Note on some Scenes of Land-measurement*, JEA 20, 1934, 54ff.; Gardiner, *Ramesside Texts Relating to the Taxation and Transport of Corn*, JEA 27, 1941, 19ff.; *idem*, *The Wilbour Papyrus* II, 24f., where the two terms are *ps* and *šmw*. For *šmw* "harvest tax," see also Goedicke, *The Report about the Dispute of a Man with His Ba*, 133.

96 Gardiner, *loc. cit.*, 103, "Up, my heart and bewail this land"; Erman, *loc. cit.*, 153, "Rühre dich (?), mein Herz, dass du dieses Land beweinst"; Lefèbvre, *loc. cit.*, 99, "Emens-toi, mon coeur, et pleure sur ce pays"; Wilson, *loc. cit.*, 444, "Reconstruct, O my heart, (how) thou bewailest this land"; Posener, *loc. cit.*, 150, "secoue-toi, mon coeur"; Faulkner, *loc. cit.*, 236, "stir yourself, my heart, weep for this land"; Helck, *loc. cit.*, 18, "Rege dich, mein Herz, dass du dieses Land beweinst"; M. Lichtheim, *loc. cit.*, 140, "stir, my heart, bewail this land."

97 Addressing the heart is an attested literary device, but only as metaphor for an inner dialogue; cf. Khakheperre^{c}-seneb rt. 7; vs. 1.

98 Although both constructions are acceptable in principle, the infinitival formulation of O DeM 1187 seems superior, despite Helck's evaluation to the contrary.

99 Urk.IV 1154,5 *ḥws ᶜwy.ṯn rḥw* is quoted Wb.III 249,4, further by Posener, *loc. cit.*, 150; and Faulkner, *A Concise Dictionary*, 186, as an example where a part of the body serves as object to *ḥws*, and it is rendered "to stir the arms." However, as Grapow, *Anreden* III, 21, already pointed out, *ᶜwy.ṯn* is not object in this instance. *Ḥws* is rather to be recognized as a *sḏm.f* with *ᶜwy.ṯn* as subject, so that the address should be read "may your arms pound, O comrades!"

100 Cf. Piankoff, *Le "coeur" dans les textes égyptiens*, 83ff.

101 M. Lichtheim, similarly Helck and Gardiner; Erman, Wilson and Faulkner keep closer to the basic meaning of *šꜣᶜ* by rendering "this land in which you began." A compromise is Lefèbvre's rendering "ce pays où tu as commencé (d'être)."

102 According to the Manetho epitomes the Fourth Dynasty was "of Memphis."

103 Wb.IV 407,6 has a misleading entry, because *šꜣᶜ* in *ḫft šꜣᶜ* "according to his beginning" is a nominally used infinitive.

104 Wb.IV 407, 5; cf. also Caminos, *Literary Fragments in the Hieratic Script*, 7.

105 *Loc. cit.*, 103, "He who is silent is a transgressor (??). Behold, that exists whereof men spoke as a thing to be dreaded (??). Behold, the great one is fallen <in the land> whence thou art sprung. Be thou not weary. Behold, these things are before thee; rise up against what is in thy presence. Behold, princes hold sway in the land, things made are . . ."; Erman, *op. cit.*, 154, ". . . Ruhe nicht, sieh, es liegt vor deinem Antlitz; stehe auf gegen das, was vor dir ist . . ."; Lefèbvre, *op. cit.*, 99, "Celui qui se tait dans les calamités (?), vois, il y a quelque chose qui peut être dit à son sujet en manière de réprobation. Vois donc, le grand est (maintenant) abaissé dans le pays où tu as commencé (d'être). Ne te montre pas mou. Vois, ces choses sont devant toi. Lève-toi contre ce qui est en ta présence. Vois donc, les grands sont dans le même état que le pays (lui-même); Wilson, *loc. cit.*, 444f., "To be silent is *repression*. Behold, there is something about which men speak as terrifying, for, behold, the great man is a thing passed away (in the land) where thou didst begin. Be not lax; behold, it is before thy face! Mayest thou rise up against what is before thee, for, behold, although great men are concerned with the land, what has been done . . ."; S. Herrmann, *Untersuchungen zur Überlieferungsgestalt mittelägyptischer Literaturwerke*, 22, "Der Schweigende ist vernichtet, siehe, der etwas dazu sagen könnte, ist verscheucht (?). Siehe, der Beamte ist niedergeworfen. Du hast den Anfang gemacht mit dem Land. Sei nicht müde. Siehe, es steht bei dir, dass du aufstehest gegen das, was vor dir ist. Siehe, die Grossen entsprechen der Art und Weise im Lande"; Faulkner, *loc. cit.*, 236, ". . . for he who is silent is a wrong doer. See, that

(now) exists which was spoken of as something dreadful. See, the great one is overthrown in the land in which you began. Do not become weary; see, they are before your eyes; rise up against what is before you. See, there are great men in the governance of the land . . ."; Helck, *op. cit.*, ". . . denn Schweigen wäre Begünstigung. Siehe es gab etwas, wovon man in Respekt sprach; doch siehe, der Beamte ist nun ein Niedergestreckter im Lande. Sei nicht müde, denn siehe, es ist dir gegenüber. Du sollst dich erheben gegen das, was vor dir ist. Siehe, es gibt nicht mehr Beamte in den Angelegenheiten des Landes"; M. Lichtheim, *op. cit.*, 140f., "When there is silence before evil, and when what should be chided is feared, then the great man is overthrown in the land of your birth. Tire not while this is before you, rise against what is before you! Lo, the great no longer rule the land. . . ."

106 See also Barta, MDIK 27, 1971, 37, who renders "Schweigen ist (jetzt etwas) Verwerfliches."

107 The syntactical position of *m wrḏ* is demonstrated by the fact that Pap. Ermitage writes it as a *rubrum* and that in O DeM 1188 it is the first word written.

108 Cf. also CT V 10g; 14f.

109 Cf. Wb.V 620,5-6.

110 See above note 105; further Barta, *ibid.*, "Siehe doch, ein (feindlicher) Fürst wirft das Land nieder."

111 For the meaning of *sr* see Goedicke, *Königliche Dokumente aus dem Alten Reich*, 186.

112 Among recent translators only Faulkner prefers the latter, while Helck and Lichtheim choose the former.

113 See also Ḥeḳanakhte II 34. The specific connotation would seem the loss of properly owned property.

114 *Der Gebrauch des Passivs in der klassischen Literatur der Ägypter*, AIO 18, 9; 13.

115 Gardiner, JEA 1, 1914, 105, gave for it "the land is utterly perished"; Erman, *Literatur*, 154, "dieses Land wird verderbt"; Lefèbvre, *Romans et contes*, 99, "le pays est complètement ruiné"; Wilson *loc. cit.*, "this land is (so) damaged"; S. Hermann, *loc. cit.*, 40, "zerstört ist dies Land"; Faulkner, in Simpson, *The Literature of Ancient Egypt*, 236, "This land is destroyed"; Helck, *loc. cit.*, "das Land wird zerstört"; M. Lichtheim, *loc. cit.*, 141, "(yet) while the land suffers"; Barta, MDIK 27, 1971, 38, "dieses Land wird zerstört werden." The translations range from passive present to passive future, including a stative.

116 Barta, *ibid.*, speaks of "substantivierte, prospektive Partizipien," although they are clearly perfective.

117 For *mh hr*, cf. Sinuhe B 199 and Suicidal 32; 78; cf. Goedicke, *The Report about the Dispute of a Man with His* Ba, 111; 138. Faulkner, *op. cit.*, 113, renders it "to ponder on," in which he is followed by Helck.

118 As the context makes a reference to speaking unlikely at this point, especially since no addressee is mentioned, it seems tempting to take *ḏd* here to mean "to anticipate," "to answer"; cf. Wb.V 623,7; Suicidal 30; Sinuhe B 45.

119 O Michelides pl. 8 has instead *wn t3 pn*. The question has a striking parallel in Sinuhe B 44 *wnn ỉr.f t3 pf mỉ m-ʿ* "How indeed will that land be. . . ."

120 Wb.I 309,2; Urk.I 105,17; Ptahhotep 119.

121 Cf. Grapow, *Anreden* IV 38; cf. also Gardiner, *Egyptian Grammar*^{3} §496.

122 S. Herrmann, *op. cit.*, 40f., conceived the structure differently and rendered "Aton ist verhüllt, er scheint nicht, damit die Menschen sehen; man kann nicht leben, die Wolke verhüllt (ihn)." Aside from the need to make emendations, it also disregards the last part.

123 Others resorted to more or less extensive emendations: Erman, *Literatur*, 154, "Man lebt nicht, wenn das Unwetter (sie) verhüllt"; Lefèbvre, *Romans et contes*, 99, "on ne vivra plus, car les nuages (le) recouvriront," Wilson, *ibid.*, "no one can live when clouds cover over (the sun)"; Posener, *Littérature et politique*, 41, "on ne vivra plus, car les nuages voileront le soleil"; Helck, *op. cit.*, 23, "Nicht kann man leben, wenn die Wolke (sie) verdeckt"; Gardiner, JEA 1, 1914, 103, emended <*ỉw ỉtn*> *ḥbs* <*m*> *šn* and rendered "None can live <when the sun (??)> is veiled <by (??)> clouds (?)," which is followed by Faulkner, in *The Literature of Ancient Egypt*, 236, "none will live when <the sun> is veiled <by> cloud."

124 See in particular Lefèbvre, *ibid.*, note 22.

125 So already Gardiner, *loc. cit.*, 103, note 10; Helck, *op. cit.*, 23.

126 A sentence **wn.ỉn ḥr-nb ỉdw* could only be rendered "and then every face was numb," as in Peasant B 2,117, *wn.ỉn sẖty pn snḏ* "and then this peasant was afraid"; cf. Gardiner, *Egyptian Grammar*^{3} §429; Lefèbvre, *Grammaire*^{2} §665.

127 Cf. also *ỉnsyt* "the red one" as term for the eye-of-Horus, Wb.I 100, 14; Grapow, Die bildlichen Ausdrücke des Aegyptischen 56f.; cf. also Pyr. 285a-d *m3.k Rʿ m ỉnṯt.f ḏw3.k Rʿ m prwt.f m z3-wr ỉmy ỉns.f* "may you see Re in his fetters and may you praise Re in his ascendance as *z3-wr*, who is in his redness"; cf. also Sethe, *Übersetzung und Kommentar zu den altägyptischen Pyramidentexten* I, 326f.

128 Cf. also below l. 38, where *ỉd* is used in its normal meaning.

129 See Satzinger, *op. cit.*, §§30ff.; Gardiner, *Egyptian Grammar*^{3} §418. The construction certainly has no prospective meaning, as Faulkner ("I will never foretell what is not to come") conceives; see also Morenz, *Untersuchungen zur Rolle des Schicksals*, Leipzig AAW 52,1, 1960, 12; *idem*, *Ägyptische Religion*, 72.

130 See also Urk.I 149,2-3, "who pronounces in the council the coming of the day of storming."

131 So explicitly Lefèbvre, *op. cit.*, 100, note 34, "le Nil, les bras et les branches du Nil" and Posener, *op. cit.*, 41.

132 For *kmt* in this sense, see Wb.V 126f., in particular also Adm. 3,1 and Urk.IV 4,3, which concerns an area possibly related to the one concerned here.

133 A. de Buck, *Orientalia Neerlandica* I, 1, confirms the generally held opinion that *ỉtrw* denotes the Nile, which is also considered the meaning of *ỉtrw-ꜥꜣ*; see Gardiner, *Ancient Egyptian Onomastica* II, 159*ff. The form of qualification indicates the existence of a multitude of *ỉtrw*, which curtails its applicability to the Nile proper. The difficulties vanish when taking *ỉtrw* to denote a navigable watercourse, natural or artificial, as distinguished from man-made "canals." Siut V 3 supports this interpretation with the mention of an *ỉtrw* of ten cubits, which was man-made (*šꜣd*). That the particular feature of *ỉtrw* is its navigability explains also the extended use of the term for a measure of distance; see A. Schlott, *Die Ausmasse Ägyptens nach altägyptischen Texten*, 132ff.

134 Though determined differently, *šw* "to be dry" (Wb.IV 429) might also be implied here.

135 The suffix *.f* refers to *mw* and not to *ꜥḥꜥw* as Helck, *op. cit.*, 26, assumes.

136 See also Hammamat 113,13, *ỉrỉ.n(.ỉ) ḫꜣst m ỉtrw ỉnwt ḥrywt m* 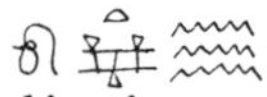 "I made the desert in a navigable water and the high-lying wadis in a riverbed."

137 In its composition it corresponds to the aforegoing group of sentences where the prevailing low water level in the watercourses is juxtaposed with the prospect of seeking water to sail on.

138 Gardiner, JEA 1, 1914, 103, "Their course is become a sand-bank. And the sand-bank shall be stream . . ."; Erman, *Literatur*, 154, "sein Weg ist zum Ufer geworden und das Ufer wird zum Wasser . . ."; Lefèbvre, *Romans et contes*, 100, "Le lit (où elle coulait) étant devenue la rive; la rive (à son tour se transformera) en eau, et l'eau fera place (de nouveau) à la rive"; Wilson, *op. cit.*, 445, "Its course is [become] a sandbank. The sandbank is against the flood; the place of water is against the [flood]--(both) the place of water and the sandbank"; Helck, *op. cit.*, 26, "Denn sein Weg ist eine Sandbank geworden und die Sandbank zur Flut; Wässriges (wurde) zu Sandigem"; Barta, *loc. cit.*, 38, "Sein (des Flusses) Lauf ist zum Uferland geworden; denn das Uferland wird zu dem werden, was im Wasser ist, nämlich zum Flussbett (wörtl. zum Ort des Wassers), und das, was im Wasser ist, nämlich das Flussbett, wird zum Uferland werden"; Faulkner, *op. cit.*, 236, "For their course has become the riverbank, and the bank (serves) for water; the place of water 'has become' a riverbank"; M. Lichtheim, *op. cit.*, 141, "Its course having turned into shoreland. Shoreland will turn into water, watercourse back into shoreland"; cf. also Posener, *Littérature et politique*, 41, "Le lit se transformera en rive, et la rive sera recouverte l'eau."

139 Cf. Volten, *Zwei altägyptische politische Schriften, Analecta Aegyptiaca*

IV, 69; the passage is rendered by Faulkner, *loc. cit.*, 191, "the mud flat is replaced with water" and by M. Lichtheim, *op. cit.*, 106, "As watercourse is replaced by watercourse," neither one tenable.

140 It seems probable that  is etymologically to be understood as *nit-mw*, i.e., derived from *ni* with *mw* as its object, "that which repels water."

141 JEA 1, 1914, 105, "The sky shall not have one wind alone"; Lefèbvre, *op. cit.*, 100, "Le ciel n'appartiendra plus à un vent unique"; Wilson, *loc. cit.*, 445, "The skies are no (longer) in a single wind"; Helck, *op. cit.*, 26, "Und der Himmel wird nicht ein einziger Wind sein"; Faulkner, *loc. cit.*, 237, "And the sky will not be with one single wind"; M. Lichtheim, *op. cit.*, 141, "Sky will lack the single wind." The only exception is Erman, *op. cit.*, 154, "Und der Himmel hat nur noch einen Wind."

142 See Satzinger, *op. cit.*, §53; cf. also Gunn, *Studies in Egyptian Syntax*, 146 and 153, especially nos. 110 and 111. *Nn pt m ṯ3w wᶜ* could be rendered "there was never a sky with only one wind," which would also be meaningful as part of the allegorical concern of the passage discussed below.

143 Cf. Baedeker, *Egypt and the Sudan*, 8th ed., 1929, LXXXI.

144 The movement of the migratory birds as reflected in ancient Egyptian records is discussed by Edel, *Zu den Inschriften auf den Jahreszeitenreliefs der "Weltkammer" aus dem Sonnenheiligtum des Niuserreᶜ*, II. Teil, NGAW 1963, 4, 105ff.; see also Goedicke, *The Report of Wenamun*, 119f.

145 Gardiner, *Egyptian Grammar*[3] §178.

146 Gardiner, JEA 1, 1914, 103, "the people have caused it to approach through want of it"; Erman, *op. cit.*, 154, "und lasst sie in seiner Not an sich herankommen"; Lefèbvre, *op. cit.*, 100, "les hommes le laisseront s'approcher, dans (leur) détresse"; Wilson, *loc. cit.*, 445, "and people have let it approach through want of it"; S. Herrmann, *op. cit.*, 43, note 1, "und man lasst ihn in seiner Not sich nähern"; Helck, *op. cit.*, 26, "und sogar die Menschen aus Not heranlässt"; Faulkner, *loc. cit.*, 237, "for men have caused it to approach through want"; Barta, *loc. cit.*, 38, "und er lässt die Menschen herankommen aus Not"; M. Lichtheim, *op. cit.*, 141, "the people having let it approach by default."

147 Kuban-Stela 1. 11; also ASAE 38, 1939, 223, 1. 16.

148 So in particular by Wilson and S. Herrmann.

149 He was followed by Wilson, S. Herrmann, and M. Lichtheim, while Faulkner interprets the "foreign bird" as an ill omen.

150 Pap. Anastasi VI 51ff.; cf. Caminos, *Late-Egyptian Miscellanies*, 293ff.

151 Cf. v. Beckerath, *Tanis und Theben*, Äg. Forsch. 16, 13f.

152 Gardiner, *Egyptian Grammar*[3] §253; Helck, *op. cit.*, 30; Barta, *loc. cit.*, 39. This interpretation is apparently influenced by Peasant B 1,197, *ḥd bw-nfr* "goodness ceased."

153 Posener, *Catalogue des ostraca hiératiques littéraires de Deir el Medineh*, Doc. de fouilles I, I, pl. 41.

154 Gardiner, JEA 1, 1914, 103, "Perished are those good things (of yore)"; Erman, *op. cit.*, 154, "Auch jene guten Dinge sind verdebt"; Lefèbvre, *Romans et contes*, 100, "Assurément ces bonnes choses (d'autrefois) ont péri"; Wilson, *loc. cit.*, 445, "Damaged indeed are those good things"; S. Herrmann, *op. cit.*, 39, "Es fehlt auch an jenen guten Dingen"; Helck, *op. cit.*, 30, "Doch vergangen sind jene glücklichen Zeiten der Fischteiche"; Barta, *loc. cit.*, 38, "jene guten Dinge aber werden zerstört sein"; Faulkner, *loc.cit.*, 237, "Perished are those erstwhile good things"; M. Lichtheim, *op. cit.*, 141, "Then perish those delightful things."

155 Lefèbvre, *Grammaire*[2] §97; Westendorf, *Grammatik der medizinischen Texte* p. 58. See also Suicidal 37; cf. Goedicke, *The Report about the Dispute of a Man with His* Ba, 114.

156 Gardiner, *Admonitions of an Egyptian Sage*, 44, renders "Forsooth, that has perished, which yesterday was seen (?)." Similarly, Erman, *op. cit.*, 138, "Es ist doch so: jenes ist zugrunde gegangen, was gestern noch gesehen wurde"; Faulkner, JEA 51, 1965, 56, "Indeed, that has perished which yesterday was seen"; M. Lichtheim, *op. cit.*, 154, "Lo, gone is what yesterday was seen."

157 So Sethe, *Erläuterungen zu den Lesestücken für den akademischen Gebrauch*, followed by Barns, *The Ashmolean Ostracon* p. 24. *N ḏd.f ḥꜥw.ỉ* is *n* + *sḏm.f*; cf. Gardiner, *Egyptian Grammar*[3] §455.

158 Notes on the Story of Sinuhe 87.

159 Also BD 125,10.

160 Gardiner, JEA 1, 1914, 103, "the ponds of those (?) who slit fish, teeming with fish and fowl"; Erman, *op. cit.*, 154, "die Fischseen (?) wo die Schlachtungen waren und die von Fischen und Vögeln leucheten"; Wilson, *loc. cit.*, 445, "those fish-ponds, (where there were) those who clean fish, overflowing with fish and fowl"; Lefèbvre, *op. cit.*, 100, "ces étangs poissoneux qui étaient le théâtre de massacres et qui resplendissaient des poissons et riseaux qu'ils portaient"; S. Herrmann, *op. cit.*, 39, "Fischseen, wo die Schlachtungen waren, die da leuchteten von Fischen and Vogeln"; Helck, *op. cit.*, 30, "jene glücklichen Zeiten der Fischteiche, die für das Fischaufschlitzen bestimmt sind, übervoll an Fischen und Vogeln"; Barta, *loc. cit.*, 39, "nämlich die fischreichen Gewässer der Schlächter (wörtl.: der unter Schlachtungen Seienden, d.h. deren, die die Fische schlachten), die (gemeint sind die Gewässer) glänzen von Fischen und Vögeln"; Faulkner, *loc. cit.*, 237, "⌜the fish ponds⌝ of those who carry slit fish, teeming with fish and fowl"; M. Lichtheim, *op. cit.*, 141, "the fishponds full of fish-eaters, teeming with fish and fowl."

161 For *n3* in Old Egyptian, see Edel, *Altägyptische Grammatik* §201; see also James, *The Ḥeḳanakhte Papers*, 107.

162 Also Faulkner, *Concise Dictionary*, 277.

163 Cf. also Urk.I 126,1, where *kꜥḥt* is used for the "corner" of heaven, i.e., the very distant.

164 The  is a misreading by Golenischeff, the hieratic sign being , i.e., , which conforms with the spelling in O Petrie 38,4.

165 Already Gardiner, JEA 1, 1914, 103, note 16; also Helck, *op. cit.*, 30 and Barta, *loc. cit.*, 39, "die beim Schlachten Seienden." Lefèbvre, *Romans et contes* 100, note 27, renders it literally "qui étaient sous les massacres," while M. Lichtheim sees in it "fish-eating birds," referring to Peasant R 29, where the word is better understood as "gutted birds."

166 Wb.I 294f.; Breasted, *The Surgical Papyrus Edwin Smith*, 523; v. Deines and Westendorf, *Wörterbuch der Medizinischen Texte*, 172ff.

167 Wb.I 387,23; Gardiner, *Egyptian Grammar*^{3} §166.

168 *Wbn* "to shine" of objects, see Wb.I 293 C; Peasant B 1,294; for *ḥr* introducing the cause of shining, see Wb.III 387,22.

169 Cf. L. Klebs, *Die Reliefs des alten Reiches*, 78f.

170 Cf. Goedicke, CdE 45, 1970, 247.

171 Gardiner, JEA 1, 1914, 103f., "The earth is fallen into misery for the sake of yon food of the Beduins"; Erman, *op. cit.*, 154, "Das Land wird hingestreckt aus Elend durch jene Speise der Beduinen"; Lefèbvre, *op. cit.*, 100, "Le pays est prostré dans la misère, à cause de cette nourriture des Bédouines"; Wilson, *loc. cit.*, 445, "The land is prostrate because of woes from that food, the Asiatics," who are considered "a bitter diet for the Egyptians"; Helck, *op. cit.*, 30, "die Welt (ist) in Elend durch jene Versorgung der Asiaten"; Barta, *op. cit.*, 39, "Alles Gute ist gewichen, indem es zu Boden geworfen worden ist im Land wegen des Unglücks durch jene Speise der Beduinen"; Faulkner, in *The Literature of Ancient Egypt*, 237, "The land being cast away through trouble by means of that food of the Asiatics"; M. Lichtheim, *op. cit.*, 142, "The land is bowed down in distress, owing to those feeders, Asiatics who roam the land."

172 Proposed first by Gardiner, *ibid.*, note 17, and Helck; Barta retained the extant reading.

173 O Petrie 38,4 is different and should be restored *ptḫ t3 nty m ḳsnt m-ꜥ nf3* . . . "the land, which is in misery by those aiming for food . . . is collapsing." In this formulation *ptḫ* is a *sḏm.f*, whose subject is qualified by a relative expression.

174 For the two ways to render the compound preposition, cf. Gardiner, *Egyptian Grammar*^{3} §178; they are basically identical, one meaning literally "in the hand of," the other "by the hand of."

175 M. Lichtheim, *op. cit.*, 144, renders "feeders" and cites Wb.V 571,8-10 in support; *ḏf3y*, the term quoted, denotes "someone fed" (Hatnub Gr. 23,9), i.e., a nominally used passive participle.

176
Sinuhe B 1,245 also refers to bedouin and not to Asiatics, which also applies to Admonitions 14,11, as well as Hammamat no. 17.

177
Some Notes on the Easternmost Nomes of the Delta in the Old and Middle Kingdom, JNES 18, 1959, 129ff., especially 135ff.; *idem*, *Dendera in the Third Millenium B.C.*, 5.

178
Kleines Wörterbuch der Ägyptologie, 112; Helck, *Die altägyptischen Gaue*, 187ff.; cf. also Sethe, NGAW 1922, 234f.; Kees, *Das alte Ägypten* 105; *idem*, ZÄS 81, 1956, 39.

179
The events under Pepi I in which Weni participated are another indication of the political situation along the eastern fringes of the Delta in the Old Kingdom; see Goedicke, *The Alleged Military Campaign in Southern Palestine in the Reign of Pepi I*, Revista Studi Orientali 38, 1963, 187ff.

180
See Fischer, JNES 18, 1959, 137ff., fig. 3. In the scene on an altar of Amenemhet I (MMA 09.180.526 = Hayes, Scepter of Egypt I 175, fig. 105) *ʾI3btt*, different from and (*km-wr*), is not indicated as a "nome," because there is no "nome-sign" ( ) in this case!

181
ʾI3btt does not appear in the geographical list of Sesostris I. *Ḫntt ʾI3btt* denotes the area of Tanis and thus is not identical with *ʾI3btt*; cf. Lauer, *Une chapelle de Sesostris Ier*, 235f.; A. Schlott, *Die Ausmasse nach altägyptischen Texten*, Tf. VII, 105ff.

182
It seems feasible that *ʿ3m* is originally a designation of the Sinai Peninsula and that the term was later reapplied, possibly due to geographical changes there.

183
O Petrie has instead *ng3.tw ḫnrt ky-r-gs.f*, which is virtually identical.

184
Gardiner, JEA 1, 1914, 104 ". . . is in want, though (?) another is beside him; no protector hears"; Lefèbvre, *op. cit.*, 101, "Le palais (?) sera dans la détresse; <personne> ne (le) secourra; aucun protecteur n'entendra (?)"; Posener, *Littérature et politique*, 151, "[la fortresse] sera trop étroite, et lorsqu'un nouveau réfugié (litt. "un autre") sera à côté, les défenseurs n'écouteront pas (ses appels)"; Helck, *op. cit.*, 30, "Man zerbricht die Grenzsperre, auch wenn eine andere daneben liegt, da die Wache nicht(s) hören kann"; Barta, *loc. cit.*, 39, "und die Grenzfestung wird bedrängt werden, indem einer neben dem anderen angreift (wörtl. indem ein Anderer an seiner Seite ist), ohne dass ein Helfer hört"; Faulkner, *loc. cit.*, 237, "for a fortress lack another beside it, and no guard will hear." Erman, Wilson, and M. Lichtheim leave the section untranslated.

185
The existence of fortification is reflected in the inscription of *Nswt-nfr*, Junker, Gîza III 172ff. and *K3-ʿpr*, Fischer, JNES 18, 1959, 233ff.

186
Cf. Scharff, *Der historische Abschnitt der Lehre für König Merikarê*, SAW München 1936,8, 32; also Ward, *Egypt and the East Mediterranean*, World 34.

187
Kommentar zu den Klagen des Bauern, Unters. VI, 62.

188 Similarly, Lefèbvre, *op. cit.*, 50., "Il s'agit probablement d'un de ses oasiens qui est venu vers un autre que lui"; M. Lichtheim, *op. cit.*, 171, "Surely it is a peasant of his who has gone to someone else beside him."

189 This does not apply to the inscription Berlin 8163; see Engelbach and Gunn, BIFAO 30, 1930, 809.

190 Also Siut III 3; Pap. Mill. 2,2; the term is probably related to the more common *mnfyt;* cf. Fakhry, ASAE 46, 1947, 26, pl. 5; Fischer, JNES 18, 1959, 269; Faulkner, JEA 39, 1963, 39; Gardiner, *Ancient Egyptian Onomastica* I, 112*; Schulman, *Military Rank, Title and Organization,* MÄS 6, 13f.

191 Erman, *op. cit.*, 155, guessed the meaning as "Nachts wird man überfallen (?) werden"; Lefèbvre, *op. cit.*, 101, finding no sense in the signs following *isk,* read "on s'attardera . . . pendant la nuit"; S. Herrmann, *op. cit.*, 42, offers as translation "man wird davor zurückschrecken, ein Gesicht anzusehen bei Nacht"; Posener, *op. cit.*, 151, gives "on fera attendre [l'homme avec (l'ouverture)] du portail"; Helck, *op. cit.*, 30, "man wird auf die (Sturmleiter in der Nacht warten"; Barta, *op. cit.*, 39, "man (d.h. der Gegner) wird die Sturmleiter in der Nacht noch warten lassen (d.h. micht angreifen)"; Faulkner, in *The Literature of Ancient Egypt,* 237, "men will hold back and look out by night"; M. Lichtheim leaves it untranslated.

192 Cf. the scenes showing the storming of a fortified place in Petrie, Deshasheh pl. IV; Quibell, *Teti Pyramid North Side,* frontispiece; W. St. Smith, *Interconnections in the Ancient Near East,* 148, fig. 185; Newberry, *Beni Hasan I,* pl. XLVIII; II, pls. V, XVI; Arnold and Settgast, MDIK 20, 1965, 50, fig. 2; cf. also Yadin, *The Art of Warfare in Biblical Lands,* 167; Schulman, *Siege Warfare in Pharaonic Egypt,* Natural History 73, 3, 1964, 12ff.

193 See Blackman, *Middle Egyptian Stories,* 8; Caminos, *Literary Fragments in the Hieratic Script,* pl. 24.

194 Cf. Gardiner, *Notes on the Story of Sinuhe,* 14f.; *idem, Admonitions of an Egyptian Sage,* 41. *ʾIkṣ* is possibly related to *kȝs* "rope-ladder," Wb.V 13,17.

195 Sethe, *Ägyptische Lesestücke,* 79,16. Pap. An. VI 83 might have the same meaning.

196 A feasible etymology of *ἰsk* is an extension of an original (Old Kingdom = vernacular) imperative of **skȝ* "to make high," namely the ladders for the assault. A comparable development of an original military command is *ἰsi ḥȝk* "go plunder!"; see Lorton, JARCE 11, 1974, 57ff.

197 See Goedicke, *Studies in the First Intermediate Period* (in press).

198 JEA 1, 1914, 104, note 1; his view is quoted Wb.IV 161,6; Faulkner, *Concise Dictionary,* 231. Barta, *loc. cit.*, 40, takes it as causative of *nbi* "to melt."

199 Gardiner, *ibid.*, "Sleep shall be banished (?) from my eyes"; Erman,

op. cit., 155, "Man wird den Schlaf aus meinen Augen scheuchen (?)"; Lefèbvre, *op. cit.*, 101, "On chassera le sommeil de mes yeux"; Wilson, *op. cit.*, 445, "Sleep will be banished from my eyes"; S. Herrmann, *op. cit.*, 42 and Helck, *op. cit.*, 30, "Man wird den Schlaf aus den Augen vertreiben"; Barta, *ibid.*, "Man wird den Schlaf aus meinen Augen vertreiben (wörtl. schmelzen machen)"; Faulkner, in *The Literature of Ancient Egypt*, 237, "And sleep will be banished from my eyes."

200 For this type of expression, cf. Gardiner, *Egyptian Grammar*[3] §194; Lefèbvre, *Grammaire*[2] §162; Edel, *Altägyptische Grammatik*, §§258ff.; Erman, *Ägyptische Grammatik*[4] §186.

201 The determination by  in O Petrie 38 suits this meaning extremely well, as in *ꜥḫ* in Sinuhe R 21.

202 Gardiner, JEA 1, 1914, 104, "(so that) I pass the night wakeful," deleting *ḥr*; Erman, *Literatur*, 156, "und ich liege da und sage: 'ich bin wach'" expecting an attack; Lefèbvre, *Romans et contes*, 101, "tandis que je demeurerai couché, disant: 'Je suis éveillé'" with *ḏd* emended after *ḥr*; Wilson, *loc. cit.*, 445, "as I spend the night wakeful"; Helck, *op. cit.*, 30, "Der Schläfer aber sagt 'Ich bin wach gewesen'" reading an unattested *sḏr.ti*; Barta, *loc. cit.*, 40, "indem ich die Nacht wachend (wörtl. bei einem 'ich bin wach') verbringe"; Faulkner, *loc. cit.*, 237, "so that I spend the night wakeful."

203 Golenischeff, *Les papyrus hiératiques*, pl. XXIV.

204 Cf. Gardiner, *Egyptian Grammar*[3] §464, who lists only *iw sḏm.n.f*; cf. also Lefèbvre, *Grammaire*[2] §323, but Edel, *Altägyptische Grammatik* §890, lists this form; the two examples quoted (Pyr. 959c and LD II 104) are probably to be taken differently. The sentence as it stands here could be rendered "may you go to rest because I have been watchful."

205 Cf. Goedicke, CdE 45, 1970, 246; cf. also *idem*, *The Report of Wenamun*, 129.

206 A similar stylistic arrangement occurs in Merikareꜥ P. 80, where the admonitions to the new king are concluded with *šms-ỉb.k m ỉrt.n.ỉ nn ẖry m ḳ3b t3š.k* "follow your conscience with what I have done and there will be no enemy within your border"; for the translation see Lorton, JARCE 7, 1968, 50f.

207 Wb.I 171,1; cf. also Spiegelberg, ZÄS 64, 1929, 89; Blackman, JEA 16, 1930, 66f.; Hintze, ZÄS 78, 1942, 55f. Additional occurrences are Berlin 7317,3; Urk.VII 55,19; CT I 154e; Horus and Seth XIV,12.

208 Spiegelberg, *Die sogenannte demotische Chronik* (Demotische Studien VII); cf. Malinine, BIFAO 34, 1934, 68f.

209 Gardiner, JEA 1, 1914, 104.

210 Barta, *loc. cit.*, 40, renders "sie werden sich kühlen an ihren Ufern," as is also the view of Wb.V 23,2.

211 Cf. Scharff, SAW München 1936,8, 17.

212 James, *The Ḥekanakhte Papers*, 21.

213 See in particular Barta, *ibid.*

214 Cf. Posener, *Catalogue des ostraca hiératiques littéraires* I, pl. 41.

215 Cf. Möller, *Hieratische Paläographie* I, L and LV.

216 The reading is based on O DeM 1074 and Cairo 25224, while Pap. Ermitage has no preposition. This is not necessarily faulty but could be taken as Old Perfectives.

217 See the discussion by Gardiner, *The Idiom ἰṯ ἰn*, JEA 24, 1938, 124f.; see also Vandier *La famine dans l'Egypte ancienne*, 71ff.

218 Gardiner, JEA 1, 1914, 104, "for this land shall be (?) in perturbation (?)"; *idem*, JEA 24, 1938, 125, "this land will waver"; Weman, *op. cit.*, 155, "dieses Land ist fortgenommen und zugefügt"; Lefèbvre, *op. cit.*, 101, "ce pays sera dans l'agitation"; Wilson, *loc. cit.*, 445, "this land is helter-skelter"; S. Herrmann, *op. cit.*, 44, "dieses Land ist in Verworrenheit"; Helck, *op. cit.*, 33, "dieses Land ist weggenommen und ist weggeholt"; Barta, *op. cit.*, 40, "dieses Land wird im Zustand der Verwirrung sein (wörtl. wird fortgenommen und hingebracht sein)"; Faulkner, *loc. cit.*, 237, "this land is in commotion"; M. Lichtheim, *op. cit.*, 141, "For this land is to-and-fro."

219 So Westendorf, *Der Gebrauch des Passivs*, 63, "nicht wird gekannt (= ist erfahren worden) das Ende, das eintreten wird." The passive construction was also recognized by Helck "indem das Resultat, das geschehen wird, nicht bekannt ist" and Barta "man kennt das Ereignis, das eintreten wird nicht," which follows Lefèbvre, *op. cit.*, 101, "le dénouement qui doit survenir ne sera pas connu." Gardiner, JEA 1, 1914, 104, has "none knows the issue that shall be"; similarly Erman, *op. cit.*, 155, "man weiss nicht, was der Ausgang sein wird"; S. Herrmann, *op. cit.*, 44, "Nicht weiss man, worauf es hinaus will (?)"; Faulkner, *op. cit.*, 237, "no one knows what the result may be"; and M. Lichtheim, *op. cit.*, 141, "knowing not what comes."

220 *Notes on the Story of Sinuhe*, 71. Wb.IV 474 C lists the meaning "sich ereignen" under *bs* "to flow forth," but the equation with the idiom "ein Ereignis tritt ein" would have led to a different attribution.

221 See Czermak, *Die Lokalvorstellung und ihre Bedeutung für den grammatischen Aufbau afrikanischer Sprachen*, *Festschrift Meinhof* 1927, 204ff.

222 Zandee, *De Hymen aan Amon van Papyrus Leiden* I, 350,72.

223 See above note 219. The exception is M. Lichtheim, *op. cit.*, 142, who renders "What-will-be being hidden according as one says."

224 I wonder whether the choice of *ἰmn* at this point is not an anticipation of the *ʾImny* mentioned in l. 58. Needless to say, this is not a material link, but rather an intonation of a theme.

225 Gardiner left the passage untranslated, while Erman, *op. cit.*, 155, suggested "der ist verborgen und man kann ihn nicht sagen, sehen und hören . . .", which was to some degree followed by Lefèbvre, *op. cit.*, 101, "restant caché pour (?) la parole, la vue, l'ouie"; Wilson, *loc. cit.*, 445, apparently takes *ỉmn* to qualify *bsw* and renders "which is hidden from speech, sight, or hearing"; S. Herrmann, *op. cit.*, 44, "Das, was geschehen wird, ist verborgen dem Sagen, Sehen oder Hören"; Helck, *op. cit.*, 33, translates "indem das Resultat, das geschehen wird, nicht bekannt ist, verborgen nach dem Sprichwort"; Faulkner, in *The Literature of Ancient Egypt*, 237, "for it is hidden from speech, sight and hearing"; M. Lichtheim, *op. cit.*, 142, "What-will-be being hidden according as one says."

226 O DeM 1074 has  as determinative, which is common with the interrogative *ptr;* for the latter, see Admonitions 3,7.

227 Cf. Lefèbvre, *Grammaire*^{2} §680; Westendorf, *Grammatik der Medizinischen Texte*, §430.1; cf. also Grapow, *Anreden* IV 32.

228 *H̱f*[*t*]-*ḥr* does not necessarily refer to a person, but can equally have any masculine word as antecedent. This makes it possible to connect it with *ỉd* "deafness."

229 Despite the placing of the verse-point in Cairo 25224, it might seem possible to consider *sḏm ḥr ỉdw* as a pseudoverbal clause "a hearer is being deaf."

230 JEA 1, 1914, 104, "I show thee the land upside down." He had discussed the expression in conjunction with Khaʿkheperreʿ-seneb rt. 11 in his *Admonitions of an Egyptian Sage*, 103.

231 Erman, *op. cit.*, 155, "Ich zeige dir das Land in Jammer und Leid"; Lefèbvre, *op. cit.*, 101, "Je te montre le pays sens dessus dessous"; Wilson, *loc. cit.*, 445, "I show thee the land topsy-turvy" explaining the literal meaning of *sny-mny* as "is passed-by-and-sick"; Helck, *op. cit.*, 33, "Ich zeige dir das Land durchseinander"; Faulkner, *loc. cit.*, 237, "I show you the land in calamity"; M. Lichtheim, *op. cit.*, 142, "I show you the land in turmoil."

232 This interpretation is followed by Barta, *loc. cit.*, 41, "Ich will dir das Land zeigen beim Durchmachen einer Krankheit," It also suits the other occurrences of *sny-mny*. For Khaʿkheperreʿ-seneb rt. 11, cf. Kadish, JEA 59, 1973, 78, "The land is in continuous distress"; Urk.IV 2027,11, "the land was passing through a sickness" is a reference to the Amarna period; LD III 256a,8, "the temples are passing through (a) malady"; cf. Caminos, *The Chronicle of Prince Osorkon*, Analecta Orientalia 37, 92f. See further Klasens, *A Magical Statue Base (Socle Behague)*, 96, who renders the expression as "to go through an illness."

233 Cairo 25224 seems to be the only complete version and superior to Pap. Ermitage 39 *tm ḫpr ḫpr*, although this can be rendered "the not-to-happen has happened," with *tm* as an infinitive; cf. Lefèbvre, *Grammaire*^{2} §403.

234 Although the passage is generally rendered correctly, its syntactical place is not fully realized in the translations; e.g., M. Lichtheim,

op. cit., 142, "I show you the land in turmoil, what should not be has come to pass."

235 Gardiner, JEA 1, 1914, 104, "the land lives in uproar"; Erman, *op. cit.*, 155, "dass das Land vom Aufruhr lebe"; Lefèbvre, *op. cit.*, 101, "et le pays vivra dans le désordre"; Wilson, *loc. cit.*, 445, "(so that) the land lives in confusion"; S. Herrmann, *op. cit.*, 42, who disregards the division into sections and renders "das Land lebt im Aufruhr"; Helck, *op. cit.*, 33, "indem das Land in Unruhe lebt"; Faulkner, *loc. cit.*, 237 and M. Lichtheim, *op. cit.*, 142, "and the land will live in confusion."

236 Faulkner, *Concise Dictionary*, 237, follows Gardiner's views.

237 For this rendering, cf. Goedicke, JARCE 11, 1975, 36ff.

238 A possibly better rendering might be "An attack is it! May you cause the land to retire and the lawbreakers to be called out."

239 Cf. Giveon, *Les bédouins Shosou des documents Egyptiens*, 47ff.

240 See Massart, *The Leiden Magical Papyrus I 343 + I 345*, 76, who retains Gardiner's rendering "the sky is in confusion." In rt. VII, 2, *ibid.* 74, he renders *hnn* with "roaring," although "investigate his (i.e., Seth's) attack" would be better.

241 ASAE 2, 1901, 219; cf. also Gauthier, *Dictionnaire géographique*, I 49.

242 See Sandman-Holmberg, *The God Ptah*, 214f.

243 See Spiegel, *Die Götter von Abydos*, 16f.

244 See Brunner, Die Lehre des Cheti, Äg. Unters. 13, 38; Helck, *Die Lehre des Dw3-Ḫtjj* II, 89; Piankoff, RdE 1, 1933, 63f.; Jequier, BIFAO 19, 1922, 210.

245 Petrie, *Tools and Weapons*, 34; Wolf, *Die Bewaffnung des altägyptischen Heeres*, 50. Posener, *Littérature et politique*, 43, note 7, poses the possibility that the use of metal for arrowheads was invented or first introduced in the Eastern Delta; see also Yadin, *The Art of Warfare in Biblical Lands* 167.

246 Although "copper" is the common meaning of *bi3* (cf. J. R. Harris, *Lexicographical Studies in Ancient Egyptian Materials* 50ff.), a more general meaning "metal" (cf. Graefe, *Untersuchungen zur Wortfamilie bj3*, 26ff.) suits here at least equally well.

247 Edel, *Untersuchungen zur Phraseologie der Inschriften des Alten Reichs*, §33; Polotsky, *Zu den Inschriften der 11. Dynastie*, 25f.; Janssen, *De traditioneele Egyptische Autobiografie* II, Bm 14ff.

248 Gardiner, JEA 1, 1914, 104, rendered "they crave for the bread of blood"; Erman, *op. cit.*, 155, "dass man mit Blut um Brot bettele"; Lefèbvre, *Romans et contes*, 101, "et on demandera du pain avec du sang"; Wilson, *loc. cit.*, 445, "beg for the bread of blood"; S. Herrmann, *op. cit.*, 42, "man bettelt ums Brot mit Blut"; Posener, *op. cit.*,

43, "on demande du pain dans le sang"; Helck, *op. cit.*, 36, "und Brot mit Blut fordern"; Faulkner, *loc. cit.*, 237, "men will beg for the bread of blood"; M. Lichtheim, *op. cit.*, 142, "will crave blood for bread."

249 Gardiner, *ibid.*, "Men laugh with the laughter of pain"; Erman, *ibid.*, "Man lacht mit einem krankhaften Lachen"; Lefèbvre, *ibid.*, "On rira d'un rire douloureux"; Wilson, *ibid.*, "and laugh with the laughter of sickness," considering it as "hysteria"; Posener, *op. cit.*, 151, "On rira d'un rire de douleur," questioning Wilson's interpretation; S. Herrmann, *op. cit.*, 41, "Man lacht mit dem Lachen des Schmerzes"; Helck, *ibid.*, "Man lacht über eine Krankheit"; Barta, *op. cit.*, 41, "Man lacht mit einem Lachen über die Krankheit"; Faulkner, *ibid.*, "men will laugh aloud at pain"; M. Lichtheim, *ibid.*, "Will laugh aloud at distress."

250 Shipwrecked Sailor 149; see Goedicke, *Die Geschichte des Schiffbrüchigen*, Äg. Abh. 30, 58f.

251 Wb.IV 90f.; especially for pains (90,11, as in Sinuhe B 139) and for mourning (90,12, as in Peasant B 1,30; furthermore Wb.IV 91,5; cf. Sethe, *Übersetzung und Kommentar zu den altägyptischen Pyramidentexten* III, 346).

252 Wb.II 96,1ff. lists the masculine *mr* only from the medical literature on, but it occurs in Peasant B 1,25 *n mr n ỉryt r.f* "for the affliction of what was done to him." The word is, of course, the infinitive of *mr* "to be painful"; cf. Gardiner/Sethe, *Letters to the Dead*, p. 19. See further Grapow, *Die Medizin der alten Ägypter* III, 22-24.

253 See Goedicke, *The Report about the Dispute of a Man with His* Ba, 137; Wb.II 417,8.

254 Pap. Kahun 30,19; CT II 211b.

255 So in particular Posener, *op. cit.*, 151, "on ne pleurera pas devant la mort"; he is followed by Barta, *loc. cit.*, 41, "man weint nicht (mehr) über den Tod"; Helck, *ibid.*, "und kann nicht über den Tod weinen."

256 Erman, *op. cit.*, 155, "man schläft nicht mehr hungrig wegen des Sterbens"; Lefèbvre, *op. cit.*, 101, "on ne se couchera plus, affamé à cause de la mort"; Wilson, *loc. cit.*, 445, "there is no one who spends the night fasting because of death"; Posener, *ibid.*, "on ne passera plus la nuit à jeûner en raison de la mort"; S. Herrmann, *op. cit.*, 41, "man liegt nicht hungrig wegen des Todes"; Helck, *op. cit.*, 36, "Nicht verbringt man die Nacht hungrig wegen des Todes"; Faulkner, *loc. cit.*, 237, "none will lie down hungry at death"; M. Lichtheim, *op. cit.*, 142, "none will wake fasting for death."

257 See Edel, *Untersuchungen zur Phraseologie*, §29.

258 Egoism is a problem of particular concern in the early Twelfth Dynasty; see Goedicke, *op. cit.*, 179f. It is, of course, also the theme of social concern reflected in the tomb inscriptions of the late Old Kingdom and continuing into the Middle Kingdom; cf. Junker, *Pyramiden-*

zeit, 55ff. Posener, *op. cit.*, 151f., renders the passage "l'esprit de l'homme étant absorbé par ses propres soucis" and sees in it a reference to "l'inobservence du jeûne et non une attitude égoïste."

259 Wb.IV 18,10; Faulkner, *Concise Dictionary*, 210, gives for it "lock of hair."

260 Gardiner and Černý, *Hieratic Ostraca* I, pl. LXXXIV.

261 Gardiner, JEA 1, 1914, 104, "No dishevelled (?) locks are made today"; Wilson, *ibid.*, "(Dishevelled) mourning is no (longer) carried out today"; S. Herrmann, *op. cit.*, 41, "Man veranstaltet nicht Trauer heute"; Helck, *op. cit.*, 36, "Nicht will man heutzutage die Trauerfrisur anlegen"; Barta, *op. cit.*, 41, "Trauer wird nicht (mehr) durchgeführt heute"; Faulkner, in *The Literature of Ancient Egypt*, 237, "None will dress hair today"; M. Lichtheim, *op. cit.*, 142, "Mourning is not done today."

262 Lefèbvre, *Romans et contes*, 101f., rendered "on ne fera plus de cérémonies de denil alors," followed by Posener, *op. cit.*, 152, "on n'observera plus la (coutume) *š3m.t* alors."

263 See Kitchen, *The Instruction by a Man for his Son*, Oriens Antiquus 8, 1969, 193; my discussion of the text in ZÄS 94, 1967, 62ff. floundered by an erroneous omission in the text.

264 Cf. Otto, *Die Verben Iae inf. und die ihnen verwandten im Ägyptischen*, ZÄS 79, 1954, 41-52.

265 Gardiner, *ibid.*, "A man sits in his corner careless (?) while one slayeth another"; Erman, *op. cit.*, 155, ". . . und einer mordet den anderen"; Lefèbvre, *op. cit.*, 102, "Un homme restera assis dans son coin, n'ayant de pensées que pour lui-même (?), pendant qu'un individu sera entrain d'entuer un autre," proposing an emendation *<ỉb.f m-ʿ>s3.f*; Wilson, *ibid.*, "A man sits *in his corner*, (turning) his back while one man kills another"; Posener, *op. cit.*, 152f., "Un homme se tiendra coi et courbera l'échine, pendant qu'un autre tuera quelqu'un"; Helck, *ibid.*, "In jeder sitzt da, indem er sich abwendet, wenn einer den andern totet"; Barta, *ibid.*, "Ein Mann sitzt da, indem er seinen Rücken wendet, wird einer den anderen töten"; Faulkner, *loc. cit.*, 238, "and a man sits quiet, turning his back, while one kills another"; M. Lichtheim, *ibid.*, "A man sits with his back turned, while one slays another."

266 The use of the *sḏm.f* form to state an ability is insufficiently recognized; cf., however, Shipwrecked Sailor 17f.; Admonitions 5,7.

267 Cf. Gardiner, *Egyptian Grammar*^{3} §163.11a; Lefèbvre, *Grammaire*^{2} §743; Westendorf, *Grammatik der Medizinschen Texte*, §218, 1b.

268 For *kʿḥ* as a verb, especially in reference to "bending the arms in an angle" as a gesture of greeting, cf. Wb.V 18f., also Müller-Feldman, MDIK 7, 1937, 93ff.

269 Wb.II 390,3; cf. in particular Urk.IV 389,15, although Gardiner, JEA 32, 1946, 54, restores *nṯr nb* instead of *r3 nb*. Otherwise, *r3 nb*

appears to be attested only late.

270 Erman, *op. cit.*, 155, voiced the possibility that the passage reflects the call of beggars for alms, in which Lefèbvre, *op. cit.*, 102, note 38, would be willing to follow him. Principal doubts were expressed by Helck, who did not offer an alternate interpretation. M. Lichtheim, *op. cit.*, 144, rejects *mr wi* as meaning "love me" and conjectures it an idiom like "I wish I had," for which there is neither grammatical nor lexicographical support.

271 The term seems to substitute for *tp-r3*, which has legal connotations; cf. Goedicke, *Königliche Dokumente aus dem Alten Reich*, 74.

272 Erichsen, *Demotisches Glossar*, 172.

273 See Urk.I 39,6; cf. also Sinuhe B 237. The formula disappears with the Middle Kingdom, so that O Gardiner 90,1 has the meaningless *mrwt*.

274 Cf. Goedicke, *The Report about the Dispute of a Man with His* Ba, 136.

275 So Barta, *ibid.*, who renders "man erlasst (zwar noch) Gesetze," which is imprecise, while M. Lichtheim, *ibid.*, gives an untenable "its fate (is) decreed."

276 Cf. Gardiner, *Egyptian Grammar*[3] §358; Lefèbvre, *Grammaire*[2] §434b.

277 Most translators divide the text differently: Gardiner, JEA 1, 1914, 104, "there is a paucity (?) of things done"; Lefèbvre, *Romans et contes*, 102, "il y a manque (?) d'objets fabriqués"; Wilson, *op. cit.*, 445, "the damaging of what had been done"; Helck, *op. cit.*, 41, "Verfall ist bereits im Geschaffenen"; Faulkner, *op. cit.*, 238, "Men wreak destruction on what has been made"; M. Lichtheim, *op. cit.*, 142, "deprived of produce," An exception is Barta, *op. cit.*, 42, "man erlässt (zwar noch) Gesetze, die (dann jedoch) verletzt werden durch das, was getan wird."

278 Most translators combine the two: Gardiner, *ibid.*, "men are bereft of what was found"; Lefèbvre, *ibid.*, "on est privé de ce qu'on trouvait (autrefois)"; Helck, *ibid.*, "Zerstörung im Gefundenen"; Faulkner, *ibid.*, "make a desolation of what has been found"; M. Lichtheim, *ibid.*, "lacking in crops." The exception again is Barta, *ibid.*, "man geht leer aus bei dem, was gefunden wird (d.h. man findet nichts)," without realizing its juridical content.

279 Pap. Kahun 13,23,28.

280 Wb.I 368; cf. also Helck, *Altägyptische Aktenkunde*, MÄS 31, 62; Goedicke, *The Report about the Dispute of a Man with His* Ba, 127.

281 *Beni Hasan I* 26, 126; JEA 39, 1953, 20.

282 Wb.V 168 C II.

283 He renders it "und Schöpfung in dem, was nicht geschaffen werden sollte," which lacks satisfactory meaning. The same applies to M. Lichtheim, *op cit.*, 142, "What was made has been unmade."

[284] Cf. Gardiner, *op. cit.*, 104, "things are as though they had never been made"; similarly Lefèbvre, *op. cit.*, 102, "Ce qui a été fait est comme ce qui n'a (jamais) été fait" and Barta, *ibid.*, "das, was getan wird, ist wie das, was nicht getan wird," although with an untenable prospective meaning.

[285] Helck, *op. cit.*, 38, wrongly places *tw* after *irw*.

[286] Cf. Goedicke, *Königliche Dokumente aus dem Alten Reich*, 201.

[287] Cf. Gardiner, *Egyptian Grammar*[3] §92.2, who lists *ḫt* "property" only as feminine. Siut I 288, 301, 321 are clearly masculine; cf. also Schenkel, *Frühmittelägyptische Studien*, §25.

[288] The reason for the unusual position of the particle is the necessary separation of it from *z* as part of the compound, because *rdw* defines *ḫt*.

[289] See Goedicke, *Papyrus Berlin 9010*, ZÄS 101, 1974, 90ff.

[290] See Goedicke, *The Berlin Leather Roll* (P. Berlin 3029), *Festschrift zum 150jährigen Bestehen des Berliner Ägyptischen Museums*, 87ff.

[291] Gardiner, JEA 1, 1914, 104, "Men take a man's possessions from him; they are given to him who is a stranger"; Erman, *op. cit.*, 155, "Man raubt die Habe eines (angesehenen) Mannes und gibt sie einem von draussen"; Lefèbvre, *op. cit.*, 102, "On prend à un homme ses biens, qui sont donnés à celui qui est étranger"; Wilson, *op. cit.*, 445, "Men take a man's property away from him, and it is given to him who is from outside"; Posener, *op. cit.*, 43, "on enlève les biens de l'un et on les donne à un autre qui vient du dehors"; Helck, *Die Prophezeiung des Nfr.tj*, 41, "Der Besitz eines Menschen wird ihm geraubt und dem gegeben, der draussen ist"; Faulkner, *loc. cit.*, 238, "a man's possessions are taken from him and given to an outsider"; M. Lichtheim, *op. cit.*, 142, "One seizes a man's goods, gives them to an outsider."

[292] See Wb.II 400, 407, Ptahhotep 220; 227; Gardiner, JEA 37, 1951, 108.

[293] It is tempting to conjecture a phonetic pun with **n hpw* "without laws," although grammatically *nhpw* is, of course, a noun; cf. Sethe, *Übersetzung und Kommentar zu den altägyptischen Pyramidentexten* I, 85.

[294] Cf. Cairo 20498; also ZÄS 47, 1910, 163.

[295] Wb.II 283f. lists *nhp* with the following meanings: "to escape," "to jump," "to pulsate," "to copulate," "to rise early in the morning," "to mourn," "to care."

[296] The seemingly pleonastic term *pḏwt rwty* appears to denote people with whom Egyptians had no prior contact; for the passage, cf. Posener, *Littérature et politique*, 156f.; Fecht, *Der Vorwurf an Gott*, 26; Ward, *Egypt and the East Mediterranean World*, 37.

[297] Cf. Faulkner, *Concise Dictionary*, 27; concerning Suicidal 116, see Goedicke, *The Report about the Dispute of a Man with His* Ba, 166; cf. also CT I 9c; 13c.

298
The previous translations interpret the passage as concerning material enrichment, which leads to very little sense. Gardiner, JEA 1, 1914, 104, renders "He who never was one who filled for himself is one who is empty"; Lefèbvre, *Romans et contes*, 102, "Celui qui n'avait pas à remplir pour lui-même (see greniers) est (maintenant) dénué de resources"; Wilson, *op. cit.*, 445, "He who never filled for himself (now) empties"; Helck, *op. cit.*, 41, "Einer, der für sich nicht anfüllte, leert nun aus"; Barta, *op. cit.*, 42, "Der, der nichts getan hat, bereichert sich (wörtl. füllt sich), und der, der (etwas) getan hat, geht leer aus"; Faulkner, in *The Literature of Ancient Egypt*, 238, "He who did not fill for himself now goes empty"; M. Lichtheim, *op. cit.*, 142, "The lazy stuffs himself, the active is needy."

299
See Janssen *De traditioneele Egyptische Autobiografie vóór het Nieuwe Rijk II Bm 7-13;* I, 112.

300
Dunham, *op. cit.*, 86, renders *rdi ḫt n tp nfr* "who acts rightly," which disregards the basic meaning of *rdi*. For *n tp nfr*, cf. also Wb.V 286,7.

301
Cf. also Moᶜalla I β 2.

302
Posener, *op. cit.*, 153, established the reading of the previously incomplete sentence and rendered it "On donnera quelque chose par haine pour faire taire la bouche qui parle"; cf. also Helck, *op. cit.*, 41, "Man wird nur ungern etwas geben, um den Mund eines Redenden zum Schweigen zu bringen"; Barta, *op. cit.*, 42, "Man wird Bestachungen ausführen (wörtl. wird Dinge geben aus Widerwillen), um einen Mund, der reden will, schweigen zu machen"; Faulkner, *op. cit.*, 238, "Men give (something) unwillingly, so as to silence a talking mouth"; M. Lichtheim, *op. cit.*, 142, "One gives only with hatred, to silence the mouth that speaks."

303
Whereas this process is accepted in certain forms of tribal law, it is inacceptable in a legal system based on an absolute principle of law.

304
The previous translations take it differently. Gardiner, JEA 1, 1914, 104, "A word is answered, and an arm goes forth with a stick"; Erman, *op. cit.*, 156, "einen Spruch beantwortet man, indem die Hand mit dem Stock herausfährt"; Lefèbvre, *op. cit.*, 102, "on répond à une parole, un bras sortant armé d'un bâton"; Wilson, *op. cit.*, 445, "If a statement is answered, an arm goes out with a stick"; Posener, *op. cit.*, 42, paraphrases "devenus irascibles, ils répondent à la parole par des coups"; Helck, *op. cit.*, 41, "Man antwortet auf eine Anrede, indem der Arm mit dem Stock herausgeht"; Faulkner, *op. cit.*, 238, "A sentence is answered and a hand goes out with a stick"; M. Lichtheim, *op. cit.*, 142, "To answer a speech the arm thrusts a stick."

305
Cf. Shipwrecked Sailor 15; Peasant B 1,220.

306
Cf. Goedicke, *The Report about the Dispute of a Man with His* Ba, 88.

307
N sḏm.i ṯz ḥwr "Not did I hear the verdict: 'Criminal!,'" where *ḥwr* is a quotation of the verdict and not an adjective, as it is generally taken.

308 The formulation reminds one of the practice in Pap. Edwin Smith of formulating a verdict or an opinion about a case; see Breasted, *The Edwin Smith Sugrical Papyrus*, 45ff.; Grapow, *Die Medizin der alten Ägypter* III, 80.

309 Grapow, *Anreden* IV, 163, renders it "Frechheit."

310 For the use of *ẖr*, cf. also Fischer, MDIK 16, 1958, 137.

311 The parallel in P. 100 has *ẖt*, just as in our case, though reversed; cf. also Scharff, *Der historische Abschnitt der Lehre für König Merikarê*, SAW München 1936, 8, 35.

312 So already Gardiner, *loc. cit.*, "people speak, 'Slay him not!'"; similarly Lefèbvre, *loc. cit.*, "les gens [disent (?):] 'Ne le tue pas'" and Faulkner, *loc. cit.*, "[men say]: 'Do not kill him'"; an entirely different rendering was introduced by Wilson, *loc. cit.*, "and men speak with: 'kill him!'"; similarly, Helck, *loc. cit.*, "und man redet durch Mord" and M. Lichtheim, *loc. cit.*, "one speaks by killing him."

313 A possible reference to a death penalty in the Old Kingdom might be contained in Urk.I 305,18; cf. Goedicke, *Königliche Dokumente aus dem Alten Reich*, 221.

314 The text is preserved in O DeM 1261, which is not included in Helck's synoptic edition; cf. Posener, *Catalogue des Ostraca hiératiques littéraires de Deir el Médineh* II, 3, pl. 68.

315 *Littérature et politique*, 153; he renders "Une tirade est ressentie comme du feu." Other renderings are less explicit concerning the nuance of the wording. Gardiner, *loc. cit.*, translated, "The discourse of speech in (men's) heart is as a fire," followed by Wilson and Faulkner. Lefèbvre, *loc. cit.*, rendered "Un entretien est pour le coeur comme du feu" and Helck, *loc. cit.*, gives "Eine Rede (wirkt) auf das Herz wie Feuer."

316 The comparison with fire recurs in O Michaelides 16,1; see Goedicke and Wente, *Ostraka Michaelides*, pl. XXXVIII; and Kitchen, *Studies in Egyptian Wisdom Literature* II, Oriens Antiquus 9, 1970, 203ff.

317 Daressy, Ostraca p. 54, had transcribed  .

318 Cf. Kadish, *op. cit.*, 78.

319 See James, *The Ḥekanakhte Papers*, 38, 140. In Hekanakhte II 5, I would suggest reading *wḫd mi rnw* "which (scil. the size of the inundation) is suffered like names."

320 *Wḫd b3kt r ms.t.s* "who suffered a pregnant one until she gave birth." Cf. also Anthes, *Die Felseninschriften von Hatnub*, 51; in Hatnub Gr. 22,7,9, the object of *wḫd* is *ḥst* "favor," which establishes that *wḫd* cannot have the painful connotation of suffering as stressed in Wb.I 356,1ff., where the meaning in Neferyt 50 is defined as "eine unerwünschte Äusserung nicht ertragen können."

321 Cf. Gunn, *Studies in Egyptian Syntax*, 127ff.; Satzinger, *op. cit.*, §60;

Gardiner, *Egyptian Grammar*[3] §418 A; Lefèbvre, *Grammaire*[2] §283, Obs. 2.

322 Cf. Goedicke, *The Report about the Dispute of a Man with His* Ba, 125f.

323 Gardiner, *loc. cit.*, rendered, "No utterance of the mouth is tolerated," disregarding the final sign. Similarly, Erman, *op. cit.*, 156, "und man erträgt nicht, was ein Mund äussert"; Helck, *op. cit.*, 45, "und nicht will man einen Ausspruch dulden" and Faulkner, *op. cit.*, 238, "and none can endure utterance"; Lefèbvre, *Romans et contes*, 102, translated "on n'endure pas ce qui sort de la bouche (d'un autre)" reading *n wḫd.tw* instead of *nn wḫd.tw;* M. Lichtheim, *op. cit.*, 142, gave for it "one cannot endure the word of mouth."

324 Cf. Gardiner, *Egyptian Grammar*[3] §194; Lefèbvre, *Grammaire*[2] §599 bis.

325 Cf. also Admonitions 2,13 "People have diminished. The one who inters his brother (lit. gives his brother into the ground) is everywhere" and Siut IV 9 *sꜥḥ ꜥnḏ mityw* "a nobleman, rare of equals."

326 Gardiner, JEA 1, 1914, 104, "The land is diminished, its rulers are multiplied"; Wilson, *loc. cit.*, 445, "The land is diminished, (but) its administrators are many"; Lefèbvre, *Romans et contes*, 102, "Le pays est appauvri, mais ses dirigeants sont nombreux"; Posener, *op. cit.*, 154, "Le pays est diminué et ses dirigeants sont nombreux"; Helck, *op. cit.*, 45, "Gering ist das Land, aber die Regierenden viel"; Faulkner, *op. cit.*, 238, "The land is diminished, though its controllers are many"; M. Lichtheim, *op. cit.*, 142, "The land is shrunk--its rulers are many".

327 Cf. also Urk.IV 973,3.

328 Cf. Erman, *Zur ägyptischen Wortforschung* II, SAW Berlin 1912, 913.

329 Posener, who was the first to utilize O Gardiner 331, rendered "il est dénudé." Barta, *op. cit.*, 42, reads *wš.tw.f* "Es (das Land) wird zerstört," which is not supported by the text, nor is Helck's rendering, *loc. cit.*, "Es ist verwüstet" or M. Lichtheim's "It is bare."

330 Cairo 25224 has *b3kw* (); the term denotes, not imposts, but "trade goods"; see Lorton, *The Juridical Terminology of International Relations in Egyptian Texts*, 104f. Posener, *loc. cit.*, accepts Cairo 25224 as superior and renders "les impôts qui le frappent sont grands" as Barta, "gross sind seine Abgaben" and M. Lichtheim, "its taxes are great."

331 In one case *ꜥ3* is used parallel to *špsi*, in the other to *wsr;* cf. Blackman, JEA 17, 1931, 57.

332 O DeM 1261 has *tw r ḫ3y.sn m wbn.*

333 Gardiner, *loc. cit.*, took it conditionally "(If) he shines, it is (but) an hour (?)," followed by Wilson. Erman, *op. cit.*, 156, translated "Sie geht auf, wenn es die Stunde ist (?)," followed by Lefèbvre; similarly S. Herrmann, *op. cit.*, 41, "Er geht auf zu seiner Zeit" and M. Lichtheim, *op. cit.*, 142, "Though he will rise at his hour." A somewhat different view was taken by Blackman, JEA 10, 1924, 198, trans-

lating "He rises, and the hour passes," which is to some degree the basis for Posener's discussion (*op. cit.*, 154f.). He reads *wbn.f wn wnwt* and renders it "Quand il se lève, il existe l'heure," interpreting it as "on a l'heure." His view was accepted by Barta, *op. cit.*, 43, "(Aber nur wenn) er erscheint, existiert die Stunde (d.h. kann man die Zeit messen)" and Helck, *op. cit.*, 45, "Geht er auf und wäre (dadurch) die Stundenrechnung möglich."

334 O DeM 1261 has *n[n] b3g.tw.f*, which appears to reflect an auditory error.

335 Similarly also Lefèbvre, *op. cit.*, 156, "La visage ne sera pas ébloui"; Helck, *op. cit.*, 45, "nicht kann das Gesicht geblendet werden"; Faulkner, in *The Literature of Ancient Egypt*, 143, "No face will be dazzled by seeing [him]"; M. Lichtheim, *loc. cit.*, "no one is dazzled when [he] is seen." A different approach was taken by Erman, *op. cit.*, 156, "kein Gesicht wird mehr hell" and Wilson, *loc. cit.*, "There is no one bright of face when seeing [him]."

336 Cf. Assmann, *Liturgische Lieder an den Sonnengott*, MÄS 19, 172f.; cf. also Pyr. 245a et al.

337 O DeM 1261 has an erroneous *ỉb.tw mw n.f m ỉrty*.

338 *Op. cit.*, 45, "wie der Mond, dessen Nachtzeit doch nicht überschritten werden kann. Sind doch seine Strahlen im Gesicht, wie es seine Art war unter den Vorfahren."

339 *Op. cit.*, 143, "his nightly course unchanged, his rays on the face as before," taking it to describe "a limited punitive action" by the sun-god, "without . . . altering his regular course."

340 O DeM 1261 is too fragmentary to be of any help in establishing the original wording.

341 Posener, *Catalogue des ostraka hiératiques littéraires* II, pl. 68.

342 Cf. below l. 67; Khaᶜkheperreᶜ-seneb vs. 3; Shipwrecked Sailor 139; Sinuhe B 33; Suicidal 84; cf. also Goedicke, *Die Geschichte des Schiffbrüchigen*, 56, where the particular nuance of "experience inherent in the word is pointed out.

343 Similarly Faulkner, *Concise Dictionary*, 300, with his rendering "transgressor."

344 Cf. Suicidal 35; Admonitions 9,2-3; 12,1; Ptahhotep 202.

345 This meaning is not listed before the Eighteenth Dynasty in Wb.II 220, 16ff., but see CT II 973 "you have returned those belonging to heaven and earth."

346 Cf. Goedicke, *The Report about the Dispute of a Man with His* Ba, 139ff.

347 The variant *nn thw nw.f ib šs3w* in Cairo 25224 has a similar message as "there is not one who misses his time when the heart is experienced."

348
Lefèbvre, *Sur l'âge du grand prêtre d'Amon, Bakenkhonsou,* REA 1, 1927, 138ff.

350
Cf. Polotsky, JEA 16, 1930, 199; Siut V 29; Sinuhe B 218; cf. also E. Blumenthal, *Untersuchungen zum ägyptischen Königtum des Mittleren Reiches,* AAW Leipzig 61,1, 218.

351
Vandier, Moꜥalla 208, renders *ỉr ḥḳ3 nb . . . ỉr.ty.fy* ꜥ *ḏw bin* "quant à tout nomarque . . . qui agira avec méchanceté et avec malveillance," but ꜥ clearly is the object of *ỉri*.

352
The former is *nn ḫst* ꜥ *(n) nb-ḏrt* "There is no warding off the action of the Lord-of-the-hand," and the other is *r ḫsf* ꜥ *n ḫpryt* "to ward off the action of the happenings."

353
Cf. Scharff, *Der historische Abschnitt der Lehre für König Merikare*ꜥ, 58.

354
See above p. 54f. Gardiner, *op. cit.,* 105, rendered "Men do the bidding of him who (once) did (other men's) bidding"; Wilson, *op. cit.,* 445, "Men salute (respectfully) him who (formerly) saluted"; Lefèbvre, *Romans et contes,* 103, "On saluera celui qui (autrefois vous) saluait"; Posener, *op. cit.,* 43, "On salue qui saluait"; Helck, *op. cit.,* 48, "Man grüsst den, der (eigentlich) grüssen sollte"; Faulkner, *op. cit.,* 239, "Men salute one who used to do the saluting"; M. Lichtheim, *loc. cit.,* "One salutes him who saluted."

355
It is, of course, possible to take the second infinitive as complementary and to render "One will consult a consulting," but such a translation does not capture the continuous futility so typical of endless administrative meetings.

356
Golenischeff's reading  is to be improved into  in the light of O Gardiner 331,8.

357
For unexplained reasons he transcribed *pẖrt* and *pẖr.tj,* although the first clearly has *pẖr.ti,* while the second has no ending.

358
For the formation, see Edel, *Altägyptische Grammatik* §§246f.

359
Pẖr combined with terms for parts of the body, such as *pẖr-ḥr, pẖr tp, pẖr ỉd,* has different meanings, derived from *pẖr* "to turn around."

360
Sinuhe B 162 could be cited in support of such a view, and also Admonitions 4,2, "great and small say 'I wish I were dead'." Suicidal 130ff. states a yearning for death, but the motifs are different; cf. Goedicke, *The Report about the Dispute of a Man with His* Ba, 172ff.

361
Cf. Goedicke, *Königliche Dokumente aus dem Alten Reich,* 217.

362
Cf. Varille, BIFAO 35, 1935, 157,5; Garnot, *L'Appel aux vivants,* 32.

363
Cf. also Sethe, *Übersetzung und Kommentar zu den altägyptischen Pyramidentexten* II, 151; IV 58.

364
Gardiner, *loc. cit.,* "The poor man will make (his) hoard"; Erman, *loc.*

cit., "Der Arme wird Schätze erwerben"; Wilson, *loc. cit.*, "The poor man will make wealth"; Lefèbvre, *loc. cit.*, "Le pauvre acquera de grands trésors"; Posener, *op. cit.*, 143, "Le pauvre fait fortune"; Helck, *loc. cit.*, "Arme werden sehr Schätze erwerben"; Faulkner, *loc. cit.*, "The poor man will achieve wealth"; Barta, *op. cit.*, 44, "Der Elende wird grossen Besitz erwerben"; M. Lichtheim, *loc. cit.*, "The beggar will gain riches."

Cairo 20542 a 19 *ỉr.n(.ỉ) n.s ꜥḥꜥ ꜥꜣ m špss nb* "I made for it a great heap/amount of all kind of treasures" could be quoted in support of a rendering "riches" as well as the idiom *nb- ꜥḥꜥw* in Suicidal 33; Admonitions 2,5,9; 7,12; 8,1; Siut I 247; cf. Goedicke, *The Report about the Dispute of a Man with His* Ba, 111. In Admonitions 2,4-5 it is not entirely clear whether *nb ꜥḥꜥw* should not be taken as "social standing" as in BM 574, because of the parallelism between *nb-ꜥḥꜥw* and *nb-špss*.

365
Cf. Gardiner, *Notes on the Story of Sinuhe*, 34; 157.

366
Cf. also Möller, *Hieratische Paläographie* I, 33 B.

367
Cf. also Urk.I 201,6; Khentika D 10,8; Sinuhe B 11.

368
Cf. in particular the discussion of the passage by Posener, *op. cit.*, 156, where he renders it "Ce sont les pauvres qui seront nourris."

369
For *ḳꜣꜣ* "height" as a descriptive term for the mundane abode see Goedicke, *op. cit.*, 125.

370
An interchange of *h* and *ḥ* is not attested, so the spelling is probably to be seen as an orthographic error in an unfamiliar word; the omission of the determinative points in the same direction.

371
M. Lichtheim, *loc. cit.*, similarly, Helck, *loc. cit.*, "Es gibt für die Welt kein Heliopolis mehr, den Geburtsort jedes Gottes" and Erman, *op. cit.*, 156, "Der Gau von Heliopolis wird nicht mehr ein Land sein (?), er, die Geburtsstätte jedes Gottes"; Wilson, *loc. cit.*, "The Heliopolitan nome, the birthplace of every god, will no (longer) be on earth."

372
Gardiner, *op. cit.*, 105, "The nome of Heliopolis will not be the land of birth (?) of any god," which would be worded as *nn ꜥnḏ-ḥḳꜣ m tꜣ*. Lefèbvre, *op. cit.*, 103, note 59, translates literally "Il est exclu (*nn wn*) que le nome Héliopolite doive être (*r*) le pays . . .," but *nn wn* expresses nonexistence. Faulkner, *loc. cit.*, "There will be no Heliopolitan nome to be the birth-land of every god" omits *tꜣ*. Some discussion is offered by Barta, *op. cit.*, 44, who considers the preposition *r* to have here the meaning "in bezug auf," "entsprechend," but renders "Der unversehrte Szeptergau wird nicht (mehr) existieren als Land der Geburtsstätte irgendeines Gottes (d.h. eines Königs)," which would, however, require a construction with the preposition *m*.

373
Cf. Goedicke, *Die Geschichte des Schiffbrüchigen*, 8.

374
Cf. Goedicke, Zu *ỉmy-rꜣ šmꜥ* und *tp-šmꜥ* im Alten Reich, MIO 4, 1956, 1ff.; Gardiner, *The Reading of the Geographical Term* 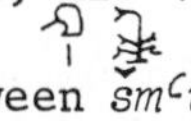, JEA 43, 1957, 6ff. It seems that there is a vacillation between *šmꜥw* and *rsy* reflecting preferences dictated by political circumstances.

375 Cf. in particular Posener, *op. cit.*, 51; Newberry, *Beni Hasan* I, tomb no. 2, which belongs to an *ʾImn-m-ḥ3t*, who also calls himself *ʾImny* and *ʾImny-m-ḥ3t*; see Urk.VII 19,6; 14,9; 19,9,15.

376 Posener, *op. cit.*, 47, note 3. It should be noted that Golenischeff's transcription 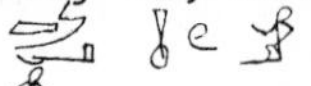, which is retained by Helck, should be corrected 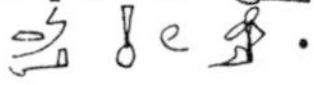.

377 In this connection the formulation *Ḥr-m3ᶜ-ḫrw* (e.g. Louvre [43]), as well as the epithet *ỉkr m3ᶜ-ḫrw* concerning royal followers, has to be taken into consideration; for the latter cf. Polotsky, *Zu den Inschriften der 11. Dynastie*, §81; Vandier, *Moᶜalla* 256; Fischer, *Dendera in the Third Millenium B.C.*, 131; Schenkel, *Frühmittelägyptische Studien*, 76.

378 A reflection of this tradition is found in a reference contained in a fragment of the Book of the Dead; cf. Griffith, PSBA 14, 1892, 41f. and Luft, *Das Verhältnis zur Tradition in der frühen Ramessidenzeit*, FuF 14, 1972, 59ff.

379 Cf. also Polotsky, *op. cit.*, §71; Schenkel, *op. cit.*, 75; Edel, *Die Felsengräber der Qubbet el Hawa bei Assuan* II, 1, 2, 72 quotes two instances from the late Old Kingdom. It appears that this form of indication is specifically Upper Egyptian.

380 See Vandier, Moᶜalla V β 1; cf. also Helck, *Die altägyptischen Gaue*, 69. *T3-Sti* is mentioned by King *W3ḥ-ᶜnḫ* Intef II (= TPPI §12).

381 Gardiner, JEA 1, 1914, 105; Erman, *op. cit.*, 157; Wilson, *op. cit.*, 445; Junker, JEA 7, 1921, 124, note 2; Stock, *Die Erste Zwischenzeit* 88. Objections were voiced by Lefèbvre, *op. cit.*, 104, note 61; Säve-Söderbergh, *Ägypten und Nubien*, 64; Posener, *op. cit.*, 47f.; Hayes, *The Middle Kingdom* (CAH), 34.

382 Cairo 25224 writes 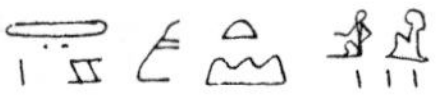 as if it referred to Nubia.

383 It would be tempting to conjecture a relation between Sarenput and the royal family.

384 Pap. Ermitage is partially destroyed as .

385 See also Gauthier, *Dictionnaire géographique* IV, 197f.; Sethe, *Urgeschichte und älteste Religion Ägyptens*, §199; Posener, *op. cit.*, 48.

386 For its dating to the Eleventh Dynasty cf. Fischer, JAOS 74, 1954, 32, note 53.

387 *Ḥ3 ḏd mdw n tp-rsy sḏm.f* [*ḏdt*]  "Wish that words could be said to the Head-of-the-South and that it would hear what 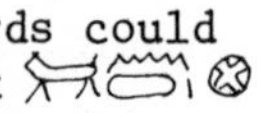 [says]." The restoration follows Schenkel, *Memphis--Hierakonpolis--Theben* 80, note n; Brunner, *Die Texte aus den Gräbern der Herakleopolitenzeit von Siut*, Äg. Forsch. 5, did not offer a translation.

388 The title *ỉmy-r sp3wt*  has a Saitic parallel 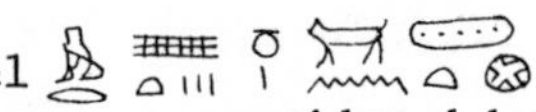 cited by Kees, ZÄS 70, 1934, 86. A further occurrence considered by Junker, ZÄS 75, 1939, 68, is rather problematic and is better omitted

from the discussion; but, cf. also Urk.III 6,8.

389 Peet, *Great Tomb Robberies* 9,2, quotes Pap. Abbott 5,17 and 6,9-11, 18 as New Kingdom instances of the term, but confuses them with *ẖnw-ḫni*, Wb.I 370,1, denoting a part of the Thebais; cf. Černý, *A Community of Workmen at Thebes* 96.

390 See also the nisbe *ẖnwyw* "people of the Residence," JEA 47, 1961, 6; Urk.I 78,5.

391 It is not certain whether the Heracleopolitan kings resided at Ehnas or whether they had another residence. The available material is not sufficient to answer this question.

392 Cf. E. Blumenthal, *Untersuchungen zum ägyptischen Königtum des Mittleren Reiches*, I, 47.

393 Wb.IV 539,13.

394 Wb.I 383,3,8; cf. Pyr. 295d.

395 For Sesostris I the idiom *ẖnm sḫmt(y)* is used; cf. Lacau and Chevrier, *Une chapelle de Sesostris Ier à Karnak*, 68; 263.

396 There is no reason to presume an erroneous determination [hieroglyphs], as repeatedly expressed.

397 For the construction, cf. Gardiner, *Egyptian Grammar*^{3} §303, concerning the use of the infinitive after *mr*.

398 Wb.I 120,11-12; cf. Grapow, *Anreden* I, 37; Hintze, *Untersuchungen zu Stil und Sprache neuägyptischer Erzählungen*, 179.

399 LD II 104; cf. Boreux, *Etudes de nautique égyptienne*, MIFAO 50, 458.

400 Cf. also Lutz, *Egyptian Tomb Steles and Offering Stones*, pl. 34,11. An alternative for the restoration is *ḥmw* "steering oar"; cf. Peasant B 1,90-1; Sinuhe B 13.

401 The older form of the word is possibly *nwd* as in Pyr. 2112a; cf. Goedicke, *Private Rechtsinschriften aus dem Alten Reich*, 115, 93.

402 Cf. Goedicke, *Die Geschichte des Schiffbrüchigen*, 43.

403 For *n h3w.f*, cf. Sinuhe B 150 *wʿr wʿrw n h3w.f* "a fugitive of his time fled."

404 As *nḏs* does not imply legal dependence or lack of freedom, the passage should be taken to reflect not social stratification, but a differentiation by age; i.e., not to distinguish the young man from the older, but to consider everyone for his merits; for *nḏs*, cf. Goedicke, *The Report about the Dispute of a Man with His* Ba, 131f.; *idem.*, *Die Geschichte des Schiffbrüchigen*, 35.

405 Similarly Pap. Chester Beatty VII, rt. 5,8 *s3 s rḫ rn.f* "the son of a man whose name is known."

406 Piankoff, *The Litany of Re*ᶜ, 3ff.

407 Gardiner, JEA 1, 1914, 105, "those who turn to mischief" was generally followed except for minor restylings; cf. also E. Blumenthal, *op. cit.*, 209.

408 Edel, *Altägyptische Grammatik*, §541, lists a future usage of the *sḏm.n.f*-form in Pyr. 1327ab, *nṯr nb šzp.ty.fy* ᶜ *ny M. pn ỉr pt* 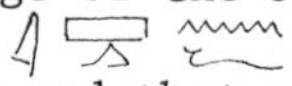 *ỉr Ḥwt-Ḥrw*. However, different from his interpretation and that of Sethe, *Übersetzung und Kommentar zu den altägyptischen Pyramidentexten* V, 235, 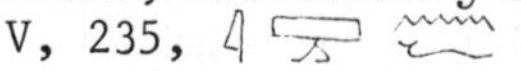 should be understood as *ỉ(w) šm.nf*, indicating a conditional clause and rendered "as for any god who takes the arm/writ of this M. to heaven, after he has come to the estate of Horus. . . ." The same applies to the cases cited by Westendorf, *Grammatik der Medizinischen Texte*, §244, as the specific uses of *rdi* in the so-called "divine promises" are actually conditional clauses and are relative past to the prospective context in which they occur. Brunner's explanation (ZÄS 85, 1960, 77) as "synchrones Praesens" misses the interaction of the syntactical process; see Goedicke, JNES 22, 1963, 189.

409 Cf. Vogelsang, *Kommentar zu den Klagen des Bauern*, 69ff.

410 For *nswt*, cf. also Fischer, *Inscriptions from the Coptite Nome*, 112ff., fig. 16(b) x + 7; Caminos, *Literary Fragments in the Hieratic Script*, 40ff.

411 Pap. Ermitage 64 has *nḏnḏ*, which makes no sense here; the superiority of *dndn* was first pointed out by Gardiner, *loc. cit.*, note 5. Only E. Blumenthal, *op. cit.*, 213, prefers *nḏnḏ* and translates "Die Rebellen fallen (*ḫr*) vor seiner Entschlusskraft (?)."

412 Gardiner, *loc. cit.*, "The Libyans shall fall before his flame, and the rebels before his wrath . . ."; Helck, *op. cit.*, 55, "die Libyer werden durch seine Flamme fallen, die Feinde durch seine Wut . . ."; similarly also Faulkner and M. Lichtheim. The genitival construction was observed by Lefèbvre, *op. cit.*, 104, "Les ennemis appartiendront à sa colère . . ." and Wilson, *op. cit.*, 446, "The rebels belong to his wrath . . .".

413 So Gardiner, *loc. cit.*, "to go down into Egypt, that they may beg for water"; similarly Wilson and Faulkner. The separation of the sentences is due to Lefèbvre; cf. also Posener, *op. cit.*, 157 and Helck, *op. cit.*, 58.

414 Pap. Ermitage has wrongly 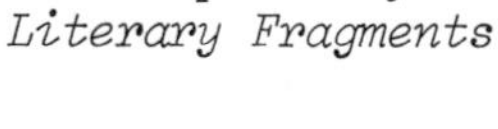, but the superiority of 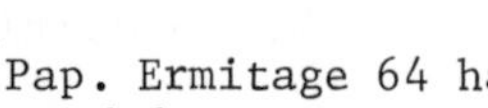 was pointed out by Posener, *ibid.*

415 Cf. Goedicke, *Die Geschichte des Schiffbrüchigen*, 46.

416 Griffith, *The Inscriptions of Sîut and Der Rifeh*, pl. XVI.

417 A philosophical interpretation of the designation prevails in the Suicidal; see Goedicke, *The Report about the Dispute of a Man with His* Ba, 131. This does not necessarily corroborate the view proposed by Brunner, *Die "Weisen," ihre "Lehren" und Prophezeiungen" in alt-*

ägyptischer Sicht, ZÄS 93, 1966, 29-35, who narrows the meaning of the term to "sage" and renders the passage under discussion (p. 32), "Ein Weiser wird mir Wasser sprengen, wenn er sieht, dass das, was ich gesagt habe, geschehen ist," while realizing that a *rḫ-iḫt* is principally "ein Mann, der etwas weiss."

418 Cf. Junker, Gîza XII, 93.

419 Gardiner and Sethe, *Letters to the Dead,* 19.

420 Pap. Millingen 1,9 states the converse *sṯi mw ẖry* (or *mẖr.i*) "those who were annointed with my myrrh are pouring lower (stable) water for me"; cf. E. Blumenthal, *op. cit.,* 248.

421 Cf. Goedicke, *Die Geschichte des Schiffbrüchigen,* 18.

TRANSLATION

I. The Royal council and the king's request

I[1] It happened, when the majesty of King Snofru, the blessed, was benevolent
king in this entire country;

On one [2] among those days it happened that the administrative council of the
Residence entered the Palace to discuss business [3] and that they went
forth, when they had discussed business as well as their daily
obligations.

And then his majesty said to a nobleman [4] on duty: 'Rush and bring me back
the administrative council of the Residence, which has left here
after discussing the business on this day!'

And they were promptly ushered in [5] at once.

And then they were prostrate before his majesty, l.p.h., again and then his
majesty, l.p.h., said to them:

[6] 'Fellows, see, I have summoned you that you seek for me
a son of yours who is an experienced one,
a brother of yours in excellence,
[7] a friend of yours whom good fortune favored,
(one) who can tell me some true words and choice [8] opinions,
which should extend the view of my majesty for hearing them!'

II. The courtiers' answer

And then they prostrated before his majesty again and II[9] then they said
vis-à-vis his majesty:

'There is a renowned lector-priest of Bastet, O Sovereign, our Lord,

Neferyt [10] is his name:
a citizen is he, valiant with his arm,
a writer is he, excellent with his fingers,
a wealthy one is he, who has greater wealth [11] than any peer of his.
May he be permitted to see his majesty!'

III. Introduction of Neferyt

Then said his majesty, l.p.h.: 'Hasten and bring him to me!'
And he was [12] introduced to him at once.
Then he was prostrate before his majesty, l.p.h.
Then said his majesty, l.p.h.: 'Come, now, Neferyt, [13] my friend! May you tell me some true words and choice opinions, which could extend the view of my majesty for [14] hearing them!'

IV. Neferyt's reply

Then said the lector-priest Neferyt: 'Something that happened or something that is bound to happen, O Sovereign, l.p.h., [my] lord?'

V. The king's charge

[15] Then said his majesty, l.p.h.: 'Something that is happening! It is (still) today and the passing of it already happens!'

VI. The king writes down Neferyt's pronouncements

And then he stretched out his hand to a case [16] of writing equipment and then he took for him a scroll and palette.
And then he was putting in writing what the lector-priest [17] Neferyt said:

VII. The king's transcript: Identification of Neferyt

A knowledgeable one of the East is he,
One belonging to Bastet is he when she appears,
A child of the Heliopolitan district is he

[III] He, indeed, [18] is concerned about what is happening in the land,
he, indeed, is bringing to mind the condition of the East,
that the Asiatics migrate forcefully,
[19] that they diminish the measures of what is on the harvest tax
and that they take the assignment on the plowing.

VIII. Neferyt's opening statement

[20] He says: 'May my heart stir that you bemoan this land!
Begin yourself with it, do not oppress it!
See, he who could speak for it [21] was expelled;
furthermore, the official was cast down.
Begin yourself there <with> the land!
[IV] Do not weary of what is in front of you,
[22] but stand up against that which is before you.
See, officials in the governance of the land are no longer;
what is to be done, is no longer done.
May a day begin with reorganizing, [23] as the land is entirely lost,
without that a remainder exists,
without that the black of a nail remains from its dues.'

IX. The misery of the East because of the drought

[V][24] 'While this land is destroyed, none cares about it.
No one speaks and no one sheds a tear:
"Wherewith shall this land exist?"
The sun is covered [25] and does never shine, so that people can see--
one can not live as long as clouds are always covering who is being red (i.e., the sun).
Every face is numb [26] for lack of it.
While I shall say what is before me,
I cannot foretell something that has not yet come.'

X. Effects of the drought on the East

[VI] 'The watercourses of the arable land are empty:
One can [27] cross the water on foot

and one will seek water for the ships to sail it.

Its course has become riparian land:

The riparian land [28] || will silt up the water-place until what is in the water-place will be riparian land.

The south wind will ward off the north wind, so that heaven consists of [29] || only one wind.

The migratory birds will breed in the marsh of the Delta, after they made a nest near [30] || people (i.e., Egyptians),

after the weakened people had let them come near!'

XI. The collapse of fishing and hunting

[VII] || 'Finished is the carrying off by those aiming for good fortune:

Those of the exotic lakes, they [31] || used to be in possession of gutting knives which shone from fish and fowl.

All success has gone away and is eliminated [32] || in the land of misfortune by those aiming for food

and the bedouin roaming the land.'

XII. Attacks by Asiatics

'And as strife [33] || will develop for the East and the Asiatics will descend to Egypt,

one will lack a fortification and assistance.

The garrison will not hear,

[34] || when one will scale the ladder by night,

when one will enter the fortification,

when one will surprise the drowsy one.'

[35] || "You can be at rest, because I am watchful!"

XIII. The East in foreign hands

[VIII] || 'The wild game (i.e., the desert dwellers) will drink water from the watercourses [36] | of the arable land, while they are pleased about their riparian land,

as those to chase away [37] | their coming are lacking.

When this land will be seized and recovered, is an event not known--

as what will be is hidden.
Do not say: [38] "Who can listen because of deafness, as the prospect is mute?"
I present to you the land in passing a sickness,
[39] as that which should not happen happened:
One will take up the weapons of warfare, and
the life of the land is in [40] rebellion.'

XIV. Prospects of War

IX,|| '(When) one will make arrows of copper,
one will request bread with [41] blood,
one will laugh at the outcry for pain,
one will not weep for a death,
one will not [42] spend a night hungry for a death.
(As) man's heart is concerned with himself,
one will not do the post mortem [43] presently,
(as) the mind has totally gone away from it:
A man can sit down, that he bends [44] his back,
while one is slaying another.
I can present to you a son as an enemy,
a brother as a foe, or
a man able [45] to slay his father.'

XV. Futility of administrative measures

X,|| 'Every pronouncement is completed with "As loves me!,"
but all success is gone away.
The land [46] perishes, as laws are decreed for it, which are annulled by crimes;
one will be scot-free in inquiries
as crimes are [47] something, which is as when it was never done.
One will take the very property of a man, which is given to a litigator.
I can show you a lord in worries, while an outcast is satisfied.
[48] The one who does not act will be paid for,
while the doer will be empty.

One will give things in a case of serious crime in order to silence sentencing,

(while) one rejects 49 | a sentence (about) an aggravated assault
and one says "don't kill him!"'

XVI. Demagoguery and its political effects

XI, || 'Slogans are for the mind (heart) like fire (and)
50 | not shall one endure a demagogue:
While the land diminishes,
its administrators are numerous.
While it dries up,
its servants are rich.
While the grain is little,
51 | the measure is great and
one measures it in overflow.'

XVII. Another drought

'Reʿ removed himself from men:
He shines and the daytime exists,
but one knows not that noon happened,
and one 52 | is not able to calculate his shadow.
The face is not clear when one looks,
nor do 53 | the eyes fill with water,
as he is in the sky like the moon.
(But) one who went astray, will return, when the heart is experienced,
and so 54 | his rays will be from the face (of the sun) again in the previous fashion.'

XVIII. Social upheaval for lack of leadership

XII, || 'I present to you the country in passing a sickness:
When a weakling is the master of action, one will 55 | consult and consult.
I present to you the lowly against the superior:
One who should be attentive has become self-concerned.
One lives from (the hope for the) Necropolis:

while [56] | a wretch will make a stela,
the great one will worship, in order to exist (beyond).
The beggars will eat [57] | offering cake,
while the servants abandon the heights.
The Heliopolitan district, the birthplace of every god, will no more be the burial ground.'

XIX. The need for a king to come to help

XIII, || 'It is such that a king [58] | of the South shall come, ʾImeny, the triumphant, with his name,
a son of a woman of the Elephantine district
[59] | a child is it of the Residence.
He shall assume the white crown,
he shall wear the red crown,
[60] | he shall unite the double crown.
He shall appease the Two Lords with what they desire,
(namely) to change the course by [61] | grasping the oar and by turning aside the tiller.'

XX. Outlook toward the future

XIV, || 'Rejoice! O people of his time! A freeborn man [62] | will be able to establish
his name for eternity and everlastingness!
Fall to disaster! O those contemplating treason [63] | (even) after they abandoned
their plans for fear of him
The Asiatics will fall to his terror,
and the [64] | Libyan will fall to his flame.'

XXI. Return to order

'Although the traitors belong to his wrath
and the discontented belong to [65] | his might,
XV || the Uraeus, which is on his brow, is pacifying for him the discontented.
[66] | One will (re)build the Fortification-of-the-Ruler, l.p.h.,
without allowing the Asiatics to descend [67] | to Egypt.

They shall request water in the manner of supplication
[68] in order to let their herds drink.
And order will come (back) to its place [69] and disorder will be cast away.
Rejoicing will be the one who observes [70] and he who will be serving the king.'

XXII. Neferyt will be acknowledged

'The educated one will pour [71] water for me, when he realizes that what I said, happened.'

Colophon.

It was completed by the scribe . . .

INDEX

INDEX OF EGYPTIAN WORDS

pr-šn^{c} "storehouse" 142, n. 21
pri "to attack, charge" 113, n. av
  pr-^{c} "outgoing of action" 121, n. az
pẖr "to turn, revolve" 132, n. bg
  pẖr m s3 "to serve attentively," lit. "to go behind" 122, n. ba
  pẖr-ẖt "self-concerned, selfish" 122, n. ba
ptr "who?" 97f., n. ah
ptḫ "to go to the ground, collapse, be cast down" 77, n. p; 90, n. aa
m, preposition
  partitive use 64, n. j
  m wḥm-^{c} "again" 61, n. h
  m b3ḥ "before," with retrospective connotation 77, n. q
  m grḥ "by night" 93, n. ad
m33 "to see; realize" 139, n. bn
m3^{c}*-ḫrw* "justified" indicating deceased king 11
  "triumphant," in reference to the living king 128, n. be
mi "come!" + enforcing particle *m* 63, n. i
mi, with additive meaning 55, n. c
min "at present, presently" 102, n. al
mw "water," in metaphorical sense of "loyalty" 85, n. y
mwnf "garrison" 93, n. ad
mwt "(a case of) death" 101, n. al
mny "malady" 98, n. ai
mr "affliction" 101, n. ak; 160, n. 252
mḥ "to complete" 105, n. ao
  "to pay in full" 108f., n. at
  mḥ ḥr "to be concerned about" 70, n. n
msi "to breed," of birds 84, n. y
  ms pw n "he is a child of," as legal specification of place of registration 69, n. m
msḫnt "bearing stool," as metaphor for the cemetery 125, n. bd
msḏḏ "capital crime" 109f., n. au
mk, particle 76, n. p
mtrt "noon" 116, n. ax
mdt nfrt "proper saying, true words" 59, n. g
n "for"
  expressing purpose 47, n. 118
  n g3w "for lack of" 80, n. t
n3 n "those of" 88, n. z
ny-sw, expressing professional or cult affiliation 69, n. m
nt-^{c}, lit. "what belongs to the books/activity," i.e., fixed "routine, duty" 55, n. c
nit-mw "that which repels water" 151, n. 140
nw "time" 117, n. ax
nwy "to return" 118, n. ay
nwd "to vacillate; play (the rudder)" 132, n. bg
nb "lord, master" 108, n. as
  nb-^{c} "master of action" 121, n. az
  nb-m3^{c}*t* "lord, master of law" 54, n. a

kꜥḥ s3 "to angle the back," used of relieving one's bowels 103, n. am
ḳbb "to be cool; idle" 96, n. af
ḳnbt nt Ḫnw "administration of the Residence" 54, n. b
ḳsnt "misery; famine" 90, n. aa
ḳdd-m-ỉrty "drowsy one" 94, n. ad
k3 sbỉ "to think of rebellion" 134, n. bi
ky-r-gs(.f) "assistant; assistance" 92, n. ac
kmt "arable land" 33; 47, n. 118; 82, n. v applied to the eastern Delta 10
ktt "little, trifling" 114, n. aw
gb3 "arm" 57f., n. a
gmḥ "to observe, perceive" 137, n. bm
gr "also" 76, n. p
t3 "bread; food" 101, n. ak
t3 "land," applied to the eastern Delta and Wadi Tumilat 10; 75, n. p
"arable land" 113, n. aw
T3-Stỉ "Elephantine District" 129, n. be
tw "one," absolute use 83, n. v
tp-rsy "head of the South," denoting the seven southernmost districts of Upper Egypt 128, n. be
tm-ỉrw "one who cannot act (any longer)," as victim of a crime 109, n. at
trỉ "to worship" 124, n. bb
th3 "to miss (time)" 117f., n. ay
thỉ "to disobey, go astray" 118, n. ay
ṯnw "number," in connection with time concepts 116, n. ax
ṯs "sandbank," metaphor for low water, famine, affliction 30
ṯs "legal sentence, verdict" 110, n. au
ṯsw stpw "selective of opinions/decisions" 59, n. g
dbḥ "to demand" 101, n. ak
dg "to look," without object 116, n. ax
ḏ3ỉ "to extend"
ḏ3ỉ ỉb r "to extend the heart to" 59, n. g
ḏ3ỉ m3ꜥ r "to pay heed to," lit. "to extend the temple to" 59, n. g
ḏ3ỉ ḥr "to influence, to form an opinion/outlook," lit. "to turn the face" 59, n. g
ḏ3t-ḥr, lit. "extending attention," with connotation of supervision 142, n. 35
ḏ3t "rest" 78, n. r
ḏꜥr "to seek and establish" 57, n. g
ḏwt "disaster," as the embodiment of all bad things 134, n. bi
ḏf3w "food" 90, n. aa
ḏrḏr "foreign; hostile" 84, n. y
ḏd "to anticipate; answer" 149, n. 118
ḏd ḫft "to say vis-à-vis" 61, n. h

INDEX OF TEXT PASSAGES CITED

Pap. Berlin 3029
39, n. 29; 40, n. 49
I,2-4 54, n. b
I,3 54, n. b
II,9 107, n. ar

Pap. Berlin 3038
66, n. 1

Pap. Berlin 9010
8 107, n. ar

Pap. Chester Beatty III
vs. 3,6 7f.

Pap. Chester Beatty IV
vs. 3,5ff. 42, n. 63

Pap. Chester Beatty VII
rt. 5,8 171, n. 405

Pap. Ebers
1,7 69, n. m

Pap. Kahun 13
23 162, n. 279
28 162, n. 279

Pap. Kahun 30
19 160, n. 254

Pap. Lansing
14,10 59, n. g

Pap. Leiden I 343 + I 345
rt. VII,2 159, n. 240

Pap. Leiden I 350
rt. IV, 9 97, n. ag
vs. V, 11 84, n. x

Pap. Millingen
1,6 124, n. bc
1,9 173, n. 420
1,11 88, n. z
1,12 94, n. ae
2,2 155, n. 190
2,4 98, n. aj

Pap. Sallier I
6,2 145, n. 80

Pap. Sallier II
7,4 100, n. ak
9,1f. 114, n. aw
10,1 110, n. au
10,2 116, n. ax

Pap. Sallier IV
1,2 143, n. 39

Pap. Westcar
3,3 55, n. c
4,11 77, n. q
5,1 143, n. 43
6,5 127, n. be
6,15 88, n. z
6,16 77, n. q
7,9 63, n. i
8,9 56, n. d
8,10 56, n. e
9,23 143, n. 43
11,20 88, n. z
12,2 78, n. q

Petrie, Abydos I
Pl. 54 129, n. be

Shipwrecked Sailor

28f. 139, n. bn
51 84, n. y
54 66, n. 1
85 84, n. y
89 127, n. be
124 133, n. bh
128 70, n. n
129 137, n. bl
139 167, n. 342
142 64, n. j
149 160, n. 250
170 57, n. g
186 58, n. g

Sinuhe

Ashmoleon Ostracon, vs. 30 84, n. y
Ashmoleon Ostracon, vs. 33 88, n. z
B 11 169, n. 367
B 13 171, n. 400
B 17 47, n. 114; 90, n. aa; 137, n. bl
B 17ff. 37
B 25 47, n. 114; 90, n. aa
B 33 167, n. 342
B 35 64, n. j
B 44 149, n. 119
B 45 149, n. 118
B 46-75 10
B 48 58, n. g
B 52 110, n. au
B 54f. 91, n. ab
B 63 125, n. bc
B 70 133, n. bh
B 73 56, n. d
B 73ff. 49, n. 142
B 75 61, n. h
B 89 95, n. af
B 96 70, n. n
B 104 88, n. z; 107, n. ar
B 139 160, n. 251
B 141 92, n. ab
B 150 171, n. 403
B 160 58, n. g
B 162 168, n. 360
B 171 138, n. bm
B 178 96, n. ag
B 181ff. 42, n. 71
B 184 110, n. au
B 189 65, n. k
B 199 70, n. n; 148, n. 117
B 218 168, n. 350
B 222 70, n. n
B 226 84, n. y
B 227 110, n. au; 142, n. 32
B 228 88, n. z
B 237 162, n. 273
B 245 154, n. 176
B 248 57, n. g
B 253 56, n. f
B 264 56, n. e
B 265 92, n. ab
B 266 61, n. h
B 272f. 49, n. 138
B 273 134, n. bi
B 274 56, n. d
B 293 94, n. ae
B 309 124, n. bc
G 15 93, n. ad
R 12-16 135, n. bj
R 21 156, n. 201
R 28 115, n. ax
R 66 84, n. y
R 67 61, n. h

Urk. IV

Urk. VII